Shadowman

Records of a Life Corrupted

Johnny Daukes

A RedDoor book
Published by Ember Press 2022
www.emberpress.co.uk

ISBN 978-1-9997701-3-6   LIMITED EDITION
ISBN 978-1-9997701-4-3   PAPERBACK EDITION

A CIP catalogue record for this book is available from the British Library

Cover design: Rawshock Design
Typesetting: Megan Sheer

Printed and bound in Poland by B.Z. Graf

Contents

With love to my sister Jo for her unerring support through the writing of this, and to my brother Nick who, more than anyone, knows what it all felt like.

Prologue

It's the evening of 18 April 1995, and I'm onstage at the Anson Rooms in Bristol. My band, FIN, is the opening act on the bill for Radio 1's Sound City and we're being broadcast live. We've played around 100 gigs since we started out in early '93 and have become a powerful live act. We've a twenty-minute spot and the first four songs have all received a fair amount of radio and press attention. By the last song, the crowd are on our side and, as far as winning over the radio listeners, we've done ourselves justice.

So why do we finish with a new song that I've only introduced to the rest of the band in rehearsal that week? For two reasons that I can identify. Firstly, I have (and will continue to have for the next twenty-five years) a tendency to shoot myself in the foot whenever a hard-earned opportunity presents itself because, to my mind, I don't deserve that opportunity as I am: a) a chancer b) a fraud c) a liar d) unworthy e) any and all of these. Secondly, because the song we play, 'Seed', is yet another attempt to express something that I haven't even slightly acknowledged to myself: that I was sexually abused between the ages of eleven and sixteen.

> I wrap you round and hold you tight - and let you strangle me in spite
> I get no warmth beyond a brief release
> And you are here and I fear you - 'cause you do things I could not do
> Like make me feel that I am someone, someone good.
> 'Seed', 1995

The song has a loping, slowly building intensity and as I'm singing, my skin prickles with what feels like nervous embarrassment. I have to close my eyes as they're filling with tears. These words that I've written just days before, in what I think is an academic examination of a warped power dynamic, are a covert attempt to vocalise events that I'm still years from acknowledging. Yet I've chosen to sing them on a night when we're being broadcast into hundreds of thousands of homes.

As the song builds to a crescendo the audience, who've been bouncing along to the previous tracks, have been stunned into a slightly confused yet reverential stillness. The last words seem to be a defiant repudiation of what I've suffered, addressed to someone or *something* inside me.

> I am the king of all you see and it belongs to me.
> And I can provide all that you need, if you just give it back to me.
> I am the king - and I'll give you everything.
> 'Seed', 1995

The final line decays over and over and we're given a generous send-off by the crowd who, though most of them are there for headliners Elastica, realise they've just witnessed something a little out of the ordinary. The lyrics of 'Seed' are part of a strange and unconscious dialogue with the man who has corrupted my past. It has been creeping into my songs over the years and will find its way into all of my creative output; from solo albums to comedy sketches, radio shows, screenplays and a feature film. Without my being aware, his actions throughout my formative years will exert a terrible influence. These distortions will continue to cast a shadow over my life, until well beyond the time the realisation of what he has done has eventually dawned on me.

As I sit here in the spring of 2022, just over a year after I began to write what has become this book, it occurs to me that what I'm doing is reassembling the mangled fragments and clues that I scatttered in the two and a half decades between the end of the abuse and my eventual acknowledgement of it.

The process of sifting this wreckage, of decoding these broadcasts and simultaneously reassessing – by taking possession of some of the songs and re-recording them in the full knowledge of their meaning – is a means of reconnecting and exploring what might have been.

Throughout this manuscript, I'll be quoting from lyrics and scripts that I wrote over a period of around thirty years. These documents were both

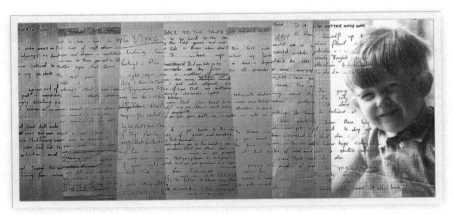

an unconscious recording of what I'd undergone and a similarly inadvertent attempt to explain to myself what was inexplicable.

Like the twisted remnants of a crashed airliner, being painstakingly reassembled into a facsimile of its undistorted form, I'm attempting to find a route back to the uncorrupted me.

Back to the Towers

I'd like to go, back to The Towers
To play the old games and use the old names
And I'd like to know, when did the dream sour?
Did you take us by force or as a matter of course?
'Back To The Towers', 1997

My mum, Tess Shanks, grew up with her five siblings and parents in a flat within a Victorian five-storey house in Camberwell, south-east London. It was known as The Towers. The Shanks family were working class; my grandad had various jobs, from bread-roundsman to concierge at the Berners Hotel, and the kids were all brought up with a Roman Catholic ethos discharged by swivel-eyed priests and malicious teachers rather than anything that went on in the home. It was a belief system that was Sunday-best (at best), observing the major feast days, and rarely impinged on a post-war life that was influenced more by the social club and extended family ties. Mum left school at sixteen, working variously for a boxing promoter, dentist and as a receptionist for a sporting publishing company.

Tess was good-looking and vivacious, making the most of the increasing freedoms of the late 50s and, according to her brothers, observing a fairly loose interpretation of Catholic dogma. One sunny autumn lunchtime she was working behind the central London reception of *The Autocar* and *The MotorCycle*, hungry and about to head out. Just then, through the doors came a smartly dressed and rather dashing young man carrying a motorcycle helmet. As Colin Daukes approached the reception desk, he quickly abandoned his intended request for a back issue of *The MotorCycle* and instead, unusually emboldened, asked the beautiful young receptionist whether she'd like to go for lunch. She would retrospectively claim she'd not found him all that attractive and had only agreed to his request because she was broke and hungry (a state of affairs that she was consequently to remain familiar with for years to come).

4

Mum and Dad (as they were later to be called) must have seemed an odd couple. Dad was still in the army and from a military family, his father having been an army pathologist in India. Colin had been a boarder at public school whilst his parents were overseas and had a pretty miserable time. Very occasionally if we stayed up chatting (which would necessitate a couple of stiff scotches for him) he'd let some of this out. Anything that ever passed between us which might have led to a deepening of our bond would invariably not be mentioned the following day. Dad's upper lip was even stiffer than the scotch.

Although Mum would always be at pains to stress that the lunch with Dad was a purely practical decision, there was clearly more to it, a fact supported by their engagement not three weeks later. Dad was smitten and remained so throughout their lives together. I've a lot to thank him for; his selflessness, decency and fairness were exemplary and though he could be quite awkward with us kids, his warmth and affection for Mum was always very obvious – very, very obvious – like, 'get a room' obvious. I'm not altogether sure Mum was as convinced, and, at least in the early flush of their relationship, I think she saw in the well-spoken,

meticulously polite lieutenant an antidote to her more rowdy and vulgar family and surroundings. To a certain extent, he represented *a way out*.

They married in October 1959 and Francis appeared the following July. Meantime, the dashing lieutenant had left the army and become a brewery rep, en route to computer sales and thence selling life insurance. He was a man of honesty and principle, so consequently struggled to hit sales targets. If his less-than-stellar career trajectory was giving Mum cause for alarm, she had little time to think about it, as into their tiny one-bedroom flat with shared toilet and tin bath three more children arrived. Janet, Joely and Jonathan illustrated several things:

Firstly, that having four children in five years might be what the Lord had chosen for you, but he wasn't having to wash the nappies.

Secondly, that six people living in a tiny one-bedroom flat was not, in any way, shape or form, 'a way out'.

And lastly, that someone had stolen most of the pages from the baby name book.

There was only one thing for it (there were actually two things for it but, as Mum seemed opposed to offering Joely and I up for adoption, there was only one thing for it) so, Dad went out and bought a map. The 'thing' wasn't buying a map, but the first step in order to *do* the thing needed a map, a map with the main railway lines out of London. By process of elimination – commutable, new low-cost housing stock, proximity to a huge power station – my parents arrived at Didcot and consequently arrived *in* Didcot, where they were shown a three-bedroom semi-detached house at 11 Freeman Road.

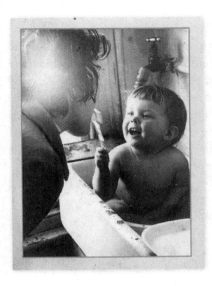 

It was to become our home for the next eight years. Shortly after we had left London, one of my uncles bought The Towers and, for the next decade, we would return regularly as it became a focal point for family parties and get-togethers at weekends and holidays.

I'd like to go, back to the times
Fields of green and smoking on screen.
'Back To The Towers', 1997

The verses of 'Back To The Towers' are a yearning for a halcyon past, embodied by the house in London and the time in our lives when it was our fulcrum. But the song is also harking back to a time for me, the time before my childhood was polluted and brought to a premature end.

The snakes that you know, and the ladders you climb
And the dreams that you steal from a man in his prime
'Back to the Towers', 1997

When I wrote this song, I was still several years from acknowledging the events that had inspired it. The imagery that was forefront in my mind was an elegiac reflection of a lost world and not even one I particularly remembered. The visions I was evoking were partly borrowed and clouded the actual recollections of things more painful – *I can't see the truth for all that cigarette smoke.*

If that sounds confusing, I guess what I'm trying to say – and to unravel in this book – is that I was clearly undergoing some kind of unconscious process as I began to tease these memories to the surface. But I'm getting ahead of myself, when I should actually be in Didcot.

Didcot
(change for Oxford)

My earliest memory is from Christmas 1966. Our gran had come over from New Zealand and I'd had to vacate my bunk in the bedroom I shared with Francis. I was just two and had been demoted to a hastily assembled cot. The bedroom door was adorned with posters of the Manchester United Holy Trinity of George Best, Dennis Law and Bobby Charlton. It was early on Christmas morning and I was gazing between the bars of my cot at Charlton, who was prematurely bald and thus a reassuring visual presence as he looked like our dad. As I stared at this man who looked like Dad, but could kick

a football so wasn't Dad, I nonchalantly tossed my tangerine peel onto the floor. Gran picked the peel up, then tossed it back through the bars like it was an experimental domestic zoo. Which I suppose it was.

At this time, we were still six – Mum, Dad, Francis, Janet, Joely and me – but were soon joined by Hannah in '67 and Nick who ushered in the 70s, albeit unknowingly. This period for our family was, more often than not, happy – despite our living in Didcot. The town has recently been voted 'the most boring place in Britain' and even as kids we were aware that it wasn't 'where it's at'. In fact, we were pretty sure that it was as far from 'where it's at' as it was possible to be. An early joke I overheard from my older brother: 'If God gave the world an enema, he'd stick the tube in Didcot', made little sense, as I had no idea what an enema was and why it would involve a tube. But even at the age of six or seven, we realised that Didcot was essentially somewhere one travelled *through* rather than *to*, or, as we put it, 'Didcot change for Oxford'.

What Didcot did have was space. We had a huge garden and the town was surrounded by fields and woods. We'd lay out race tracks through them, then tear around on our bikes. The estate we lived on, of late 60s semis, was thronged with other kids our age and the games (which in my memory are either bathed in golden sunlight or muffled by knee-deep snow) would last all day until we'd be called in, either flushed with heat or blue with cold. Our family was relatively hard up; we wore mostly hand-me-down clothes, often had bread and jam for tea and we enjoyed few of the things that most mates took for granted – trainers, jeans and orange squash come to mind. Dad left for London every morning around 06:30 and wouldn't arrive back until around 8:00 in the evening. He must have been exhausted and was more often than not greeted by a screaming baby and a litany of stuff that we'd broken.

What we lacked in stuff, we were compensated for amply by an irreverent and spontaneous home where most things were acceptable. There was a whole-lotta-love, we had joy (we had fun) and an occasional Friday-night treat of fish and chips or a Sunday lunchtime trip to the Barley Mow beer garden.

At this point, the religion in our lives was driven by a similar Catholic ethos to the one that had governed the generation before us. We went to Mass on Sundays, said our prayers every night: 'God Bless Mummy, Daddy,

Francis, Janet, Joely, Me, Hannah and Nicholas, Nanny, Grandad, Gran, aunties, uncles and little cousins. Please help all the sick children and make them better soon. I'm sorry if I've been naughty, please help me be good tomorrow.' We'd go to confession with the local parish priest where the admissions were very general: 'I've been unkind', 'I swore', 'I wasn't helpful at home'. Although I was yet to understand what 'phoning it in' meant, I was definitely already doing it.

The worst it got was during Easter. On Good Friday afternoon, when all the other kids would be playing an endless game of football in the park, we'd have to sit in church from 1:00 until 4:00 for the Easter Vigil. This was a real-time re-enactment of the Passion of the Christ which contained some quite remarkably scary shit. At the point just before Jesus gave up the Holy Ghost, he (quite reasonably) got a bit testy with his omniscient, omnipotent father (God) and yelled '*Eli, Eli, lama sabachthani?*' Which means, 'My God, my God, why have you forsaken me?' When screamed across the reverberant expanse of Didcot's Church of the English Martyrs, this was the most terrifying phrase I'd ever heard. Normally, at the consecration of communion – at the moment the wafer turned into Jesus's *actual body* – it was customary to ring a bell. Which is kind of understatement really – 'bread becoming flesh' should warrant some heraldic trumpets at the very least. At the Easter Vigil, the bell was dispensed with and instead, there was the dry, staccato ratchet of a football rattle. It was close to being comical but was actually hideous – like a clown's face.

When 1970s childhoods are evoked, everything is brown apart from Space Hoppers (which are orange) and Raleigh Choppers (which are red). There were a couple of Space Hoppers in Didcot (one of which was actually blue) but they quickly punctured, and a kid from a nearby village had a Chopper but he was always last on our grass-track scrambling course so we all thought his bike was a bit shit. In our 1970s there was green grass, yellow straw and magnolia walls. There was actually a lot of yellow. Most people's kitchens were yellow Formica, as was the Tupperware we'd take on picnics to the river at Clifton Hampden.

As well as being a transport hub, thanks to its pivotal position on the Great Western Railway and proximity to the M4, Didcot also sported a power station that dominated the entire Thames Valley. If the cathedrals of the Middle Ages were seen as priapic (which according to my A-level study of William Golding's *The Spire*, they were) then Didcot Power Station was the Ron Jeremy of industrial architecture. Other people would always make a bigger deal of this massive erection than we did. For us, the collection of cooling towers and the chimney

were just...*there*. Far more important was *why* they were there. The nearby river Thames cooled this coal-powered behemoth and we spent endless days in its meandering depths (which actually *were* brown, albeit greeney). Summer afternoons would be spent with other families in the meadows by the river. We'd jump off the bridge, mess about in inflatable boats, play rounders, step in cow shit, get stung by nettles – and eat (yellow) cheese rolls from yellow Tupperware plates. Then on Mondays it was back to school.

St Amand's in the nearby village of East Hendred was a small primary school of fewer than 100 kids, at least four of whom were my own siblings. Mr and Mrs Tonge, the headmaster and headmistress, were an elderly couple with an extraordinary capacity for fun and a sixth sense for how to engage their pupils. Every subject or activity involved us doing practical things and in lessons we were frequently on our feet, or outside of the classroom altogether. School plays were elaborate and Mr Tonge would construct flying scenery and staging that wouldn't have shamed a provincial theatre. Everyone was encouraged to play music. I started on the sopranino recorder, but threw it out of the bus window and the driver refused to stop and collect it. At the end of one summer term there was a raffle for who got to take the school guinea pig home and Mr Tonge conspired with Mum for me to win. I somehow got to keep her and proudly named my first pet 'Fruity'. Sadly, when we went to Cornwall for a week, we left her with the Daveys, whose Dalmatian got into the enclosure and bit her to death. A terrible event, the worst aspect of which is that anyone who reads this now knows the answer to my security question.

We spent most of our time at school playing football, tennis and cricket. There was the constant smell of Dettol, so we were sick too. Chief culprit was the obligatory half-pint of full-cream milk that had been sat in the sun all morning. We did what all 70s primary school kids did: sharpened pencils, did Music & Movement in our pants and vests, learned to count with coloured wooden rods, ate boiled fish and mash for lunch, sang songs about birds and Jesus and sharpened more pencils. It was hardly idyllic by modern standards; most of us wore patched clothes, everyone seemed to have a wart and at least one lunchtime a week, Gordon McAteer threw up the boiled fish.

But there were heady highlights too:

> Winter mornings when Mr Tonge would prepare the playground with a hose to make a thirty-five-yard slide of clear black ice and cancel all lessons!

> Summer afternoons when Mr Tonge would mow the field to a perfect wicket and cancel all lessons!

> Bus trips home when Jackie Walsh would allow the boys to form an orderly queue and granted them a stealthy glance down her knickers (which Mr Tonge got wind of and until he found out who was involved, cancelled all playtimes!).

Our family expanded again and in 1974 we moved across Didcot to another three-bedroom semi that had been extended above the garage with a further two bedrooms and bathroom, providing (just) enough room for the arrival of Sofia and then Kathy. We were ten. For years our family transport had been an old Bedford bus and this was upgraded to a twelve-seater Ford Transit. It was actually an ex-rental, bought from Aylesbury Van Hire, which we only partly scraped the letters from, so, for months, it was emblazoned 'To Hire A lesb y'. Mum frequently drove through Didcot with my five sisters in the back and this explains a rich seam of Didcot folklore.

My life until I was ten was football, bicycles, mates, school and a slightly chaotic but fun family. It was an unremarkable and quite predictable existence and I would trade huge amounts of very valuable things for it to have stayed that way. But it didn't.

The Work

During the period between 1972 and 1974, a gradual change began to ripple through the foundations of our family unit. I think you can see it in some of the photographs of the time, but that might be post-rationalisation. Maybe my Mum and Dad were tired – I mean, why *wouldn't* they have been? A division slowly crept in as a result of a religious organisation my Mum had begun to devote more time to. At first, this was seen as *supporting her role as a wife and mother*, but that wasn't the wife and mother that my dad had been a partner to. The creeping division very subtly began to shift the functionality and foundations of our lives. It was a weakening, which compromised the implicit trust and structure that offered protection to the children within our family and left us vulnerable. The cause of that imbalance was Opus Dei.

> If blessed is he who comes in the name of the Lord
> Then why is he always so fundamentally flawed?
> 'Lamb Of God', 1995

Opus Dei is a religious organisation that was founded in Spain by a Catholic priest called Josemaría Escrivá De Balaguer in 1928. Its name means 'The Work of God'. On its surface (and in countless online blogs by members who purport to be endeavouring to sanctify their daily lives) Opus Dei is about individuals being able to dedicate their everyday existence to the glorification of God. You don't have to dig very deeply to reveal that these people frequently seem borderline fascistic and have an extraordinarily patronising and narrow world view. They are also *obsessed* with sexual propriety and convinced that if men and women are allowed in close proximity for more than five minutes, there'll be an orgy. Unsurprisingly, they are keen advocates of anything and everything that opposes women's rights. My mum was introduced to Opus Dei whilst we still lived in London. Her brother (my Uncle Mik) had been recruited when a student by a family friend called Vladimir Felzmann. The now Father Felzmann, a Catholic priest who was a favourite son of the Opus Dei founder, left the organisation

in 1981 and once said to me that the greatest regret of his life was 'introducing Opus Dei to the Shanks family'. Amen to that, Father.

Opus Dei encourages some quite weird behaviours: members tie a spiked metal chain called a cilis around their upper thigh until it draws blood, and flagellate themselves with a small whip called (without a great deal of imagination) a 'discipline'. So far, so Max Mosley. If people want to hurt their upper thighs and backs to the greater glory of God, I guess it's their business.

Where Opus Dei becomes much more problematic is in the way it insists on itself and God being the primary relationship and responsibility of its members. When Mum started engaging in occasional Opus Dei activities it had little effect on our family. We'd go to the odd Christmas carol service at one of their extremely well-appointed and immaculately decorated and invariably huge properties, where the softly spoken inhabitants would all smell of very expensive cologne and seemed to float about rather than actually walk.

They referred to these properties as 'houses'.
They were very big houses.
Very big houses with leather-bound (religious) books that smelled of rich mahogany.

Mum then started visiting a women's house of Opus Dei for her increasingly frequent confessions and to meet and talk with her spiritual advisor. This person becomes a combination of confessor (they begin to know every detail of your life), advisor (they are generally single, celibate and have not one iota of a clue about family life), and offer you 'fraternal correction', which is basically shitty advice that makes you feel bad, but you have to smile and take it because it's sort of coming through them from God. There was a spiritual

advisor when we were in London, a Spanish woman called Maria, but at that stage I think it was all a bit vanilla and I suspect Mum was taking it with a pinch of salt. When we moved to Didcot, Maria would visit (imagine taking a train sixty miles to give someone shitty advice that makes them feel bad?) but after a few years a women's house called Winton opened in Oxford.

What happened, at first gradually – then increasingly – in the decade between 66 and 76 is that my dad's position as Mum's confidante (and consequently their ability to function as a unit at the heart of our family) was undermined. Shortly after my mum died in 2007, I put it to my dad that, for him, Mum's increasing devotion to various other males (who were either dead or simply didn't exist) must have been akin to her having an affair. His eyes welled up (he'd moistened on the odd occasion when discussing boarding school, but these were real tears that needed wiping away) and said, 'When your mother found Opus Dei, I lost my best friend...' I put an arm round his shoulder and, for at least seven or eight seconds, my dad didn't move.

Unfortunately, when I began to be preyed upon as a child, my dad didn't move then, either. But probably because he wasn't alert to seeing it, because in some way he didn't feel like I was allowed to be his responsibility – or he was just too fucking tired.

Welcome to the Club

On an October Friday afternoon in 1974, Mum arrived at school in the Transit, picking up me and a bunch of mates to take us into Oxford. As we zoomed along the A34 past Abingdon we were busy thinking up smutty conjunctions: a new Japanese motorbike 'Itchifani 500', dirty footballers 'Terry Veinyballs', and the Russian torturer 'Ivan Kutabolokov'. We were passionately debating the England front line of Mick Channon vs Sniffer Clarke and had this been full-on 'Wonder Years' territory, 'Jean Genie' would have been thrumming away in the background. Sadly, the van radio was jammed on long wave and we were listening to an indecipherable French pop station mulched together with a local mini-cab firm.

We were on our way into Oxford for an inaugural session of Grandpont Boys' Club. What we didn't know (as we had no knowledge of Opus Dei with its apparently obsessive adherence to sexual propriety and exploitatively divisive methods) was that Boys' Club was an embryonic version of other feeder streams to Opus Dei that exist in almost every city in every country across the world. These Boys' Clubs had much to recommend them. Activities including sports, film-making, camping, car mechanics and lots of other things appealing to teenage male youth without the requirement to wear a cap or a woggle. They did, however (much like a fruitcake that's ruined by the liberal addition of mixed peel), have a key component, disguised by the attractions of tents, balls and grease, of praying. Just as local churches invite non-believers for 'coffee', so Boys' Club was a Trojan horse to ensnare unsuspecting youth in the religious activities of Opus Dei. The clubs were (and still are) attached to men's houses of The Work that were inhabited by adult students and Opus Dei members.

When we arrived, I don't know where my mum went (in retrospect, I'm quite sure it involved some form of prayer) and we were handed over to one such student. He was a ruddy-faced, chubby and enthusiastic nineteen-year-old and an inhabitant of Grandpont House, Oxford's Opus Dei residence for men.

This student, who I was to get to know far too well over the following years, I'm going to henceforth refer to as 'Bananas'. Having read that Dennis Potter called his cancer 'Rupert' (after his disgust for Rupert Murdoch) and as I was once described in the music press as 'the Dennis Potter of indie rock' – and I find bananas disgusting – the label seems as appropriate as any.

My memories of this first meeting with him don't extend much beyond 'ruddy-faced, chubby and enthusiastic' because the two hours was disorganised mayhem. We met in the grounds of Grandpont House, a stately Georgian property built on two small bridges that spanned tributaries of the Cherwell, and our focal point was a millstone sunk into the lawn beneath a huge mulberry tree.

Our activities, such as they were, all took place outdoors, other than some obligatory 'prayer'. This was either benediction or the rosary – which was carried out in the oratory, an incense-clouded room with deep-swagged curtains and much oak panelling. Once we'd done the praying, the student continued trying to corral us likes rats into a sack as we ran around hitting things (and each other) with sticks and he would attempt to impose some order whilst barely keeping his temper. He was quite overweight and asthmatic, which loaned him a near-permanent film of sweat.

For two hours (including the praying) Bananas engaged us in some extreme British Bull Dog and then gave us beakers of orange squash and huge slices of McVitie's chocolate sponge, an impossibly exotic treat that we gorged on without any thought as to what might be required in return. With the benefit of hindsight, this last sentence rings alarm bells loud enough to wake Sleeping Beauty after a massive Bank Holiday bender. But the benefit of hindsight (like Tory compassion or myrrh) is something that never, in any practical sense, seems to exist.

Awakenings

Bananas had already met my older brother Francis a year or so before, in an abortive attempt to get the Boys' Club established. This had foundered largely I think because Francis, who was four years my senior, was too close in age for Bananas to exert any authority. Francis was already fourteen and was powerful, physically and in terms of his assured character and outspoken nature. Soon after I met Bananas, he began to bad-mouth my brother. He found him quite abrasive and arrogant and told me that no one liked Francis, that he was a 'big-head and a loudmouth'.

As our Boys' Club meetings became more frequent, my parents began to invite Bananas to our house for the occasional meal and it wasn't long before he became a regular visitor. When he was sat round our family dining table, he was never less than respectful of my parents, bordering on sycophantic. Yet away from them, he would subtly criticise our family unit to me.

There was a weird snobbery about Bananas, who was from a background that he regarded as more 'proper' than ours. He talked about his elderly relatives as if they were a team of Manners Superheroes, whose powers were wielded through an antimacassar, an armoire and a doily. In later life when I'd met most of his family, it occurred to me that they were actually The Munsters, put together in a hurry by Madame Tussaud – in the dark. But at ten, I was also in the dark and couldn't see what was in front of me.

He was obsessive about the strangest things. We were reasonably polite as a family; please and thank you were regular currency, but rubbed up against sod it and bugger off in the same pocket. He could just about turn a blind ear to this, but taking jam or marmalade directly from a jar with your knife? 'Nurse! The Epsom salts!'

The undermining of my family occurred simultaneously with the increasing attention he devoted towards me and I'm sure as one of seven (about to become eight) siblings, it felt gratifying on some level. It was a classic case of 'grooming' and his technique was to shepherd me away from the flock that offered me protection. The fact that the foundations of that unit were already becoming unsteady through my mum's devotion to Opus Dei made his efforts all the easier. If the Germans have a word that means 'Irony with the addition of a Supercharger', this would be an appropriate time to use it.

In the summer holiday between primary school and middle school, the criticism of my family and the establishment of a belief that I was boastful and over-confident was compounded, as Bananas became my Spiritual Advisor. I'm not sure this was ever an official appointment; I certainly can't remember any form of investiture and he didn't start wearing a hat or anything. He *did* however start asking me lots of intrusive questions, some of which concerned 'impure thoughts'.

I was a late developer and until the last term of primary school (when I suddenly wanted to sit next to Sarah Robinson in class – for reasons I knew not) girls were pretty much either my sisters or things that occasionally got in the way of the ball in the playground. That summer, something began to awaken in me and Bananas' sixth sense was alert to it.

Every week Francis read *Autosport,* a weekly magazine of all-things motor-racing. Our uncles were all car-racing fans and we'd inherited the passion. Our bedroom walls were adorned with posters of my brother's heroes: Jochen Rindt, Ronnie Peterson and Gilles Villeneuve, who all inevitably became my heroes and sadly, but equally inevitably, all died in horrible crashes.

Autosport carried reports on Grand Prix races and also carried a weekly advert in the inside back cover for a company called Grand Prix Racewear. They sold overalls and helmets to racing drivers and shiny jackets to men who wanted to pretend they were racing drivers. Strangely, in the advert, rather than racing drivers (or men) wearing the outfits, the pictures were of a lady who didn't seem to have anything on underneath the unzipped outfits other than her pants. And they were really tiny pants. And I liked looking at them. To this day I have absolutely no idea how Bananas knew; it's likely he didn't but simply went on a fishing expedition as to the nature of my 'impure thoughts'. But sure enough, in the course of a conversation where I was encouraged to share any thoughts that might have been 'impure', I spilled the beans.

I expected Bananas to affect a countenance of heavy piety, for his brow to furrow and, at the very least, to heave a sigh of disapproval. Instead there was a change in his demeanour that I was to recognise too many times from thereon. It was a creeping, slightly sickly curiosity that I now recognise as arousal. I don't know if I was the first child that he'd been attracted to, maybe these first instances were as confusing to him as they were me. Maybe my explaining to him how I felt when I looked at the lady in the tiny pants gave him a similarly inexplicable feeling? Who knows

What I do know is that the lady in the tiny pants was likely in her early twenties and not really in any danger from the adoring gaze of a trembling eleven-year-old with a flutter in his heart and a stirring in his underwear. When I described these feelings to a twenty-one-year-old man – in the belief that I had to tell him so that I might begin to be forgiven by God – I was putting myself in a lot of danger because of what was stirring in his warped ego and, more threateningly, in *his* underwear.

A Lamb to the Slaughter

Living in Didcot and attending a Catholic primary school had meant a four-mile bus journey with siblings and mates. But the nearest Catholic secondary school was in Oxford, which meant a mile by bike to the station, fifteen miles by train to Oxford, then three miles by bus to Cowley. A journey of 1h 20m if it all went smoothly, which meant leaving home around 07:20. So far, so much – a bit of a pain in the arse.

What made things a little trickier for me was that Oxford used the Middle School system, so I was entering a new school in Year 3 that all the other kids had joined, aged nine, in Year 1. What made things a great deal trickier for me was that Bananas (who I was now spending much more time in the company of) had begun to widen his remit as spiritual advisor in ways that were feeling oddly intrusive. When I started at St John Bosco RC Middle School, I had a constant and overwhelming discomfort that felt like an ill-fitting set of clothes – beneath my ill-fitting set of clothes.

The first week was shocking. I was small for my age and I'd been kitted out in grey trousers, white shirt, blue V-neck, stripey tie, a blazer, Clarks Attackers and a massive brown leather satchel, and I walked into a playground of giants wearing ox-blood DMs, patch-pocket bags, mohair jumpers, Harrington jackets, with tie-knots the size of small pillows, and sports bags variously Adidas, Gola or Puma. It's a cliché to say, 'I might as well have had a target on my back', closer to the truth is that I might as well have carried a sign saying 'pre-pubescent weed – won't fight back if hit'.

I'm not for a minute trying to claim that the dawning of Bananas' depravity caused me to be bullied. I think any kid being put into the situation I was would have felt a bit lamb-to-the-slaughtery and, as time went on, I learned my own way of dealing with it. But the following year was to be polluted and adulterated through Bananas' systematic destruction of my barely formed character. And that was to make everything I was negotiating, at the onset of the most formative period of my life, impossibly complicated and contradictory.

The Apostolate

A fundamental required of all Opus Dei members and their acolytes is to do 'apostolate', or to spread the word about Opus Dei and attempt to attract any and all of your contacts towards it. So pretty much the opposite of Fight Club. In the early days of Grandpont Boys' Club this was a natural and organic process; who wouldn't want to tell their mates about a place where you could play bulldog, smash through undergrowth with sticks and then get a massive slice of McVitie's chocolate cake and gallons of orange squash (even if the 'saying the rosary' bit seemed to have slipped your mind)? And for the first year the numbers grew. Once primary school was over, it dwindled as most of my mates went to the local senior school in Didcot and so Oxford was off their radar. Oxford was very much on my radar and as the long, hot summer melted into the long and still quite hot autumn, I entered the new term at my new school with the following agenda:

1. Get to Oxford and back every day.

2. Negotiate dramatically different peer group.

I entered the second week of the new term with the following, adjusted, agenda:

1. Try to avoid Seamus O'Carrol, Joe Curran and Shaun Keane.

2. Disguise your leather satchel with white and red Humbrol paint so it looks less like a satchel and more like a sports bag. (It actually still looked like a leather satchel that had been badly painted with the words 'Manchester United' and 'The Who'.) Mum went ballistic: 'You've defaced a perfectly decent hold-all!' It didn't look in the slightest bit like a sports bag – it looked like Richard Hammond looks like Ferris Bueller.

3. Don't hang around on your own by the arches reading during break and lunch; it seems to attract the attention of too many people.

These agendas are faced by every child who has a change in circumstances, and our ability to face and overcome these challenges is key to the developmental shift we make on the path from childhood to adulthood. You could compare it to climbing a steep and rocky hill, jagged rocks and loose gravel underfoot with perilous falls on either side. Throw some sexual abuse and character destabilisation into the mix and you're doing that same climb with no shoes and socks – on a skateboard.

Over the previous six months, Bananas' attention toward me had begun to very subtly change. His interest in me had always felt rewarding and it's almost impossible to pinpoint exact moments where that interest felt awkward or strange. The 'success' of a man with his impulses relies on building trust and progressing a situation with a potential prey in such a manner that they suspect nothing. And what was it that I would have suspected? I didn't have the first idea what 'it' was. That's the role of an attentive parent, to be alert to a situation that their child can't possibly imagine.

Through the summer holiday we had spent more time together and no doubt my parents were glad that I was occupied. As the new term began, I was now in Oxford every day and as he was still living at Grandpont House, I would often meet him after school. As the term progressed, I was encouraged to do 'apostolate' and to spread the word about the Boys' Club to my new and dramatically different peer group.

After a couple of weeks at St John Bosco, I'd begun to form the odd connection to a group of boys who were, if not themselves odd, idiosyncratic. They were united by their inability to be invited to any other tribe. Not sporty, not cool, not 'hard', not swots, they were the young male equivalent of the kitchen pot wherein every household dumps the odds and ends that are unidentifiable, without purpose and spare, yet not so useless as to warrant throwing away. I met them on a lunchtime trip to the toilet where they would hang out (literally) playing a game called Bogollen, which was a fairly standard form of tag with the very un-standard variation that required it to be played exclusively in the toilets without touching the floor. What this meant was a great deal of touching the toilets, but I was so grateful to have been given the opportunity to play that I grabbed it with both hands. So to speak.

Being invited into the Fellowship of Oddbods was progress of sorts, in that breaks and lunchtimes were no longer exercises in pretending to look busy and occupied. For two weeks my best friend had been a hand-painted satchel, so a group of toilet-dwelling noobs quickly became, if not my BFFs, certainly my BFSF.

Emboldened as I was by this incipient social network and feeling the weight of responsibility to fulfil my duty of apostolate, I extended them all an invitation to Boys' Club. My village primary school mates and I had found Bulldog, plant destruction and chocolate cake fantastically exotic – but I had woefully miscalculated the lived experience and expectations of the Fellowship.

Yes, in the jungle of a city middle school, they were at the lower end of the feeding chain, but they lived in Cowley and Blackbird Leys where they rode bikes with cow-horn handlebars, bought their own sweets and drank Coke. Not only were they nonplussed and unimpressed by the 'activities', but the obligatory visit to the oratory to say the rosary was worse than if I'd invited them to play dress-up with me and some dollies.

To consequently find myself persona non grata with the John Bosco Year 3 outcasts was troubling. It was troubling as if you were a member of India's Chamar caste, the lowest of the low and only worthy of cleaning sewers, disposing of dead animals and tanning leather, and the other Chamars said that *you weren't allowed to clean the sewers, dispose of the dead animals and tan the leather because your Boys' Club was really weird and the bloke you knew who ran it seemed a bit weird, too. And fuck the praying while you're at it.*

I'd like to think that I gave constructive thought as to how I needed to adjust my agenda in the light of recent events, but actually what I did was to stare out of the train window – either dreading getting to school or replaying the misery of the day that had just passed. Then salvation appeared in its coat of many colours.

Jacob, Jacob & Sons!

In my last year at St Amand's our school play had been *Joseph and His Amazing Technicolor Dreamcoat*, a title that, with hindsight, is so laughably contrived, it would sit comfortably in *VIZ*. Except it's actually from the 'Book of Genesis' (which isn't as funny as *VIZ* but is *way* more far-fetched). At primary school, I'd played the part of Joseph and it had seemed a happy story about some shepherds and I'd gotten to wear a coat that someone's mum had made out of lots of glittery material – of many colours.

Back in Oxford one autumn morning, a few days after being dis-invited from the Bogollen Brotherhood, I was in a music lesson that was drawing to a close when Mrs Ryan announced, 'OK, 3S, the school play this Christmas is *Joseph and His Amazing Technicolor Dreamcoat* and auditions will be taking place in the gym on Friday lunchtime.'

Time stood still, the hairs on the back of my neck stood up and I felt a heat rising within me. It was the unmistakable onrush of opportunity. This was a tiny leak of light, shining through a miniscule crack in a barely open door. As I sat at a lunch table listening in to the surrounding chatter, my heart sank. It seemed that the leading parts were for the fourth years, and Year Three were expected to make up the chorus line.

Two days flew by and at least during breaks and lunch, I was able to wander about on my own, convincingly looking like I was thinking about something – because I was. Then it was Friday lunchtime. I didn't go to the lunch hall – I was sick with nerves – and, instead, loitered near the gym entrance. After about fifteen minutes, a queue began to form. A queue that was a 'Who's Who?' of the gods of Year 4. Girls with long blonde hair, radiant complexions, pearly teeth – and bosoms! Boys who were tall, had the best bikes and scored all the goals! It was a photo shoot from *Mates* forming in front of my eyes and the queue was growing. Tagging onto the rear now were the Economy Class Year 4s, likely more dramatically talented but lacking the entitlement and un-burstable confidence that they simply *deserved* a main part.

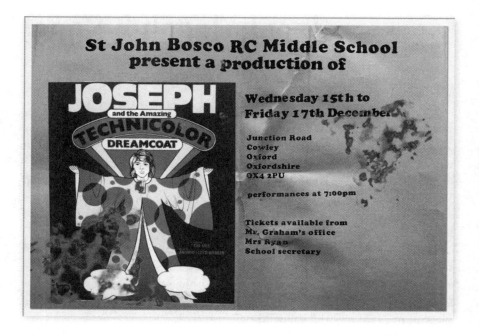

St John Bosco RC Middle School present a production of

JOSEPH and the Amazing TECHNICOLOR DREAMCOAT

Wednesday 15th to
Friday 17th December

Junction Road
Cowley
Oxford
Oxfordshire
OX4 2PU

performances at 7:00pm

Tickets available from
Mr. Graham's office
Mrs Ryan
School secretary

The doors opened and the queue snaked into the gym. I waited and before too many Year 3s joined, snuck on the end and was soon inside. The gym had full-length doors at one end that were always closed but today had been slid back to reveal – a stage! Near to the stage on the floor was Mrs Ryan's piano, various chairs with musical instruments next to them and there, right at the front just below the stage, a full drum kit! This was nothing like anything I'd seen before. Mrs Ryan clapped her hands and from various parts of the room walked pupils carrying violins, violas, a cello, clarinets and – wait, what??!! An electric guitar and a bass!!! These were objects of wonder that I'd only ever seen in magazines or on television. Mrs Ryan clapped her hands again. 'OK, over here can I have all the Jacobs? Over here Potiphar and Potiphar's wife. Over here all the brothers except Joseph.'

Nearly all of the pupils had spread out into various groups that Mrs Ryan had indicated, leaving four boys still waiting. They were Alain Delon, Johnny Depp, Brad Pitt and Paul Newman. Or they might as well have been. '…and Josephs over here.'

She pointed and the Four Musketeers made their way insouciantly across the hall, assembling under a neon sign that said 'Cool Boys Only – No Twats'. My legs were cast in lead and the floor was a foot deep in treacle, but I set off regardless, a tiny rowboat inching across a vast and turbulent shipping lane. There was an instant hum, but it wasn't from people humming; it was the hum of ALL the popular and cool kids whispering under their breath to each other: 'Who the fuck is that and what the fuck does he think he's doing?'

I made it across the hall and positioned myself on the end of The Fab Four; we were The Fab Four (and a half). Mrs Ryan looked quizzical, then tilted her head to one side as if to say: 'Really?' With a gentle smile, her eyes spoke to me: 'Are you sure you want to do this?' I did my best to smile back, but it probably looked like I was having a minor stroke.

'Right, Josephs, who's first?'

I couldn't see their eyes but could absolutely feel them – four pairs, eight eyes, boring into the top of my head, laser beams that were heating up my sticky-out ears, which were reddening and thus appearing to sticky-out even more.

With what had befallen me over the past three weeks and what was likely to happen from here on in, I somehow had no fear. I set off across the hall, climbed the stairs side-stage and walked to the centre where I looked out and FUCK ME – THIS IS HIGH AND BRIGHT AND QUIET – AND THERE'S A HALL FULL OF PEOPLE WATCHING WHO ARE GOING TO TEAR ME TO FUCKING SHREDS AFTER THIS!

'It's Jonathan, isn't it?'

I nodded, because it was.

'And what are you going to sing for us?'

'Close Every Door.'

Mrs Ryan was taken aback. The play had only been announced two days ago and she was expecting something from the charts, maybe 'Save Your Kisses For Me' or 'Fernando'?

I continued, 'I'm going to sing "Close Every Door" from *Joseph*.'

She smiled encouragingly at me. 'Would you like some music?'

I nodded as Mrs Ryan on piano and Louise Fahey on clarinet played the haunting opening bars, then I sang…

Close every door to me, hide all the world from me
Bar all the windows and shut out the light
Do what you want with me, hate me and laugh at me
Darken my daytime and torture my night

The strings joined in as the hushed crowd looked on, I continued confidently, adding some plaintive hand gestures for good measure as the song filled the hall.

By the end I'd swear there was a tear in Mrs Ryan's eye, which was maybe why she started to clap as a distracting measure, then everyone joined in and The Fab Four left the hall and I got the part and people sat next to me at lunch and Brinsley Walsh, who was the biggest kid in the school, became my friend because he thought I was funny, and things at John Bosco weren't half as bad as they could have been even though everything started to get much more confusing...

...because Bananas started to get much worse.

This is Bananas

The tablets of stone that you carry around on your back
A rod from your god as they quiver and splinter and crack.
'Lamb Of God', 1995

In a similar fashion to how my mum had been gradually brainwashed that her relationship with God and Opus Dei was more important than her relationship with her husband, I was slowly but very surely being separated not only from my family, but more damagingly for my long-term development, from the formation of my natural character.

Consider this: from the age of ten a man appeared in my life who was ten years older than me. This man was a member of Opus Dei, an organisation that my mother was in thrall to, was being influenced by and that she trusted implicitly. This organisation was simultaneously exerting a negative influence on my parents' relationship, beginning to alienate my dad from his wife and to consequently minimise Dad's influence and involvement with his own children.

This man (Bananas) was designated my spiritual advisor and I was thus encouraged to share my innermost thoughts with him. This enabled him to arbitrate as to what was 'sinful' and what I should therefore confess to – in a fortnightly trip to the Grandpont House priest, wherein my wrongdoing was ratified and penance prescribed. These 'confessions' were very different to those I'd experienced with the Didcot parish priest. I was encouraged and expected to be far more explicit and there was a conversational aspect to them that led to a much deeper level of disclosure. These were initially in a dark confessional in the nearby church, but then became face-to-face visits in the priest's room at Grandpont House.

Before long, I began to feel a sense of an inner voice that would judge not only my actions, but also my thoughts. I would travel on the train to school and make conversation with other kids, all the time mentally checking whether I was 'on-message'. Maybe I'd have developed this internal self-doubt anyway? No way of telling unless there was a clone of me made in 1974 and brought up without the presence of Bananas, but, as far as I'm aware, no such control experiment was ever established.

As my mum received regularly, so I also received regular doses of 'fraternal correction'. Shitty advice that was dispensed by Bananas as if mainlined into his head by God (or more likely some other Opus Dei nutjob with little-to-no understanding of anything other than scripture) and which I took as gospel. This system would be iniquitous under any circumstance but, as I was soon to experience, there were further depths to the iniquity – deep depths.

In Big Families

We were, by most people's standards, a big family: Mum, Dad and eight of us kids (five girls and three boys). Through our Opus Dei connections, we knew two Spanish families, with twelve and sixteen children, and would do occasional exchanges with them, not that they probably noticed. If you've got sixteen children, aside from the fact that you're likely too tired to actually see or count, unless you have a roll call you're really relying on the same kind of sensory pack behaviour more common to penguins or seals. Even with our measly eight we would occasionally go on trips in the van and have to return home for a straggler. We once went on a Sunday lunchtime pub visit about five miles from home and only realised we were *one light* when Dad got to the bar. What both of these Spanish families had in common (and it became especially obvious when we were flown to stay with one of them at their Andalusian ranch) was money. Kids cost you money (unless you're Bill Sykes) and if you have very little money and very lots of kids then something's gotta give. In our case that was time.

Dad really did his best, I think. Had it not been for Mum's religious beliefs he would have likely settled for two or three children and his relatively modest salary would have gone further. As it was, when he was working in London his days were long and must have been exhausting. When we were younger, he was more actively involved with us at weekends. Our van was a handy football team transport that took us to games all over Berkshire and Oxfordshire. Our garage became a hangar in which he'd construct elaborate, beautiful and quite huge radio-controlled gliders from balsa-wood and varnished tissue paper. These would be taken in sections to White Horse Hill in Uffington, assembled in the car park, then we'd watch in awe as he inevitably piled them into the hillside. Their gossamer wings would smash with a sickening crack which would barely mask Dad's mumbled 'bollocks'. His finest and most ambitious ever was *The Swan*, with a wingspan of nearly ten feet, which he couldn't resist taking to the nearby park for a 'shakedown' test using a rubber launch rope. As the quivering tension suddenly released, the vast delicacy of *The Swan* whooshed across the grass, arced upwards into the late summer evening, then lurched violently to one side and was obliterated against a concrete street lamp. Good times.

Mum was quick-witted and had an irreverence that was quite at odds with her religious piety. At the same time as she would implement a cast-iron code of sexual morality, she would dispense off the cuff invocations that fellow road users might 'sod off', would dismiss our efforts to do or say something with 'you silly buggers' and laughed easily and often. Billy Connolly and Dave Allen were given dispensations to say or do pretty much anything and she adored the wordplay of Tom Lehrer, Jake Thackray and Gerard Hoffnung. Mum would speak in any and every accent and we'd start breakfast in Greenock, have boiled eggs in Munich and finish our Cornflakes in Santiago. It seemed normal, especially as it came naturally to me. Dad would appear bemused at best and retreated in relief to the safe haven of the train to London and the rationality of the *Financial Times*.

> Sitting on your garden swing in honeysuckle breeze
> The rockery's a shipwreck where you fall and scrape your knees
> One of eight, you're feeling great, the company is fine
> Your body gets on good with folk and argues with your mind
> It's alright, it's alright, 'cause your daddy's coming home
> But he won't see you – he'll make us up to ten
> 'In Big Families', 1987

It's possible that my experiences with Bananas gave me a very different interpretation of the dynamics within our home. More likely, in my view, is that the dynamics in the home allowed for what happened to me. Although I describe Dad as merely 'making us up to ten', I don't blame him for the increasing distance I believe he felt. The change to the structure of their relationship, that was fostered by various members of Opus Dei, led to a clear hierarchy between my parents. The middle eight of the song is more revealing:

> You've got twenty good expressions and other people's lines
> But the cheering stops and the smiles drop
> When Jesus is knocked off the top
> And pain and guilt is all that's left to find
> 'In Big Families', 1987

There was an irreverent and adversarial, almost gladiatorial nature to much of our home life, most commonly experienced around the dining table. It was here that Dad would often struggle, appearing to have been dumped into a den of cackling hyenas who spoke a foreign language (as well as in foreign accents). He'd frequently look perplexed as conversations would, through word-association or ridicule, flip into another dimension that made no sense to him. This would often result in his slamming his fist onto the table in an attempt to wrestle some control back.

Even in our wider family (on Mum's side) there had always been a conversational style that outsiders found quite aggressive, as I now believe some of my less assertive siblings did. Sarcasm and confrontation were common currency and I quickly became adept at using impersonation and clowning to 'win' some of these exchanges, often at the expense of a less vocal sibling. It's a trait that I've only recently recognised myself employing with those I love and I blanch at the thought.

These competitions wherein I'd employ 'good expressions and other people's lines' would come to an abrupt halt when they wandered into my being not so much blasphemous as straying from the party line. This would result in swift humiliation, often from Mum's tongue with a ratifying crack round the head that Dad laughingly called a 'knuckle'. I always sat to his immediate left and these would rain down fairly frequently. I actually think that they briefly put Dad on the same page as Mum and he got caught up in administering them against his nature.

> Sit inside and think about your life and love and friends
> Comradeship and family what is real and what's pretend
> What is it you're feeling is it something of your own?
> And if it's shared with seven others why are you alone?
> 'In Big Families', 1987

It's my belief that once Opus Dei had infiltrated Mum's thought process, her desire to do 'apostolate' overrode her maternal instinct. The older girls were leaned on to do a lot of looking after of the younger ones and we'd frequently get home to an empty house as Mum was at Winton (the women's Opus Dei residence in north Oxford). Every evening around six, Mum would disappear to her room for around thirty minutes in order to 'do my prayer' and if you happened to walk in with a request, the heavy-lidded-eye-raise would have been nailed-on gold at the Piety Olympics.

As I approached my teens, there was a developing miasma about the place that said 'there's something bigger at work here' and it was The Work (of God). On top of this were daily mass, the rosary, an annual retreat to an Opus Dei manor house in Sussex and innumerable visits to help out local 'young mums' who would no doubt learn the price of this *help* when encouraged to visit Winton; that they might be taught to devote their lives to God, with an inevitable cost to their marriage.

There were many members of my extended family involved to a greater or lesser extent with Opus Dei. With one or two exceptions this involvement left their relationships and families worse off. I'm pleased to say that most of them eventually severed their ties.

Construction/
Deconstruction

Gently corrupted like sand-castles into the sea
Leaving no clues as to what they would be or had been.
'God & The Aeroplanes', 1999

Any retrospective reveal of sexual abuse attracts inevitable questions as to 'why didn't you say something at the time?' Although the answers to this are fairly well understood, it won't hurt to examine them from my point of view.

The abuser establishes a relationship that places the victim at a disadvantage; in my case this was done through the criticism of my family and the implicit belief (because of the religious structure) that Bananas had authority.

The victim is initially unsure as to what is happening. The behaviours become sexual so gradually, there's the 'boiling frog' aspect – the notion that the change is imperceptible and by the time it becomes physically injurious, it's too late to react.

At the time, the thought of sharing your discomfort seems impossible, that you won't be believed. I was trapped by Bananas in a constraint created by him, utilising the unconscious support of my parents, a priest, an organisation – and executed by him perfectly.

As time went by, I began to be very adept at living separate lives. At school, I developed a persona that was quite 'showy'. I defined myself by my achievements either on stage or as a quick-witted joker, often at the expense of teachers, which brought the approval of classmates. With Bananas I became part disciple and part carer. He was a chronic asthmatic and had spent a significant amount of time in hospital as a child. When I was with him, I was constantly on call to grab his inhaler, or to stand and watch as an attack would leave him heaving for breath. Some of these attacks were quite distressing and on the frequent occasions where I'd be staying at his house or at the club, they could render me almost paralysed as to what to do.

> Should I know what your breath-falls mean?
> An urgent call to action or to rest unseen.
> 'Fade', 1994

And I was staying with him more and more. With hindsight this all seems so strange; the thought that a teenage boy would be buddying up to a man ten years his senior to the point that he'd be staying overnight with him so frequently. It started when I was twelve or thirteen. Work had begun at the Boys' Club to renovate a stable block into a permanent centre with kitchen, showers, workshop, living room etc. As the work progressed, two things happened. Firstly, I became quite adept at helping Bananas with rudimentary carpentry, plumbing, brickwork and electrics.

Secondly, this became an excuse for our staying at the under-construction club in Oxford and/or at the lodgings he'd begun renting. My family were pretty hard up and there were none of the extras that many people took for granted. We were fed on low-cost, high-volume meals: stews, casseroles, macaroni cheese, toad in the hole, and there were no luxuries like ketchup, sugary cereal, any type of fried breakfast, anything other than water in your glass. Bananas would always offer enticing food and drink. I can recall the first time he cooked me a whole gammon steak and chips; as a pre-teen this seemed impossibly indulgent.

As I grew older, towards thirteen or fourteen, he began to take me to the Mitre, a Berni Inn in Oxford, where I was initiated into some of his ideas as to how 'proper' people ate. Always putting cutlery to the side of the plate between mouthfuls, eating peas with a knife and fork, never buttering a roll; instead, piling a wedge of butter on the rim of the side plate and applying a smear to each individually torn mouthful. These snippets would be dispensed as I greedily drank Coca-Cola or, increasingly, lager.

From his point of view, there may have been something of the 'Pygmalion' to this. Bananas *maybe* felt that he was Professor Higgins, ironing out the flaws of the potty-mouthed and unsophisticated oik, but rather than wanting to present me at a garden party he was instead moulding me into a companion to shore up his own inadequacies. Maybe. The trouble with that hypothesis is that it ignores the paucity of his intellect and the extrovert potential that I displayed and he tried to curb. He was a vampire, feeding off something within me that he lacked.

In the second year of middle school, as I began to mature, his sexual obsession and inuendo ramped up and became physical. Under the pretext of two years as spiritual advisor, having dismantled the connection to my parents and established a pattern of frequent and intimate cohabitation, Bananas' escalating yearning combined with his behavioural incontinence.

I can't recall the very first time that, in the midst of turning a conversation to sex, he was erect and masturbating. I can't remember if the first time he did this he was wearing underpants (navy blue, white waist band and Y-front), a dressing gown (white linen), trousers or maybe stepping from a shower. But I can remember the sight of his penis. Small with a very tight foreskin that wouldn't retract fully. I can feel it sticking into my back and buttocks as I gradually wake at night to realise that he's got into my bed (either because he's cold or having an asthma attack). I can remember (and this is invariably how I'm awakened from the nightmares) the pain in my bollocks as his hands gripped me tightly trying to do – god knows what? I can remember staying at his house and using the absent lodger's bedroom, then his arriving at the door, coming in and 'hey presto!' finding a porn magazine under the mattress like a malevolent Paul Daniels. He sat on the bed and leafed through the magazine with a feigned disgust at each picture, then started touching the pictures, then himself. In my memory of all of this I'm frozen – desperate for it to stop.

Silently mouthing like sailors adrift in a storm
Blindly repeating the mantras that help you feel warm
And your tears feel so wrong
But you just carry on
'God & The Aeroplanes', 1999

He'd bought a house in Didcot when I was thirteen and that made it much easier and more convenient for him to have me stay over. To this day I have no idea how my parents felt it was reasonable, necessary or in any way healthy for this to happen – *in the town where we lived* – but it did.

There were countless occasions in darkened bedrooms where I'd feel his sleeping form move and I'd know that would be the precursor to a hand sliding across towards me. Sometimes I'd pretend to be asleep – turn over with my back to him, tensing my thighs and buttocks tightly. He was around thirteen or fourteen stone and I was a whippet of seven or eight stone. The house in Didcot had two sash windows onto the street through which the streetlight flooded. On one of the nights, the wind and rain lashed the windows, making it harder to pick out the pattern of his breathing. I muttered a mantra in my mind over and over: 'Please don't, please don't, please don't'.

I'm not sure there's much point in detailing more of this. There is much more, but, as far as I was concerned, not much worse. As far as I'm aware, he never penetrated me. I only qualify that because if I mentally leaf through those years there are some memories that get somewhat hazy or just – stop.

> Chained to the ground and the sound of the footsteps at your door
> Seen – unseen, scrubbed so clean. Walk away, back for more
> 'Sold', 1996

There were a couple of weird 'chance meetings' with a man at the local college squash courts. His name was 'Ivor Thomas' and he joked that his middle name was 'John' and he had a very large penis. Why he was there at the same time as us and seemed to know Bananas – I'm blank. I'm less blank about the time Bananas had been to a work do in London where they'd screened a porno in a hotel room. That night he disgustedly described it in great detail, telling me how he'd eaten olives throughout (he hated them, so it was 'mortification' so God would be less huffy about the porno stuff) and, as he told me, he ejaculated across his bed and me.

Over the past couple of years, as I've tried to explain the mechanics of our relationship to people, I've maintained Bananas wasn't so much *trauma* for me as a systematic 're-wiring', and in the overall picture I still believe that's true. However, the sexual abuse, such as it was, was a major factor in the efficacy of that re-wiring. It felt really fucking weird but what seems even weirder, in retrospect, is that it became some component of normal.

A Lad Insane

Though starting halfway through middle school had been problematic, having a further change at age thirteen was to prove a blessing. At St Edmund Campion Upper School, my middle school merged with another Catholic middle school from north Oxford and herein, at least for a while, I found my tribe. I was immediately aware of a difference in my new classmates, a commonality that meant I could relax the sharp and defensive act I'd been protecting myself with for two years. We shared enthusiasms, music, TV, books. They wore different clothes than the Bosco kids; there were skinny ties and blazers worn ironically. We were still two years shy of trench coats,

Play with an Irish flavour

but these were the people I'd eventually wear them alongside. For now, we would recycle comedy sketches: *Python*, *Porridge* and *Rising Damp*. There were boys here with older siblings who also liked The Who, Bowie and Television. Having started playing tennis at my primary school and continued at Didcot Tennis Club, this school had courts, a team and a tournament!

There were school plays where I had much stronger rivalry for a part: *Oh What A Lovely War*, *The Plough and the Stars*, and our music lessons were a revelation. In our first year, my NBF Simeon Crace and I wrote and performed a comedy monologue, he on piano, me on words, and we won a Radio 4 competition resulting in my first BBC broadcast.

> Samuel Cesspit went to sea he had the job of a sailor
> His boat was called *The Big Black Bess*, the most enormous whaler.
> *Samuel Cesspit*, Daukes & Crace, 1977

Bananas was absolutely where he'd positioned himself as the most influential relationship in my life and I remained absolutely ensnared, but the day release had improved immeasurably. A common quote, often misattributed to Einstein: 'Insanity is doing the same thing over and over again and expecting different results.' Was I insane? I don't think so, but how else to explain the fact that, having been blessed with an upturn in my prospects at school, I then faithfully exercised my duty to the apostolate.

To be fair, the introduction of some of my new friends to the Boys' Club wasn't the disaster it was before. Simeon, in particular, came from a family who were quite high church and he seemed to delight in some of the more arcane procedures at Grandpont House. The incense-laden air of the oratory held no fear and the cravat-wearing fops who resided there seemed to represent useful fashion inspiration for a boy inspired by Waugh and Salinger. For a year or two, a few of us would attend the club without it impacting negatively on my (school) life and this reached its apotheosis in a ten-day cycle trip to Dorset. This journey was the very best and the very worst of Bananas. Three boys and two adults rode from Oxford to Seaton in Devon, a 240-mile round trip with tents in pannier bags through rain, wind and sun. We were trusted, pushed and given responsibility. Unfortunately, there were a couple of incidents in my sleeping bag I'd rather forget and a night spent in a public toilet (following our tent being flooded) that will live in my memory, at least as far as the atmosphere was concerned.

It was in Year Five that my friendship began to drift from Simeon; he distanced himself from me in the common room and, ironically, started to bond more with some of the boys from John Bosco. In recent years I've wondered whether Bananas had found any of the other boys at the club too tempting, or whether, as a few years previously, they'd just started to think it (and, by association, me) all a bit weird.

Three Chords and the Truth

My older sister Janet could play a little flamenco guitar and sometime around my being fifteen or sixteen she showed me the chords Em and Am. I was immediately able to play the first three Echo & the Bunnymen singles. G, D and C followed, and they were put to work on *Ziggy Stardust*, which sounded as good as you'd imagine played by a teenager with no experience at all on a Spanish guitar. Having cracked the chordings and most of the strummings, I was offered an electric guitar by a boy called Marius who got the train to school with me in the mornings. The guitar was an un-named semi-acoustic and it came with an amp that Marius (an electronics wizard with an account at Tandy) had made himself. Instead of speaker grille it had a flap of floral curtain material and Marius's wizardry hadn't extended beyond a single control – a volume knob that definitely didn't go to eleven. The knob was emblazoned (as all Tandy products were) 'Realistic' and as I carried the guitar and amp home through the streets of Didcot, this description seemed, if anything, 'Optimistic'.

A school band formed with a simple, direct line-up: the classic *guitar,* drums and piano. Yes, it worked for The Doors, but it's still like the classic fried breakfast of bacon, egg and grapes.

There are crucial moments in the formation of any great musician's career, moments that occur early on – before the onset of mastery, before even the onset of adequacy – where the delicate shoots of a nascent talent give the merest hint of the extraordinary fecundity and flowering to come.

We had none of these, but instead played 'My Old School' by Steely Dan using three chords. For the entire lunch hour.

There would be bands, at school and beyond, but the truth is that what was happening at home was about to dramatically alter the course of recorded music. At least for me.

Cassette Boy

The Aiwa music centre, with its satin-metal and walnut-effect fascia, its fluttering, glowing VU meters, its silky sliding controls and extraordinary ability to play records, the radio and *eyes on stalks, head flips open* COMPACT CASSETTES! had landed in our front room like an exotic, sexy spaceship from another galaxy. Amongst the woodchip, cork tiles, rented Baird TV, onyx bowl and vase of teasels it stuck out, not so much as a sore thumb, but rather an entire hand of thumbs – each of which had been struck with a mallet.

The music centre had landed in 1976 and had revolutionised the playing of (and listening to) existing music. Music that, because of the checks and balances of the record company and broadcaster paradigm, was of a certain 'merchantable quality'. Nothing emerged from the speakers that hadn't been

approved by either the marketing machine of a major label or the music programmer of a radio station. All of that was about to change as my dad, emboldened as he was by the purchase of the Aiwa three years previously, decided that he needed a further cassette deck. The intended function of the Akai standalone cassette deck which became known absolutely always by its full title 'The Auxiliary Tape Deck' was to enable Dad (who was now working in nearby Swindon in the training department of an insurance company) to be able to tape record various sales scenarios with trainee salesmen.

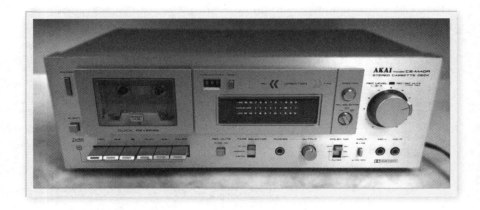

By bringing The Auxiliary Tape Deck into my world, Dad had performed the same function as the Morgan Freeman character Red performs in *The Shawshank Redemption* when he procures the rock hammer and girly poster for Andy Dufresne.

With these simple tools:

- I could tunnel relentlessly from this claustrophobic incarceration in my Didcotian prison cell!
- I could seek my redemption!
- I could hammer out my own rock!

I could have, but I didn't.

Instead, I did so much less, that (in the absence of my knowing that those were options) still felt like so much. I worked out that by 'bouncing' between the music centre and The Auxiliary Tape Deck with only one of the stereo plugs connected, and by connecting my guitar to the other connector, I could add guitar parts to each other. I had inadvertently stumbled on the alchemic process of 'overdubbing' which had actually first been stumbled on in the late 1940s and was by now commonplace throughout the entire world.

But hitherto not in mine.

It marked the first occurrence of what has become a pattern throughout my life. The acquisition of practical skills that enable the production of ideas that might otherwise not have been facilitated through traditional channels. This was summed up in *Word* magazine's review of my 2008 solo album *Promise* as 'an Orson Welles-like, mono-creator attitude'. It's a pattern that has enabled me to make music, radio, television and film that I would otherwise have been prevented from making – prompting the philosophical question: 'Just because you *can* do it, does that mean you *should* do it?'

It also set me on this path of trying to understand and explain through music, comedy and film the trauma I experienced between 1974 and 1980.

Shadowman
(excavating the toxic hazard)

In early 2020 I came across a folder in my loft emblazoned with a sticker on the spine: 'toxic hazard'. I'd applied the label at some point in the 90s as a typically self-deprecatory joke. Inside it was every lyric I'd written from the age of sixteen through to about a decade ago. Over the following few weeks I sifted through these documents and, each time, there'd be another one that would blindside me. There were songs that directly alluded to my childhood abuse and many more where I mercilessly and unflinchingly took myself to task in the present. Of all the songs in the folder, none was more direct than 'Shadowman'.

I'd written 'Shadowman' in late '92, very early in the life of my band FIN and, at the time, I believed that I was describing the intentions and actions of an imagined protagonist. This was a technique that I was to repeat on many occasions and each time seemed to follow a similar pattern. Often there would be a first verse written from a more detached perspective, looking at a condition or circumstance. Then, in the second verse or bridge, I'd revert

to a first-person narrative. I can honestly say that, at the time, I had no idea whatsoever as to why I was writing what I was. In retrospect it's unfortunate that I described the Shadowman as 'an eight-armed beast' as I was one of eight children and Dad was a kind and compassionate man whose greatest crime was to be somewhat emotionally distant. I'd hate to think that anyone might have heard the song and felt suspicious of him.

All he wants is one ambiguous touch,
a secret between you that's never discussed
He's an eight-armed beast, with blood on his hands
He's the angel of death and a family man
All he wants is one delicate kiss,
a harmless request but the problem is this
His fingers are razors and his willpower is weak
He takes the light from your eyes, puts the shoes on your feet
Shadowman - showing in his twisted smile
Shadowman - he won't let you be a child
Let me go... No - no - no
Let me go Let me grow
Love and honour's what you're taught to uphold
Respect for the man that's made your blood run cold
But its fear makes you shake when he enters the room
Then he smiles and says 'shame... that you've grown up so soon'
Shadowman - 'there's no need to be afraid'
Shadowman - memories that will never fade
Let me go No - no - no - no
Let me go... Let me grow'
'Shadowman', 1992

'Fuck Off!'

When I reached sixteen, I finally put a stop to the abuse from Bananas. It was a combination of reaching a tipping point – the compounded realisation that what he'd been doing for five years was wrong, and my getting bigger and strong enough that I could finally resist him physically. On this particular day he'd come into my bedroom, as ever, having intuited that I was getting changed. He'd always had a sixth sense for this although there were likely obvious clues (closed doors were catnip). Maybe for him it was similar to a parent sensing a toddler is up to something because they're 'too quiet'? Maybe my uncharacteristic silence was a clarion call? So many times, I would slope off requiring some privacy and just as I was at the point of maximum vulnerability, there he'd be. On this occasion, he barged in and I was just able to hurriedly pull my trousers up. The 'attacks' (at least when I was awake) were never violent or brutal but more as if he were a greedy child that couldn't resist dipping its hand into a sweet jar. As if it were a tic or behavioural incontinence (which at its least, it likely was).

As he entered the room, he dived towards me and licked my face. Actions like this would be simultaneous with a self-admonishing 'sorry', often accompanied by his smacking his own hand or face – as if the perpetrator and judge were two different people. Frequently as a precursor to a grab or squeeze he'd hum a little three-note jingle (I shit you not it was almost as if he choreographed his own sexual impropriety). This won't make much sense on the page but it was 'rrrum-pum-pum!' accompanied by a little twirl of the fingers. As I write this, I'm concerned I'm drawing up a picture of a kind of noncey Wizard of Oz, whereas he was more like a Fat Child Catcher. Apologies if anyone thinks there's a degree of body-shaming going on here, but, for my money, his flabbiness really played second fiddle to his other fiddling.

I evaded his lurch and shoved him away as hard as I could, spitting 'fuck off!' and pushing him off balance into the wall. The effect was immediate: an almost shocked indignation at my reaction, coupled with an attempt to recover some kind of decorum. From that point onwards his behaviour changed. There would still be half-hearted glances, hand movements and clumsy contrivances to ingratiate, but I'd shown an adult strength and, as such, likely made myself much less attractive to him.

Then he smiles and says 'shame...that you've grown up so soon...'
'Shadowman', 1992

At this point, five years of sexual abuse stopped and it coincided with my beginning to play the guitar and write. I think it was coincidental, but as I seem to have misunderstood why I've written almost everything, ever – then maybe it wasn't. In which case someone should initiate a study into phasing out the prescription of Prozac and Zoloft in favour of Fender and Gibson. Healthier for the patients, for sure, but huge side effects for those sharing their house, especially if the side effects become amplified.

For dramatic efficiency (golden rule: make things happen over as short a time-frame as possible) I'd probably skip over the following few years as there are no lyrics that pertain to the abuse until my early twenties. There are lots of 'songs' and they are universally dreadful. Pastiches of The Monochrome

Set, Echo & the Bunnymen, The Cure, R.E.M. – all bands that I could approximate with a handful of open chords, minimal technical ability and a very crude recording set-up. The lyrics are doggerel. Lots of people 'falling down', beauty that 'suddenly falls away', plenty of references to Jesus (but at this stage he's largely impersonal). At the time I really had no idea as to the breadth of what Bananas had done and, in all likelihood, I was numb. But the five years that followed were when I think the real lifelong issues began to germinate.

There's a song I wrote just before FIN split in 1995 and, as ever, I thought was an intellectual exercise: putting myself into the mind of two characters – a boy and a girl – who are (the title's a giveaway) sixteen and twenty-one.

> You're just a boy born in 79
> A pitiful lack of self-esteem will come in time
> Your hope and despair...repetitive waves
> There's no one to throw you out a lifeline
> Hope that Jesus saves.
> '16&21', 1995

Which is pretty much what happened. The abuse stopped around the beginning of my sixth form and it's as if that was the point where the poisonous chemical stopped being added. Then it slowly, imperceptibly reacted within me and effected a change so gradual and so insidious that no one around me was aware. I wasn't aware and it was quite separate from the flashbacks to the physical abuse; they only came out at night – in all too-regular and debilitating dreams. It was way more subtle and crept through and across me like a mould or rust.

Stock Check

Picking at your skin, picking at your feet
Scared to make your mark, slipping underneath
Make me proud of you...make me proud of you...
'Skin', 1998

I was in the summer of my sixteenth year. I'd scraped eight O levels, which included two As in English. I'd bought an unnamed semi-acoustic guitar from Marius and I'd managed to deter the physical interference from Bananas. That was *where* I was. But *who* was I?

By this time, Dad had stopped selling life insurance and was in the far more appropriate role of training life insurance salesmen. In the course of his work, Dad would run a (no doubt American-corporate inspired) character assessment on his trainees and decided it would be fun to try it out on me. It's incredibly accurate and contains many of the traits and foibles that I've carried throughout my life so far. I'm hoping I might recently have kissed at least a couple of them goodbye.

JONATHAN

Motivating Values

Tends to form opinions quickly. Feels that his instincts are right and that a great deal of investigation is not required. Emotional and tends to accept things at face value. Fairly materialistic and respects economic achievement in others. Very creative in aesthetic sense and highly individualistic. Whilst not turned on by wealth, nevertheless is concerned to get value for money. Can be less concerned than average about the wellbeing of his fellow man. Can be overhasty in judgements of others. Keen to enjoy power and authority and seeks recognition. Tries to go along with what others want unless he wants something else strongly.

JONATHAN

MOTIVATING VALUES

Tends to form opinions quickly. Feels that his instincts are right and that a great deal of investigation is not required. Emotional and tends to accept things at face value.

Fairly materialistic and respects economic achievement in others. Very creative in aesthetic sense and highly individualistic. Whilst not turned on by wealth, nevertheless is concerned to get value for money. Can be less concerned than average about the wellbeing of his fellow man. Can be overhasty in judgments of others.

Keen to enjoy power & authority and seeks recognition. Willing to go along with what others want unless he wants something else strongly.

PERSONAL STYLE

Basically a persuasive style, but could well give the impression of being a "conman". Not good at observing the rules and conventions, he is confident, self-assured, outgoing and gregarious. This is tempered with a degree of goodwill towards others.

Tends to work energetically or not at all, although when the pressure is on (or right off) he works more steadily.

Will always be popular, but must be careful not to "over-sell" and to face facts honestly.

Personal Style

Basically a persuasive style, but could well give the impression of being a 'con man'. Not good at observing the rules and conventions, he is confident, self-assured, outgoing and gregarious. This is tempered with a degree of goodwill towards others. Tends to work energetically or not at all, although when the pressure is on (or right off) he works more steadily. Will always be popular, but must be careful not to 'over-sell' and to face facts honestly.

What's striking is the observation that I'm 'confident and self-assured' as I couldn't have felt further from either. It's more than likely that the 'con man' had successfully 'over-sold' to his own father at a time when I'd have preferred him to have been asking me some very different questions. The majority of it hints very strongly at where I was drifting, anchored to nothing internal.

We're Going Up, Up, Up

September 1981 and we had returned to the sixth form as very different young men and women – and with a common room within which we could assert these differences, principally through the use of the record player. Over the summer, factions had emerged as childhood relationships fell away and we began to express our individuality through (the contradiction of) defining ourselves within tribes.

Simone LeBonBon

I wear felt floppy boots, apply eye-liner liberally, have lacy sleeves and a fringe that renders eye contact impossible. Duran Duran are my bag but I'll tolerate the Human League, Adam Ant or even Heaven 17 if I'm drunk enough.

Ian Curt Is

Fi on you, consumer of pap music! I have a raincoat, suede desert boots and possibly a little sailing cap. I also have a floppy fringe, but may have shaved the sides so as to effect the habit of having escaped a mental institution. My gods are Joy Division and Echo & the Bunnymen, but I'll dance to Haircut 100 if I'm drunk enough.

Hugh Corn Will

I'm odd. I'm really bloody odd. I have a book full of random sketches. I might ride a bicycle, though I'll take my test early, borrow my dad's Austin 1800 and be designated driver. My clothes are all black and I've some tentative facial hair which is maybe stylistic but more likely an acne-distraction. There *are no other bands* than The Stranglers, but I'll nod my head to The Doors if I'm drunk enough.

Although music was one component of our expanding lives, to me it felt all-consuming and defining. This was something that I understood, there was no second-guessing required and no element of doubt within me. I'd felt it from my early years of being played Who records by my uncle and my brother, I felt it when I first heard Bowie and I was hearing it now incredibly clearly – more clearly than I'd ever heard anything. Echo & the Bunnymen made music that I could understand and *almost* play. The first track of theirs I ever heard was 'Rescue' and, in some small way, I was already seeing music as salvation.

Dreams, journeys, flow through my mind
And the songs, you seeded. Saved my life
'The Virus', 2010

The school landscape had changed immeasurably and I had a strong sense of contradictory forces at work.

Society demanded that we were now personalities of reason, less inclined to display the erratic outbursts of teenage experiment. We were socialising at weekends and beginning to form deeper romantic relationships (or attempting to) yet were expected to study semi-permanently in order to achieve academic grades for our next transition (in my case this included English, Geography and Sociology). Maybe these things occur concurrently for most seventeen-year-olds, but I was feeling something that would become very familiar over my coming years: that I wasn't *ever* doing the right thing at the right time. Being in the here and now always felt uncomfortable and slightly alarming. I'm not talking about FOMO (Fear Of Missing Out) as this could happen at 9:30am in a Geography lesson as easily as if I were at home alone or at a packed bar on a Saturday night. It was more like a yearning to be *anywhere but here, all of the time.*

To calm this feeling, I unconsciously started doing something that I still do to this day: *balancing.* The onset of this was really quite all-consuming. It may have been in an English class. My right foot tapped against the table leg and I *had* to tap the left, except I did it three times, then tapped a further one with my right R – L – L – L – R. This needed balancing and so it was followed by L – R – R – R – L a set of ten, this felt good – but internally there was a demand that it was merely a component part of the construct that was required, which I then set about. These couldn't be alternate as (for some reason) the construct needed to be two matching sets of fifty with a distinct internal structure.

So, the century was tapped thus:

R – L – L – L – R	L – R – R – R – L	R – L – L – L – R	L – R – R – R – L
L – R – R – R – L	R – L – L – L – R	L – R – R – R – L	R – L – L – L – R
L – R – R – R – L	R – L – L – L – R	L – R – R – R – L	R – L – L – L – R
L – R – R – R – L	R – L – L – L – R	L – R – R – R – L	R – L – L – L – R
R – L – L – L – R	L – R – R – R – L	R – L – L – L – R	L – R – R – R – L

These sets became a framework that gently fluttered away at the periphery of any activity. They would be performed by feet, fingers, thumb and little finger of alternate hands, a pencil against an exercise book (padding good) or a pencil-top rubber (soft percussion – really good). Over the years these have become rhythmically and mathematically complex, though never thought out, premeditated or considered (until *very* recently). They've made me hyper-aware of: hi-hat patterns by drummers, the contrast of *finger vs pick vs felt pick* by bass players, *wooden vs felt kick-drum beaters* (with or without click-pad) and have, on occasion, made me nearly incapable of getting off a tube train in time ('I'm not *finished*!'). They've also developed to a point where they don't demand a strict decimal pattern, timings becoming dictated more by rhythm and the need for odd time signatures to then be 'encompassed' or packaged neatly by extra additional packets of beats. Simple really.

At the same time as this requirement for order appeared, I ensured that instant liberty was available and bought my first motorbike. It was a Honda 125 Twin and was de-restricted with 16.5 bhp; it felt like a rocket at the time and meant I was no longer subject to buses or trains. It also facilitated a process that was already underway: the subtle shift from my school peer group that ensured I was not part of them, but also justified to me why I wasn't fully accepted by them. I think it was a form of *getting an attack in early*; I couldn't judge myself as in any way rejected or failing if the choice to remain distant was my own. This process was aided and abetted, though not through any malevolent intent, by Bananas.

Cry Freedom

Over the past six years, Bananas had gone from being a student, to buying chairs for the Government, to buying lights for Habitat and was now stationed in Wallingford, Oxfordshire – the nearest town to our family home in Didcot. His relationship with my family had changed considerably. Over the course of the nine years he'd been acquainted with the Daukeses, Bananas had progressed from 'ruddy-faced youth club leader', through 'proxy-parent of Jonathan' and 'trusted family member' to his most recent elevation, 'potential suitor to Janet or Joely'. Which, although in retrospect seems criminal, was at least not *actually* criminal.

Though Bananas was no longer a daily physical threat, he continued to be a huge influence in my life. His job at Habitat led to my applying for a Saturday job there, which led to my meeting Mike Taylor. Wallingford was the Head Office for Habitat and the home of its flagship store on the periphery of the pretty Thameside market town. I was an assistant in the lighting department and, on my first break, walked into the staffroom to meet a young man a couple of years older than me with a ginger quiff, thick-framed round glasses, a slimly cut charcoal-grey suit and a skinny 50s-patterned tie.

Mike was a freelance graphic designer who worked weekends to supplement his income and resembled a cross between Kirk Brandon and Richard Coles from The Communards. He was also very funny and we bonded immediately over a shared love of Derek and Clive, to the distaste of all the other (predominantly female) assistants. Mike lived in Abingdon and had to drive through Didcot on his way to work, so we arranged that he'd pick me up the following Saturday. He had a green Vauxhall Victor and the smell of leather, wood and carpet mingled with thousands of red Marlboro was a (now-extinct) wonder of the post-industrial world. As he drove away from my house, I was struck by what a terrible driver he was. My family were all fast drivers, but very attentive. Dad and Mum used a gearbox pro-actively and at the speeds they drove, attention and anticipation were essential. Mike seemed to coast along, looking at me more than the road and was invariably in the wrong gear. We were immediately wrapped up in conversation as he lit the first cigarette of the journey (whilst steering with his knees), then pushed a cassette into the player and changed my life.

'Do you like Magazine?'

'Who?'

I've never had a musical baptism like it. The opening atonal notes of John McGeoch playing 'Philadelphia' on a Yamaha SG1000, the hyper-compressed smack of the kick drum (*wooden beater with click pad*) in counterpoint, Barry Adamson's flanged bass snaking in augmented by *snappy* finger clicks, Dave Formula's keyboard line straight from a 1960s spy movie.

Then the first time I heard Howard Devoto's voice…

Your clean-living, clear-eyed
Clever, level-headed brother says
He'll put all the screws
Upon your newest lover

…and his words.

Buddha's in the fireplace
The truth's in drugs from Outer Space
Maybe it's right to be nervous now

The journey was only twenty minutes long we retired to the car at break *and* lunchtime so I could listen endlessly to Magazine's *The Correct Use of Soap*, an album that remains in my top five records of all time. Meeting Mike was an eye-opener in many ways. As well as introducing me to Magazine, there was The Monochrome Set who we were to see multiple times around much of the south of the UK. Both bands influenced my playing for years to come (of more anon, not *necessarily* a good thing).

I began to help Mike with odd bits of typesetting. He lived with his parents (whom he addressed as 'Pat' and 'Ken' in what seemed the most stupefyingly progressive set-up I'd ever seen). Mike's huge bedroom/studio smelled of Spray Mount and was adorned with amazing posters, artworks and *interesting things*, not least a comprehensive collection of hardcore pornography which his parents would laughingly refer to as 'the mags' with a roll of their eyes, as if he'd left dirty plates on the floor.

I've Got a Bike

Meanwhile, back in sixth form, change was afoot. My meeting Mike had given me a get-out from my schoolmates, from whom I was feeling increasingly disenfranchised. It was Mike's dad Ken who had sold me the Honda that he no longer rode.

I was utterly reckless and not in the slightest 'risk averse'.
I had little sense of self-preservation.
I rode to school for the first time.
I hit the roundabout at Littlemore about 20mph too fast and went right over it, narrowly missing several sturdy saplings.
I'd like to say I learned a lesson…

The motorbike gave me independence and freedom, but further separated me from the common experiences of school. Things had begun to feel uncomfortable and I can't swear if I was reacting to that or in some way contributing to it. Either way, I continued to mark myself out as different. I became evasive and would seek to undermine the trust or affection of those close to me by advertising other relationships. As my schoolmates began to explore their coming of age together, I sought the company of people I met at my  Saturday job, cultivating the sense that I had *something better* going on. I'd arrive late and leave early, always apart or in some way different. To an extent this was conditional of going to school in Oxford and living in Didcot, but I had a feeling of not wanting to commit to anything.

Then he's making his excuses to the near and dear he uses...
'Homer', 1995

I've read that victims of childhood sexual abuse frequently seek escape routes whenever they find themselves in a new environment, so as to avoid being trapped or pinned down. I can recognise and understand that feeling, although I couldn't have accounted for it at the time.

On a Geography field-trip I met some students who were a couple of years older and seemed far more exotic and less parochial than my classmates. I made mental notes and within weeks had travelled to London and bought some black leather Johnson's buckle boots, German army trousers, a chunky green jumper and some bandanas. I cut my hair short at the sides, tinted it green and started using eye-liner. It coincided with many of my form group becoming markedly 'preppy' and with my becoming markedly more sullen.

At the same time, I was becoming prone to exaggeration and economical with the truth. I'd always had a capacity for storytelling and a fertile imagination, but this was different. I was altering my behaviour to second-guess and attract the approval of those around me. The first traces of a sense that, somehow, whatever and whoever I was could not be 'enough'.

Slips into an act for you as easy as you please.
Punctually late and then arrives and then he leaves.
'Homer', 1995

The darkening moods weren't connected to any sexual frustration, as this had recently been relieved on a regular basis by a clearly unfussy girl in my Geography class. Her dad was a marriage guidance counsellor and I'd like to think he found inspiration for his clients in the muffled noises through the wall that interrupted the nine o'clock news. As I sheepishly arrived back after curfew on my bike from Oxford, I'd face increasingly ferocious tirades from my mum. Looking back, it seems extraordinary that she had a sixth sense for what her seventeen-year-old son had been doing with another consenting seventeen-year-old, but had been blissfully unaware or unconcerned with what her teenage son had been subjected to when staying with a man ten years his senior.

And do you suppose, the son you gave birth to is really so low?
And I find I say yes when I want to say no
'Back To The Towers', 1997

As upper-sixth began and our workload expanded, I spent an increasing amount of time in my bedroom, smoking out of the window and playing guitar rather than doing homework. I wasn't the first teenager to become withdrawn and obnoxious, but the situation of being in a home where I was being treated with less love and respect than the man who'd sexually abused me was a recipe for conflict. In terms of my understanding what I'd been subjected to since I was eleven there was, as far as I can recall, nothing.

I walk into a room of toxic fumes and light a match
My means of self-expression seems to have no safety catch.
'Precious', 1995

My schoolwork became less important and from being a reasonably engaged or at least personable student, my teachers noticed a surliness creeping in rather than the good-natured cheek they were used to. I was able to coast through English; as long as I was reading then I could produce half-decent essays. Geography and Sociology not so much. I'd chosen Geography because, from my clutch of C-grade O levels, it seemed the least academic. Sociology was chosen out of desperation: I needed a third subject and rumours abounded that Sociology was a doss. Sociology wasn't a doss; it was actually quite taxing and, had I been even remotely engaged, I'd likely have found it quite fascinating. But I wasn't, so I didn't.

The bike meant that I could arrive just in time for lessons, go out in the lunch hour and leave immediately lessons ended. My increasing detachment must have come across as a sneering superiority, but I preferred to be considered arrogant than what I perceived as needy. I'd stop by Mike's sometimes on the way home, anything to delay returning to what was becoming non-stop confrontation at home. Aside from loving the paraphernalia of his work (scalpels, Letraset, artboards, Rotring pens, Spray Mount), he was generous with information and I'd begun to learn some of the rudiments of typography and graphic design. It was Mike who made me aware of kerning, leading, what 'rivers' were in a block of type and some of the basics of logo design. All of this was to prove very useful when I became an assistant editor and made me a tyrannical stickler with my assistants on becoming an editor.

'and this...is me'

I first saw Rik Mayall performing as 'Rik the People's Poet' on a TV special from the Comedy Store. His hysterically earnest artist persona, constantly indignant at not being treated with respect, his paper-thin ego and aggressive demeanour immediately chimed with me. Although it would be another two years until Rik from *The Young Ones* angrily announced his intention to write to 'the lead singer of Echo & the Bunnymen', this monstrous and reactionary comic confection could practically have *been* me. Shortly afterwards he played a character called Kevin Turvey: Investigative Reporter and I became obsessed. He was immediately promoted to my bedroom wall alongside Bowie.

There was something magical in his digressions, non-sequiturs and misplaced passion that I loved. There was a strange side-effect to this as, in the ongoing domestic war with my mum, I'd hear Rik's injured passion in my voice and would unconsciously find myself mimicking the cocked eye and lip sneer (stopping short of flicking the inverted Vs).

MUM

What's that face for?

JONATHAN/RIK

What face?

Jonathan looks Mum up and down with Rik face.

MUM

That! You did it again.

JONATHAN/RIK (heavy sarcasm)

Oh! Wrriight!

MUM

What?

When Rik passed away so tragically prematurely, I felt a profound sadness. I'd not continued our journey through *Bottom* or *The New Statesman* (as good as they undoubtedly were), because Rik (and Kevin) had been my friends – at that time and in that situation. I think many of the passions I adopted at that time were particularly important because they were unmolested by the presence of Bananas (he had zero musical taste or interest and wouldn't have understood Rik) and didn't rely on my having to interact with people. As well as motorbikes and making music, it was around this time I started distance running – another solitary pursuit. This tendency has remained true through most of my life in regard to creative projects. When I become immersed, I can tend to be distant from those around me because the projects become my 'company'.

In copying Rik, I was doing what countless other teenagers did, trying on a suit of clothes to see how they fit. Similarly, if I listen back to the cassette recordings of my early songs, I can hear exactly who each song is a thinly veiled copy of. There are poor facsimiles of The Monochrome Set, The Cure, Bunnymen, R.E.M., Joy Division (though no Magazine who, I think, were too musically adept and complex for my rudimentary skills). Over the next few years, in fact up until 1992 when I formed FIN, I careered through various cringe-inducing musical incarnations and the closest I came to writing anything that pertained to the pollution of my formative years were occasional diatribes about religion.

With one notable exception. A demo I came across on a cassette in the summer of 2021. From the instrumentation it must have been recorded on my four-track cassette Portastudio, with the drum track from a Roland 808 drum machine, so I would have been twenty. It's really basic, but has some rudimentary backing vocal and even some backward guitar. Until I played the tape, I had no recollection of the song which is extraordinarily direct and specific. I can remember many of the songs from this period, playing them in rehearsals or at gigs, sometimes even writing them. But not this. As such I can't recall its title, although it does repeat the line 'this heaven is hell' so maybe it was called 'Heaven is Hell', which seems as good a title as any.

I mustn't let myself relax or fall asleep
Can't escape this world. Can't escape this world.
Stay quiet, stay still, stay calm, this panic will retreat.
Can't escape this world. Can't escape this world.
This suffocating weight this struggling for breath.
Can't equate this worth. Can't equate this worth.
Another creaking sigh, another little death.
Cannot make this worse. Cannot make this worse.
This heaven is hell. This heaven is hell. (Rpts)
Can't escape this world. Can't escape this world.
Cannot make this worse. Cannot make this worse.
'Heaven is Hell', 1984 (?)

The song has a very basic rhythm and I'd obviously been listening to The Cure's 'Seventeen Seconds', but what really took me aback was the vocal. It's so much calmer and more intimate than anything else I did at the time, albeit with an affectation that sounds a bit like Ian Curtis of Joy Division. I think it's quite centred because I care about what I'm singing. Everything else before (and for a long time afterwards) was trying to learn composition and structure through impersonation. The one time I wrote a lyric, albeit in isolation, that came from a place of truth, I delivered it with a relative lack of melodrama. In terms of approaching what I'd lived through, it was as direct a song as I'd ever written, yet I wouldn't come close to the subject again until almost a decade later. It's a weirdly isolated piece of work, like a daffodil that decided to pop up in November, or an iPhone in an Ealing comedy, and I can't work out how it got there.

School's Out (forever)

Most of my upper-sixth seemed like a blur. I carried on working Saturdays (and increasingly Sundays as well) at Habitat, earning enough money to buy a new amp and keep my bike fuelled and on the road. Keeping it on the road was proving tricky as my enthusiasm consistently outpaced my skill, meaning I was frequently finding corners approaching faster than they were supposed to. Also approaching faster than they were supposed to were my A levels, revision for which was hampered by the motorbike and the new amp.

I have a common anxiety dream, which is actually not too unpleasant because at least if I'm having it, I can't be having a much more unpleasant dream about Bananas grabbing my balls. In the less unpleasant dream, I'm sitting in front of a vast array of lever-arch files which are stuffed with Geography revision modules.

In the dream, I'm explaining to a faceless authoritarian figure that there is no need for me to revise any of this stuff because I'm going to learn how to edit films, write songs for money and do a Brummie voiceover as a Belgian goose-farmer who talks about making porn. All of these things will very soon come to pass as: I will become an editor, sign a music publishing deal and be the voice-artist for Channel 4's *Eurotrash*. I didn't know I'd go on to do any of those things when I didn't do any Geography (or Sociology) revision, but my mantra in the dream, 'I'm not going to need any of this…' was certainly true. I didn't do any Geography or Sociology revision and consequently got two Es which, when added to my B in English enabled me to spell BEE with my results. So, that's good. They didn't allow me to take up my offer from Manchester to read English (although there was further hope through clearing) but, in the end, as Jeremiah 29:11 almost says: 'I know the plans I have for you declares the Lord and they will speak of much else than education…and maybe a crash or two'.

By the summer of that year I'd all but stopped seeing anyone from school and as the exams came to an end, I wasn't part of the round of parties and pub crawls.

> Another evening, another missing person
> Another cheap thrill, another pointless x-ray
> I ride my luck, I ride my bike, I ride your wave
> Reset my sight, reset my life, reset your name
> 'Coliseum', 1997

There was a camping trip to Bournemouth but I went on my motorbike, arrived late and left early. Riding home I felt as if I were escaping, fleeing from a group of people I'd decided I wanted no part of but feeling, deep-down, wanted no part of me. A familiar refrain for years, *get your attack in early*. As I rode away, I knew I'd never see any of them again. My enthusiasm to take flight was, yet again, greater than my riding skill and I drifted wide on the exit of a roundabout in Ringwood. I caught the kerb, the bike flipped and I skidded face-first across the pavement for several yards. Slamming into road, vehicle or track was to become something of a habit over the years and this was relatively low speed. Fortunately, Dad had always insisted on a decent helmet and gloves, but I'd torn my left kneecap open on impact and was badly bruised through my elbows, chest and shoulders.

The odd thing when you crash a bike is that (unless you're completely incapacitated) your first concern is for the stricken machine. In this instance the damage was all to the left side. Gear lever bent up (but still just operable), clutch lever snapped in half (but still just enough to squeeze with two fingers), headlamp and indicator smashed (but it was midday and sunny) and the left-hand fork had stoved the tank in (cosmetic damage only). Having picked it up and after fifteen minutes to assess the damage to myself and the bike and allow the flooded carburettors to clear, I was ready to go. Except I really wasn't. There was a lot of blood pouring down my shin and despite it being a hot July day, I was shivering. But I was in Ringwood and lived in Didcot, which was a good two-hour ride away. So, I got on and I rode. And my knee started to throb. And when I stopped for petrol near Whitchurch, I nearly fell over. And I was still shivering. And then it got very cloudy and there was torrential rain and I didn't have a headlight. But then I was at Newbury and then Didcot and I rode into my front garden. And then I did fall over.

Someone called Mum and Dad and they ran out of the house. Mum saw the gelatinous lump of bloody training shoe and put her hand to her mouth, 'Oh my god, Colin!'

In response, I should have said, 'It's only a fucking shoe, what about my fucking heart?' But she wouldn't have known what I meant – and neither would I.

A Man Called Rex

I may or may not have still had a mangled knee, but nevertheless, I left to see Chris in Grenobles. A sentence that an English teacher would shit themselves over if it were the opening of a piece of creative writing as it possesses back story, intrigue *and* potential.

Chris was my cousin and a year older than me. We'd spent most holidays together when we were younger but drifted apart through our teens. He was doing a French degree and somehow or other we decided I should come and spend a week with him. We had a great time: drank beer, smoked weed, listened to Joy Division bootlegs and cut each other's hair – all at the same time. But it was the journey there that stands out as I was to meet one of the best friends I've ever had: R.E.M.

I caught the train to Dover and boarded the ferry, making my way to the upper deck where I stood in my mac, buckle boots and cap, trying my best to look enigmatic. The suitcase I'd borrowed from my mum was a turquoise weave and looked like an Avon lady's bag, so the whole 'enigma' thing was struggling. Further down the deck, wearing a tribal outfit not dissimilar to mine but recognisably 'other', was a young man a year or two older than me with a really unusual bag. It quite obviously had a bicycle in because it was the exact shape of a bicycle and disguised its contents as effectively as a goat wrapped in cling film. Although I didn't yet know it, the man was Rex D West from Boulder, Colorado and he was on his way from London to visit his brother who was at the Le Coq mime school in Paris. Rex thought I was staring at him whereas I was actually staring at his shrouded bicycle and thinking: 'Why not just wheel your bicycle? Why carry a bag that is basically just a bicycle-shaped canvas shroud with a handle?'

Rex gave me a slight wave of his hand as if to say, 'Hi'. He was already the coolest person I'd ever met and I'd not yet spoken to him and heard his mumbled, sleepy drawl. Then he said, 'Hey', so I had. I wandered over, trying to look inscrutable.

I was Ian McCulloch with a bag of make-up samples. Rex's blonde quiff buffeted in the breeze that was flecked with spray like ocean rain. 'You like the Bunnymen, right?' He was, of course, right and had deduced as much from my outfit that was more a uniform than I reckoned. I half expected him to follow up with, 'Do you have an Autumn Gold blusher with a Forest Haze lip-liner?' but thankfully Avon hadn't reached Boulder (or he was just being nice). We immediately bonded over a shared musical cannon: not only did we both love Joy Division and the Bunnymen, but I'd actually seen them live, which somehow gave me a homegrown credibility that this young American respected. We went inside out of the increasingly wild wind and our conversation proceeded keenly.

Rex had been living in New York for a year on the Lower East Side and had a weekly show on college radio called *Out Of Step*. He was a huge fan of English New Wave, but referenced a stack of American music I didn't know. He was particularly enthused by Hüsker Dü and R.E.M., neither of whom I'd heard or heard of. The ferry journey passed quickly and by the time we disembarked, I'd accepted his offer to stay a day or two with him at his brother's apartment in Paris. We boarded a coach together and Rex produced a cassette Walkman. Would I like to hear some R.E.M?

As I recall, the first track I ever heard was a demo from their *Chronic Town* EP of 'Wolves', but it might have been 'Radio Free Europe'. This wasn't the same crackle of electricity I'd received from Magazine's 'Philadelphia' (though my cassette of that was shared to Rex who was unaware of them and instantly became a fan – *and so it goes*) – the murkiness of those early R.E.M. songs seeped in gradually – but it was the start of a thirty-year relationship that has been almost exclusively rewarding (and I'll forgive them *Up* because true love requires acceptance and sometimes forgiveness).

I stayed with Rex and Steve for a couple of days, then headed down to Grenobles. Chris wasn't a fan of jangly, south-Georgian swamp-pop, preferring punk and dub reggae, both of which I could take in small doses. We bonded over *Joy Division live from the Ajanta in Derby*, which had been recorded from a Walkman in someone's trouser pocket onto a C90, then re-recorded from a neighbouring flat through a sock. Ian Curtis had hung himself a few months previously and his voice seemed all the more desperate in retrospect. Hindsight is a powerful thing.

Wibble-Wibble. Tskribble

I started a band with another lad from Habitat called Andy Knowles. Andy wasn't the world's greatest bass player; in fact he wasn't Wallingford's (or likely even Habitat's), but he was a good laugh and had a Triumph Vitesse which he blew up on the Dorchester bypass.

He'd spent the best part of a year restoring the car from a wreck and I was invited on the inaugural drive. The Vitesse was visually similar to a Triumph Herald, but had a two-litre engine with an overdrive switch in the gear knob. As we hurtled along the bypass, shifting from third to fourth, the revs rising and the straight-six engine throbbing like a Spitfire, Andy turned to me with a gleeful, slightly crazed expectancy in his eyes and shouted, 'And now…OVERDRIVE!' He flicked the switch and we both prepared for the *Back To The Future*-like vortex of acceleration. There was a terrible whining from beneath the bonnet and clouds of black smoke belched out, filling the cockpit. To this day, when anything is about to happen that has any sense of expectancy or excitement, I find myself exclaiming, 'And now… OVERDRIVE!' to the bemusement of anyone in earshot (other than my kids, who've started saying it to me).

Band names are the hardest thing. Almost as hard as writing really good songs or, in the case of Tskribble, about the same hard. Andy Knowles' inaugural test drive of the Vitesse was to herald not our triumph, nor an explosive future, but there was a lot of whining and we billowed a great deal of smoke. We did so much right: we wrote, we rehearsed, we made posters, we had our pictures taken in moody poses.

And yet we did so much wrong: *what* we wrote (and then rehearsed) and then gigged. From our first live performance at The Fleur De Lys in Dorchester (carpeted function room, *huge* doll cabinet) to our next gig at The George in Dorchester ('free to all regulars' – *failed experiment by the publican*). We lit up the Dorchester-area-of-Oxfordshire like a feisty match on a wet and windy moorland. This was followed by 'The Battle of The Bands'

ALTHOUGH they've only been
together as a band, Wallingford-
based band Tskribble have already
started to plan their way to the top.
Guitarist Jonathan Deakins, bassist
Anthony Knipe, and drummer Barry
Light have written a set of 14 songs

If they want just another instrument
said some they think out's mean
cain what is in the shipping all
but our emphasis is clear. The're
at least half of the effort involve
producing a new song."
Despite a lack of experience

Tskribble ma[
out the futur

5 into 3
HOURS of LIVE MUSIC from
THE BEST
LOCAL BANDS
at
ABINGDON COLLEGE
on
MARCH 31st
at
£1·50   8·00pm   £1
from STUDENTS UNION

at Abingdon College, an event that was likely attended by the fifteen-year-old local schoolboys and members of On A Friday who would later, likely inspired by the visceral thrill of the gig, form *Radiohead*. 'Likely.'

Our drummer, a local lad called Barry Light, was the first musician I'd ever played with who could *actually* play, like, properly. He had timing, hit the drums hard and had a decent kit. Therefore, it was very obvious (to me at least) where the problem lay. This was another trait presenting itself, that was to repeat itself throughout my creative 'partnerships'. I've always assumed, whatever the medium, that we (or I) will fly with the eagles rather than scratch about on the farmyard floor. Call it arrogance, call it ambition or it might be that (as David Quantick proscribed) my 'very soul is powered by imps' (me neither). But it never occurred to me that my band *wouldn't* make records, get radio play etc. Tskribble (even the horribly zany spelling was hinting at disapproval – tsk, tsk) were going nowhere and therefore Andy had to go – somewhere. Our problem *couldn't* be that my songs were rubbish, that wasn't even a consideration. It was going to make things a bit awkward at Habitat, but things at Habitat were all set to change, too.

Sunday Girl

The ratio of girls to boys at Habitat was around 8:1 and with quite a high turnover, there would be a fresh staff intake every few months. As the summer warmed up, one Saturday morning brought an anticipatory buzz as, from the staff training room, eight newbies walked across the car park and in through the sliding doors. We watched them approach and (at the risk of sounding like I've only ever seen *The Shawshank Redemption*) it recalled the scene where Andy Dufresne and the 'fresh fish' arrive and step off the bus. We didn't rattle the fences, but only because there were no fences. There was some drooling, but before anyone brandishes a 'toxic masculinity' red card, it was mostly the girls drooling at the sight of six feet and nine inches of the Wallingford (and soon-to-be England) rower Orlando Warner.

I'd been captivated by a blonde girl with a pigtail and very short skirt called Rosetta and, as luck would have it (and as I was now designated a senior sales assistant), she was assigned to my care. Mike and I had a great laugh and pretty much did what we liked in the store. It was a huge space flooded with natural light and enlivened as few furniture shops were (or ever have been) with a music playlist comprised of The Dead Kennedys, 23 Skidoo, The Diagram Brothers, Magazine, Monochrome Set, R.E.M., Joy Division and err – Tskribble.

Our manager was a neat, earnest man who we'd managed to convince that we were utterly devoted to the Habitat career path and (in the finest sitcom tradition) had manoeuvred him to the point where *he* sought *our* approval. Thus, with a musical taste that ran all the way from Genesis to Yes, he'd fallen into our Programme of Cultural Enlightenment. This worked beautifully until the arrival of a new assistant manager from London who immediately said, 'What the fuck is this shit?' and slammed in the approved company cassette. Still, we'd had a great two months.

Whether or not Rosetta shared my musical taste I can't really recall; what I can recall is that our friendship developed very quickly and soon we were sharing pretty much everything. Rose (as she'd now become) and I would take every break and lunchtime together and if we happened to walk past Bananas in the staff canteen, she seemed like a forcefield that prevented him coming near me. The nature of our friendship must have been very obvious; when we came back from our frequent rural rambles and re-entered the store, our dishevelment was plain. I wouldn't so much have the giveaway of *jumper on back-to-front* as trousers, pants and shoes, such was our eighteen-year-old enthusiasm. In this regard I was very much more Jack Russell than Kurt Russell. If our intentions and industry were obvious to fellow employees and Bananas, then they were doubly so to my mum when, in a form of 'reverse apostolate', I invited Rose for dinner at home.

The relationship between my mum and I had deteriorated into 'Cold War in a Siberian cryogenics lab'. The underwhelming A level results were bad. The devotion to a lifestyle based around guitars and cigarettes was worse. The blatant disregard for the Opus Dei-sanctioned Pathological Criminalisation of Human Sensuality was unconscionable. As well as a MORTAL SIN. In reacting to my blatant disregard for the rule of law, an atmosphere had descended on the house (described in autocratic states as a clampdown') and led to my sisters being treated slightly worse than if it were part of *The Handmaid's Tale*. Rose, by contrast, was neither reticent nor retiring (and didn't wear a bonnet).

On the day in question she wore a very low-cut top and a lacy bra that may as well have said: SALE NOW ON! We were late for dinner and Mum was seething. Polite conversation, such as it wasn't, was hissed through clenched teeth until she couldn't contain herself any longer.

'What's that on your back?'

'Huh?'

I stood up and pulled my jumper round. There was straw on my back, quite a bit of straw. It was harvest-time and the surrounding cornfields were stacked with bales; soft, square bales that when pushed together formed a comfortable platform – not unlike a sort of bed.

In 1883 the island of Krakatoa erupted with such violence that the explosion was heard 3000 miles away in Western Australia. All that was left of the island was a vast, bowl-like crater.

Rose didn't stay for pudding.

Where the Word 'Escort' is Used Differently

During my 'relationship' with Rose I'd begun to hang out quite a lot with another girl from the same intake called Katie. She didn't hold the immediate appeal I'd responded to with Rose, preferring to wear clothes that helped her blend in as a sales assistant rather than a high-class escort. We'd chat on breaks and lunch hours where Rose and I didn't coincide and I discovered Katie had two very attractive attributes. She was funny *and* interesting. Who knew?*

* Of course, this is sarcasm about my one-dimensional eighteen-year-old self who had grown up in a system that was patriarchal but, bizarrely, run by a matriarch who had been ideologically co-opted, so not that dissimilar to Aunt Lydia in *The Handmaid's Tale* or a female feature writer at the *Daily Mail*. My point being that *I'm* not making a joke about the fact that women are funny and interesting – but that it was a revelation to my young self. And I took that opportunity for the learnings (and I did learn them).

But, before I took things any further with Katie, there was a car to crash.

Although our domestic life was organised along lines that made the average monastery look like it was a brothel run by Hugh Hefner, my parents were surprisingly permissive when it came to motor vehicles. Dad had a rule that applied to any of us borrowing Mum's Escort Estate: 'You Bend It – You Mend It'. The car was to prove significantly more bendy than my dad's interpretation of the rule as, following a shower of rain on an oily summer road, I spun and piled it headfirst into a vicarage wall, ending up against a telephone exchange. The accident wasn't completely my fault, I explained, as there had been heavy rain on the dry roads which had made them wretchedly slippery and I felt that this was at least in part, an *act of God*. To which my dad gave me a look that said: 'Oh do piss off!' and a sentence that sounded like 'Oh do piss off!' because it was. I'd Bent It – and Dad Meant It. My university plans through clearing were put on hold and the next half year would be spent earning the money to rebuild the car.

Katie was a year younger than me and still had a year to go at college where she was doing French and Photography, having decided around the age of five that she was going to be a director of photography (or movie cameraman). It was my introduction to a part of her character I was to become well versed in: that when Katie decided to do something, she did it. What she also did was say 'yes' when I asked her for a drink. Prior to meeting Katie, I had zero knowledge of the film and TV business. I'd been brought up in a home where TV was *Morecambe & Wise*, *The Two Ronnies* and *Tom and Jerry*. Though we'd been to the cinema once as a family to see *Towering Inferno*, films were mostly off-limits.

Opus Dei had lists of films and books that were 'unsuitable' and they were basically all the films and books that you wanted to watch and read. I'd found my way into Kerouac, Bukowski and Burroughs through an English teacher at school, but the movies were a foreign country. Our first drink was spent talking about music *and* movies. After our drink, we went for another drink and then decided that we wanted to do more than drink. So I told Rose that we were history and she told me that my family were freaks and somewhere inside myself I thought, 'You don't know the half of it...'

Having bent the Escort (which sounds like a sentence from a far racier book than this), Bananas arranged for me to work in a clock factory (which sounds like a sentence from a far trippier book than this). A Habitat supplier in Abingdon called Time Design needed a young and inexperienced teenager who was desperate for cash to assemble bright-red plastic clocks with a glue gun.

Bananas made the call and I began my three months of assembling bright-red clocks with a glue gun, which meant that I was in Abingdon a lot during the day. Bananas had recently bought a flat in Abingdon and I knew where he kept the key. So, when Katie and I decided we wanted to do more than drink, there was a very obvious location beckoning. That might seem weird, but really – compared to most of what's already happened, it's a bit like finding out that Fred West would sometimes wear odd socks. It definitely felt quite subversive at the time, but, in retrospect, I should probably have been more concerned about CCTV.

Unconditional,
That's What You Are

My life from ten years old until meeting Katie at eighteen had been traumatic, confusing and latterly confrontational. My storm-tossed boat was about to find a sheltering harbour, not in an *actual* harbour, ironically in the RAF town of Benson. Having embarked on a relationship basis that Americans call 'dating' but English kids of the time called 'shagging', I was invited to Katie's house one Friday evening. The home was a detached farmhouse in a rural lane, nothing fancy and a den of constantly upgrading electronic equipment, where music competed with TV (or Pink Panther films) and there was the constant industry of food being prepared and wine bottles opening. It was like living the ramshackle and benevolent generosity of a really good episode of *The Darling Buds of May*.

Katie's dad Robin was a BBC sound recordist with a voracious love for jazz, movies and wine. He'd spent years touring the world with Alan Whicker and, whatever we were watching, he'd punctuate regularly with 'I've been there', which was nowhere near as irritating as it sounds. Pat was softly spoken yet mischievous and willingly played the straight woman to Robin, who was always more outspoken. Katie's little brother Patrick was a six foot four giant, who had a great sense of humour and could play *any* Hendrix outrageously well on his Fender Stratocaster through the massive Marshall stack in his bedroom. I was welcomed into this world as if they'd been waiting for me. It was warm, comforting and immediately felt like a home. I crept into it gratefully, like an injured cat backing into a neighbour's shed. This didn't all become apparent on the first Friday evening I went for dinner, but there was lively conversation, delicious food and I heard Miles Davis for the first time.

The second time I was invited it was made obvious it was an overnight which (at this point my head flipped open) included sharing a bedroom with

Katie. In my head, as wrapped as it was in the wires of perverted guilt, this made Mike Taylor's parents acceptance of his 'mags' a pound shop gesture of parental laissez-faire in comparison.

INT: COUNTRY KITCHEN – EVENING

A brick-and-timbered kitchen with an ancient stone-flagged floor. Duke Ellington's 'Caravan' is playing and, for a second, Jonathan thinks it's 'King of the Swingers' but elects not to say anything. Smart move.

PAT

Hello, Jonathan, would you like a glass of wine?

Jonathan does want a glass of wine and knows from his previous visit that there will be many more. Robin stands at the stove, stirring a fine dice of onions, garlic and peppers.

ROBIN

Hello, mate, how are you?

Robin has a trace of a Lancashire accent. Jonathan's unaware, but will soon become familiar with Robin's Preston upbringing becoming more pronounced with every glass of wine.

JONATHAN

Good, thanks, that smells lovely... What is it?

ROBIN

Pollo al Chilindrón de Navarra.

Having worked in Spain on a few occasions, Robin has convinced himself that he's practically bilingual. His accent, when speaking Spanish, is a curious hybrid of Cheech & Chong and Ren & Stimpy.

KATIE

It's Spanish.

PATRICK

But Dad's speaking Mexican.

We dissolve to the candle-lit dining table where there are empty plates and empty wine bottles. There is easy conversation (there was always easy conversation).

INT: LIVING ROOM – NIGHT

A fire crackles in the grate and the five are illuminated by the black-and-white glow of Mel Brooks' *Young Frankenstein*. Patrick and Katie have seen the film (many times) before and know all the lines. Jonathan has tears running down his face and his stomach is aching from laughing. He's never seen the film before, but it will become his *favourite film of all time*. It will never be funnier than this first viewing.

As the film comes to a close with Marty Feldman's Igor playing the French horn in a castle window, Katie gets up and signals to Jonathan to follow. He looks at her, at the oblivious parents, back at her – then slowly, nervously gets to his feet. He crosses the room trying to be silent, unobtrusive, wearing a cloak of guilt that gives him the presence of a massive orange elephant.

PAT

Night-night, you two.

How do you take your tea in the morning?

Jonathan freezes. The game's up. He's been spotted.

He checks behind him for…something, surely there's going to be something bad. He was about to go upstairs to bed with a girl and now her mum knows and something bad is going to happen.

KATIE

He has milk and one sugar, don't you?

I did. I still do, forty years and approximately 17,500 cups of tea later.

As much as I loved Katie (and we were to spend the next eighteen years together) I owe so much to her wonderful family who took me in without realising that underneath the chatty and charmingly boyish exterior, my character was as healthy and functional as a burnt mattress.

Tskribble Rocks On Towards the Big Time

'All things must pass', originally a single by George Harrison but paraphrased in Matthew 24:6, the gist being that change is irresistible. With my debts paid and deferred university entrance a good six months away, I had my eyes on journalism. I'd always enjoyed creative writing and with time to kill before an English degree beckoned, I felt that the local free newspaper, *The Oxford Journal*, represented a good place to get some experience. I wrote to enquire about any openings they might have and soon enough was walking through one – in the front of their building.

The vacancy didn't require my doing any writing; I was supposed to sell advertising space, at least that's what Tim my advertising manager thought. I quickly formulated a cunning plan, which was that I would start selling adverts to music shops, venues and pubs in a loosely corralled classified spread called *Street Sounds*, which would require some editorial at its heart. Tim didn't seem awfully convinced, but when I saw that he had a Triumph Spitfire for sale for £600 and offered to buy it, he warmed to the idea.

Meanwhile Tskribble had recruited a new bass player in the shape of Dan O'Donnell. Dan had been in the year below me at primary school and even attended Boys' Club for a while, dropping out at a wisely early stage.

In 2008 I released a solo album under the project name 'All Our Good Friends'. The cover image was taken by Bananas and features me, aged eleven, leaping off a ramp on my bicycle. Dan can be seen in the background peering through my spokes. It's almost as if he was staring towards our shared musical future – but he was probably just peering through my spokes.

Dan was a very different proposition to the other bassists I'd played with; aside from actually being able to play bass, he understood how to work with a drummer. Some young bands make this transition naturally, some go through a very quick learning curve on their first time in a recording studio, but understanding the basic dynamics and power of bass guitar and kick drum is a vital component of a rock or pop band. There's a similar learning curve for guitarists transitioning from acoustic to electric; the penny drops that you're part of something and you can't just 'saw' your way through from start to finish. I finally learned that sometime around my fortieth birthday.

With Dan and Barry, we had (here it comes) a 'tight rhythm section' and rehearsals began to sound better. The songs were still pretty awful, but there was a certain visceral power beginning to underscore the compositional ineptitude. Around this time, we were spotted at a gig by a chap called Adrian who had a small record label in Oxford and managed a band called Colour Me Pop who were an offshoot of The Thompson Twins. An article appeared in the local paper that he was interested in us and that brought us to the attention of a brilliant local guitarist called Martin, who came and auditioned with us. The difference was immediately obvious. I was a very limited rhythm player, but Martin spun out lead-lines through a vast array of foot pedals. With the *bottom end anchored* by Dan and Barry, and Martin *painting sepulchral-sonic-cathedrals*, my lumpy sculptures, at least superficially, began to resemble slightly less lumpy sculptures. While we we're at it, Lumpy Sculptures would have been a significant upgrade on Tskribble.

Adrian contacted us to say that Colour Me Pop were playing a gig at London's Ad Lib Club in Kensington on a Saturday night a few weeks hence and would we like to support? With the benefit of hindsight (a phrase for which I should think about applying for a loyalty card) this 'opportunity' was a teen movie cliché. Our songs were terrible and we had a gauche provincial naivete, but in our eyes this was a Golden Opportunity and for the next few weeks we rehearsed as if our lives depended on it.

Rehearsals were confined to a couple of midweek evenings and Sunday afternoon. Blewbury Village Hall was in great demand from the South Oxfordshire Brass Ensemble, the am dram stylings of The Blewbury Players, and the Brownies (at least two of whom stood a better chance of signing a record deal than Tskribble). But rehearse we did, with the glow of London's Ad Lib Club shimmering at the end of our M4-length rainbow.

Meanwhile at *The Oxford Journal*, £600 had found its way from my bank account into Tim the advertising manager's pocket, *Street Sounds* had been green-lit and my embryonic journalistic career was underway. The Spitfire was also underway as I sped from the Witney offices of the paper on my way back to Didcot. This pretty little two-seater was from the designer of the Vitesse (as well as many Ferraris, Maseratis and more), Giovanni Michelotti, who would have been appalled at the fact that Tim had neglected to put any oil or water in the engine for far too long. Tim likely drove the car with care and consideration, meaning the temperature didn't rise to the point that the crankshaft seized and the engine blew just outside Marcham (I may or may not have yelled 'and now…OVERDRIVE!).

I voiced my displeasure to Tim in a characteristic manner that meant *Street Sounds* (like the car and my future at the paper) ground to a halt. The big London gig, however, was a week away and surely nothing could cause that to blow up like the hot car had?

I was in my bedroom at home when I began to feel my temperature rising, a slight prickling of my skin, an indefinable 'other-worldliness' that gradually became definable as a headache, which then became a bad headache. I told

Mum I wasn't feeling great and, as usual, the response was 'Have a glass of water'. I had a glass of water but the light through the kitchen window really hurt my eyes and then I threw the water up into the sink and almost fainted. I must have worsened as when Dad got home from work, I'd been put into their bed as the curtains blacked out the room completely and I had become intensely intolerant of any light – and very, *very* hot. Dad entered the room, took one look at me and practically ran downstairs. There were raised voices from the kitchen that didn't reassure me in the slightest, prevalent among them was Dad who clearly said the words 'ambulance' and 'hospital'. Said ambulance arrived shortly afterwards and I was wheeled from the house with a blanket over me and wearing dark glasses. I can remember thinking I looked a bit like Enzo Ferrari, but my brain was pretty much boiling so my testimony of the time is at best 'unreliable'.

A diagnosis was made as we sped towards Oxford and, having ascertained that I had an abdominal rash, I was taken to the Churchill Hospital Infectious Diseases Unit. I'd contracted meningitis and the headache was my brain being squeezed by my inflamed meninges. On arrival I was given a lumbar puncture, a procedure whereby a stud is inserted into the lower back through which a thin needle is slid into the spinal column to withdraw spinal fluid. Sounds simple enough? No it doesn't, does it – and it's not. In the process of inserting the needle, my spinal column was impinged on, causing my legs to spasm outwards like an electrocuted frog. Several times.

Sometime around my fifth day in hospital Colour Me Pop played the Ad Lib Club in Kensington with someone or other in support.

When I got home, my older brother rang to say he'd got me a job. He'd been working for a couple of years at *Autosport* magazine (home of the lady in the tiny pants!). Mum had explained to him how intolerable I'd become and they planned a mini intervention. So, I left Didcot and started work in Teddington selling advertising at *Classic & Sportscar* magazine. Tskribble split up and I wouldn't play in a band again for another decade.

'Pass the mustard, Brian...'

I was nineteen years of age, I'd been out of school a year and was now settled, living and working in London. Katie had started on the BBC Training Scheme based at Ealing Studios and was beginning lengthy attachments as a camera assistant on TV dramas, often working away for several weeks at a time. I wasn't bad at selling and before long I was going out on the road in my ad manager's Fiat 130 TC Abarth, a loan car that I was – uniquely – not to damage in any way. Most of these trips were very odd; our clients were classic car dealers and associated services. They were either 'diamond geezers' or 'terribly nice chaps', united by their adoration of classic cars and complete disinterest in Echo & the Bunnymen. I marked myself out from the cream slacks and blazers of the other sales staff, wearing a razor-sharp, skinny-fit, grey 50s two-piece Mike Taylor had gifted me that we'd christened 'the postman's suit', normally twinned with a skinny vintage tie and some Rokit brothel creepers.

A pattern began to emerge whereby I'd sell a series of ads to a client, be encouraged to do a visit and lunch and by the time I returned to the office they'd have called and cancelled the ads. I can recall the absolutely excruciating silence as I sat at a Guildford restaurant table, my mind whirring furiously, searching a conversation topic and coming out with some impersonation of what I imagined one might be expected to say to a sixty-year-old soft-top restorer.

INT. DAY – PROVINCIAL RESTAURANT

JONATHAN
So, Brian, how's business?

BRIAN
Well, comes and goes, isn't it? Seasonal, like.

A long pause as Jonathan tears his bread roll as he's been taught to by Bananas. Trying to process what effect seasonality might have on soft-tops in order to not say something that will make Brian think he's an idiot.

JONATHAN
Can you pass the mustard, please?

Brian passes the mustard pot. Jonathan puts a dob of mustard on the side of his plate like Bananas showed him, slathers some onto a piece of chicken and pops it in his mouth.
He decides to comment on the likelihood that the warm weather is leading to an upturn in business.

JONATHAN
Business must be improving with the—

The freshly made English mustard tears into his septum, the unique mustardian burn ripping through his sinuses causing his eyes to water and an involuntary gasp to escape his mouth.

JONATHAN

Oooooohhhhhhhhh…

As I drove back up the A3, I berated myself, squirming with embarrassment at the faux pas, but also for the fact that I *just didn't know what to say*. I'm sure that's not an uncommon feeling for a young man being thrown into an alien situation, but the alien situations became more common and the embarrassment was embedded in shame. In the years when I should have been working out *what I thought* and *who I was*, I had been told not to think, say or do what came naturally. This had made functioning considerably more difficult and confusing than it should have been. The one thing guaranteed to take the awkwardness and conflict away was alcohol, and now I was independent and earning money it became a readily available source of comfort.

Like the paper that you waste and the piles of food you taste
To the friends you never made, 'cause you couldn't think what to say
So you had another drink, but it didn't help you think
And your actions false and wild, only make you more reviled.
Why can't you just be you?
'Dressing Down', 1995

1984

You don't speak for me, and God makes you a fool
You've no rational case for his existence
so why would I live by his rule?
And your prejudice rains, disapproval and scorn
A universal spectacular loathing,
you thank God for where you were born

'The Emperor's Old Clothes', 2008

George Orwell's *1984* centres on the consequences of totalitarianism, mass surveillance, and repressive regimentation of persons and behaviours within society. So, in many respects, he could have been writing about Opus Dei. Not strictly totalitarian, but definite *repressive regimentation of persons and behaviours within society*, and 'observing Mass' was frequently part of it.

On 5 May 1984, my sister Janet married the man who had abused me for six years. The warning signs to his behaviour were there, had anyone chosen to look without wearing a certain pair of goggles. These goggles are the same ones that are worn by church leaders who, when an abusive priest is finally brought into the public eye, claim that they either knew nothing or felt that it had been dealt with (see the Australian Royal Commission's findings on Cardinal George Pell in regard to Gerald Ridsdale for details).

Much of this is predicated on the notion of sin (and forgiveness) versus crime. In Bananas' case, had he admitted to a priest that he was having 'impure thoughts' towards a boy, he would have been given an advisory chat by a priest and then told to do 'penance' (likely a number of prayers) and this would guarantee forgiveness from God. If you were to put this to Church authorities or the hierarchy of Opus Dei, they would no doubt point out that if a priest hears of a grave crime, they cannot offer absolution and might advise the protagonist to make themselves known to the authorities, however the sanctity of the confessional is absolute. What this allows is a huge grey area that enables, for example, a child abuser to create a framework that rewards obfuscation and minimising of their acts. With regard to Opus Dei, this confusion extends to a tendency to dismiss child abuse as an inevitable manifestation of adult sexual freedom.

In an article written in 2014, 'Will the unmasking of abusers be a catalyst for change', the current (as of 2022) chaplain of Grandpont House, Fr Andrew Byrne, makes the point that:

> ...what [Rolf] Harris has done is what unremorseful society has been doing for decades. People feel disgusted not just with him, but with themselves. Many of us are doing much the same every day, even if we keep within the bounds of the law.

This confusion as to what consenting adults do (that they believe is a sin) and the conflation of that with what an adult does to a child (which is a crime) is what creates the potential for child abuse to be such a problem for the Church and (at least in my life) members of Opus Dei. His last sentence reinforces that you can be doing something 'within the bounds of the law' (consensual sex with an adult of either sex) and it will still be against God's law. What he is doing is stretching to co-opt the disgust people feel for child abuse and attempting to weaponise that by conflating it with *any* sexual behaviours that contravene the beliefs of the Church. It gets worse as he goes on:

> So what does the law, i.e., the moral code of the Old Testament, say? 'You shall not commit adultery'. And in the New Testament Jesus explains that this law is not only external but governs one's thoughts: 'Everyone who looks at a woman lustfully has already committed adultery with her in his heart.' Christian morality holds that every fully consented action against the moral law in this matter is a serious sin, punishable with eternal damnation. Ouch! No wonder the Swinging Sixties complained about the yoke of a guilt complex. Furthermore, Christianity has no exemptions for age. 'What stains a child, also stains an old man' is a proverb of great sense.

Ouch! Indeed. I've been subject to many lectures from priests of Opus Dei. Their intellectual standpoints inevitably creak and wobble the further they try to engage in discussions as to where their 'laws' stand in terms of (and in relation to) the laws of the land. They will inevitably invoke 'eternal law' that is 'the order of creation in the mind of God'. This will then utilise any number of tortuous conceits from the pen of St Thomas Aquinas, Catholicism's pin-up philosopher. These discussions are frequently attempting to take Catholic doctrine then 'reverse engineer' it to have somehow evolved from a logical philosophical standpoint.

> Don't think, eyeball to eyeball, we don't blink
> With God on our side we define you, undermine you
> 'With God On Our Side', 1998

Aged twelve, I was at Grandpont House confessing my sins (not in a confessional to allow for anonymity) knelt in front of the priest in his sumptuously appointed and highly polished rooms. The priest's name was Fr Joseph Gabiola and I began a game of chess with him that continued until he ran out of pieces and told me that 'you must have faith' (the endgame of any true cultist or 'believer'). The game of chess wasn't strictly speaking a boardgame, but did concern my wishing to *move certain pieces around*.

Every week I would have to kneel in front of 'Father Jo' and admit to the number of occasions on which I'd masturbated. In my early days of this activity (aided and abetted by the appearance of the lady in the tiny pants) these numbers were relatively modest. I can't recall exactly, but it definitely started out feeling like *quite the event*. Within months, the numbers had shot up and his slight flinch and shrug at my admissions had become a barely concealed recoil of shock and disgust. He had an avuncular demeanour and was a cross between Walter Matthau and Ray Reardon. He was in his fifties and had a type of nasal grunt that had become a behavioural tic. As my confession 'hotted-up', the grunting became more frequent and anyone listening outside when I got to the admissions of the emissions might have imagined that maybe a pig was in the room hunting for truffles – which in some ways it was.

Father Jo explained to me that these were terrible sins and that my salvation was in grave danger. I pushed him on the doctrine and it was explained this was based on the Old Testament story where Onan had spilt his seed upon the ground and God had decided that seed was not to be spilled but rather utilised in creation etc. (This was thirteen years before Monty Python skewered it brilliantly in *The Meaning Of Life*, but I'm proud to say I reached the same comic conclusion.) I argued that the New Testament superseded this law but it was pointed out to me that the Church had ordained 'some bits' were still relevant and this got us into the whole Papal Infallibility thing where the Pope sometimes speaks ex cathedra and it's not actually him but God speaking through him and therefore he can't be wrong. Which seemed like an enormous amount of revisionist nonsense to stop you having a wank so I pushed Father Jo further (because I wanted to carry on having a wank, without endangering my salvation) and we ended up in the logical cul-de-sac of 'you must have faith'.

I was led on this journey of contorted logic in likely the same room that Fr Andrew Byrne wrote his article. I wonder what Bananas admitted to in that same room and whether, if it was a cross-over in the Venn diagram of the various priests' thinking, it contributed to the continuance of my abuse? I've no doubt that Fr Byrne's article articulates a logical compound many Church and Opus Dei members skirt dangerously close to with their thinking on child abuse.

Your ritual scenes, and this pageant demeans
If this is what you get up to in day-light
I'm damned if you live out your dreams
'The Emperor's Old Clothes', 2008

Debating this, and any related subject, with believers of an evangelical or extreme Roman Catholic point of view is becoming fraught with problems that render any sort of compromise impossible. There is almost universal support for the Republican party in the US and the Conservative Party in the UK from right across that spectrum of religious persuasion, underpinned by views that are pro-life provided that life is, as yet, unborn. When that child is born, support for it through any kind of social care or welfare disappears. Jesus' teachings are interpreted in the narrowest fashion. It's as if the believers cannot move on any single point lest their entire construct collapse. It's become bound up in a condition we see in the current political divide, whereby if a politician who is on 'your side' says or does something repugnant or at least morally questionable, you give them a free pass as they are supportive of your broad beliefs. The broadcaster James O'Brien describes it as the 'footballification' of politics and says:

'Actions are judged not by an objective assessment of their content but by the perceived allegiances of protagonists.'

Or to display it more simply:

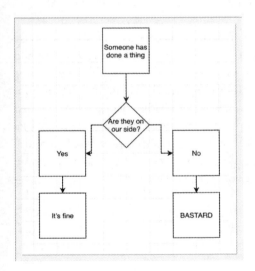

I don't think it's too much of a stretch to suggest that there was an element of this at work in our family. Certainly, as far as my mum's devotion to Opus Dei was concerned, this predisposed her to giving any of Bananas' 'foibles', as she saw them, a green light. The question of what anyone in the family did or didn't know is somewhat murky.

What's also somewhat murky, and strays to the very outer limits of forgiving foibles, is an incident that took place around this time. My point of view of this incident was from the top of the stairs, peering from behind the banister with a good view of the front door. I'd been alerted by the sound of my dad talking in a rather odd manner to what transpired to be two policemen. The conversation was slightly subdued, but clear enough that I could make out what was being said. They were going door to door with a description of a man who'd exposed himself in the area that evening. They asked if my dad had seen, or knew, a man in his mid-twenties with dark hair, wearing a tan raincoat. I knew a man who was downstairs who fitted that description. He'd been out for a walk earlier, but was now in our living room. My dad said goodbye to the officers, closed the door, stood quietly for a moment and then walked down the hallway. I looked at the coat rack, at the tan rain mac and, even after forty-five years and through the murk, I can recall the feeling of discomfort and confusion.

Before Janet and Bananas were married, there was definitely a sense throughout our family that he was a bit odd. One of my younger sisters had mentioned as much to Janet a few months before the wedding but it was brushed off as (bizarrely) jealousy. Those goggles that made anyone around him blind to his predilections (or enabled them to be dismissed as *oddities*) were definitely worn by several people that might otherwise have been able to save some other people a great deal of misery. Instead, he was taken to the bosom of my family and, with my sister, embarked on a mission to promote Abingdon over Tokyo as the most populous place on earth.

Get the Gear In

I'd realised that my primitive recording attempts on cassette players and reel-to-reel recorders were not sounding anything like the recordings of the bands I listened to. I'd seen the insides of a real recording studio once before. After I'd left school there were occasional parties that Habitat girls would invite me to, one of which was in Streatley at the home of Rachel De Freitas, sister of the Bunnymen's drummer Pete – *hallowed ground!* (Pete wasn't there).

Before the party we'd met at a pub called The Bull and that became a more frequent hang-out. One evening, we'd had a few beers with some music types who were recording up the lane at Martin Rushent's Genetic Studio. My memory tells me Marilyn was part of the entourage, but Google tells me otherwise. A few of us were invited up to the studio and, for the first time ever, I set my eyes on a control room with a vast mixing desk.

It was the most extraordinary feeling; although I didn't really know what any of the gear did, I knew it was what was required to make music. With some further reading, I began a crash-course in multitrack recording and made an investment that was the beginning of a habit, as addictive as any pill or powder. Studio tech.

A mixing desk can look incredibly complicated: a vast array of switches, control knobs and faders. They're actually reasonably simple, it's just that on

a desk there are lots of rows of them – but each row does the same thing. In 1985, for approximately £500, I bought a Tascam Portastudio which was a recorder and 4-track mixing desk in one forty-centimetre square case. It enabled me to record several parts together, then play them back varying their levels, shaping the sound and adding effects.

This alchemy took place in a first-floor Teddington bedsit within a vast Edwardian house on Gloucester Road. The other room on the floor was occupied by a City trader called Ady Fairman – who had converted his living space into a bong showroom. When Katie was working, often away for weeks at a time on location, my life revolved around selling at Haymarket, recording in the bedsit and going out drinking in Teddington with Ady. One memorable weekend I experienced my first and only rugby match, except, for reasons (booze) I don't remember much about it and therefore it's a bit of a stretch to say I experienced it. We walked the few miles to Twickenham, stopping at several pubs en route, so by the time we took our place in the stands, I was already experiencing a detachment from the roaring, stinking, rugger-buggered reality. We'd bought two four-packs of Kestrel Super, a beer that advertised itself as possessing: 'a twist of sweet toffee and hints of honey…could be paired with red meats, cheeses and rich desserts'. They should have added that it 'eliminates all sensory information from the eyes, ears and nose and affects an almost complete shutdown of the cerebellum, resulting in one being woken the next morning in one's bedsit by a hammering at the door.'

I got up off the floor, having fallen on it during an abortive attempt to get off my bed. I looked confusedly around the room for whoever it was that had thrown up on my duvet, but reasoned that they must have let themselves out after they'd thrown up on the rug. The banging continued, this time with some further clues as to who was banging.

THE POLICE

Mr Daukes? Open up, it's the police.

It was the police! Had someone called them to deal with the vomiting intruder? There was only one way to find out and that was to let them in and see what was the matter. I crawled across to the table, which I used as a frame to enable me to raise myself onto my knees. The men at the door who said they were the police were still keen to come in.

THE POLICE

Mr Daukes, is that you? We'd like you to open the door, please.

I was absolutely intent on opening the door to the police, but the door was a good ten feet away and I was now engaged in the process of getting to my feet. I briefly contemplated shuffling across on my knees, but the thought of getting a splinter from the wood floor felt awful and that made me do a little sick which I caught in my hand but at least that cleared up one mystery. That left me with only one unoccupied hand, which slowed the whole standing process down a bit so I told the police I'd be there as soon as possible.

ME (muffled)

Bin floor...mmm...bit sicky...mmm

THE POLICE

Are you OK?

Having already thrown up, the thought of shuffling to the door on my knees no longer seemed quite so terrible, so that's what I did. From the other side of the door (the policemen's perspective) this must have happened much more slowly, but eventually, after the scraping of my crossing the floor and grunting sounds produced by my straining to reach upwards for the latch, the door creaked open. Maybe, at first, I appeared to be a dwarf? A dwarf who was only wearing quite dirty boxer shorts, a T-shirt stained with many things and a cupped hand full of sick.

The policemen explained that they'd arrested a man who was found to have my wallet in his overcoat pocket. This was clearly Ady, the manybonged City trader, and I asked why they'd arrested him. He'd urinated all up the passenger window of their car, whilst they were in their car. This made me want to be sick again and so I was sick again, then the policemen tossed me my wallet and left. It can only have been a few days later that Katie's dad asked me a question that meant I also left the bedsit.

And sales.

And the last remnants of a life I still connected to home.

A Sweetheart Contract

Katie's dad Robin had an old friend called Dick Lane who was the facilities manager of a small West London post-production facility called Crow and had mentioned to Robin they were looking for a runner to service their film-cutting rooms and video edit suites. Robin called me and asked if I was interested. I knew very little about the film industry and much less about post-production, but I knew very little about most things and it had to be better than sharing awkward meals with people like Brian. So, I phoned Dick Lane.

In a world of faith and angels, a land of dust and dreams
Backpack full of boulders, you set off for the steam
Where eyes are strange relations, the streets are paved with sick and sin
'Waiting For The Lights To Change', 1997

Crow Film and Television Services was just off the Askew Rd in Shepherd's Bush, close to BBC TV Centre and myriad other TV and corporate production companies who made up its client base. The post was described as 'floating assistant' and the annual salary was £3,750, almost exactly half what I was earning at Haymarket. With Dick Lane leading the way, babbling like a slightly demented Mr Tumnus, we toured the building, from the racked camera and sound equipment warehouse to the film-cutting rooms with bins of celluloid trims, flatbed edit machines and the smell of Inhibisol cleaning solvent. It all seemed utterly alien and grubbily technical, but then I was shown into the main online video edit suite and experienced a 'halleluiah' moment, the like of which I'd never known. I think I did it quietly, but it's just possible I let out a tiny, high-pitched squeak – like air escaping from a balloon.

In front of me was a console incorporating various control surfaces and a bank of orange, gold and white illuminated switches which were reflected in the huge array of monitors, two of which were suspended from the ceiling. This was a room with the majestic potential of the studio at Genetic, but rather than being smuggled in for a quick peek, I was potentially going to be allowed to work here. I decided there and then that my immediate future was to do whatever it took to become a 'floating assistant'.

We came back to the production office which was buzzing with crews returning from shoots, dropping time-sheets and checking the huge whiteboard of forthcoming jobs. I waited for a 'nice to meet you, we'll let you know', but instead someone made me a cup of tea and a very tall and quite stodgy man in a tweed suit walked in and with an impossibly posh voice barked, 'Hello, I'm Paul Kingsley and I own this place. Who are you?' I was about to speak but Dick Lane beat me to it. 'Hello, Paul, this is Jonathan, he's our new runner.'

I'd only known Dick for approximately forty-five minutes and that would barely have given him time, even if he'd been a crack interrogator or Derren Brown, to ascertain much beyond the fact that I was a superficially confident, eager-to-please young man who was well spoken and had made a high-pitched squeak that suggested I seemed to like the look of the edit suite. Derren Brown might have had a stab at some of the 'burnt mattress' stuff on the basis of my being eager to please but, fortunately, he wasn't there.

I was asked if I could be there on Monday and immediately replied yes. (Eager to please, see? Four-week notice period at Haymarket? Nope.) *No* is a word I've struggled with. Saying it and risking displeasure can seem almost impossible. So I didn't say it, left Haymarket and was at Crow on the Monday.

A Design for Life

In March 1985 I found myself, largely through luck, employed by Crow Film and TV in West London. I was twenty years old and knew almost nothing about the industry I'd been smuggled into. The company had three distinct areas of business. There was camera and sound equipment hire (film and video), plus a pool of technicians that would utilise the fleet of Crow transit vans. These crews and equipment would be hired by production companies to shoot anything from corporate films to TV documentary. There were four film-cutting rooms that would be hired by production companies and be staffed by freelance editors. The biggest room in the building was the main video edit suite which was staffed by two editors who worked a one week on, one week off schedule, often encompassing seventy to one hundred hours. My job was to float between the film-cutting rooms and video-edit suite performing whatever tasks were required and making a lot of coffee.

I spent my first few days in a handover process with the previous assistant who was leaving Crow to become an editor at a competitor in Soho. He was a couple of years older than me, having followed the traditional route into the business by acquiring a degree in Film Studies and his easy relationship with the two video editors immediately put me on edge. There was constant conversation about films; who'd seen what and where. Names of actors and directors that I'd literally never heard of were common currency and I experienced a feeling I've had at various points over the intervening thirty-three years: that I was a bit of a philistine. I decided that the best course of action was to say as little as possible and bide my time, playing the long game and waiting for the subject to swing round to *Towering Inferno*.

The first two months at Crow were a welter of half-understood tasks and consequent mistakes. I was taught the basics of syncing film and sound rushes (film picture and sound were shot and recorded separately and the clapperboard was there to enable them to be synchronised). One of my first

jobs was synching up *One Man and His Dog*. The sound of a clapperboard across a field amidst the yelps of a sheepdog is almost indecipherable, but I quickly realised that no one really knew if it was in sync anyway. Bah humbug.

One of my duties as assistant video editor was operating the Aston character generator which applied titles, roller captions etc. I applied many of the 'rules' I'd learned from Mike Taylor in regard to typography, although these subtleties weren't much appreciated by clients whose attitude to anything graphical was 'more is more'. Bigger with brighter colours seemed the order of the day and I began to understand why many of these people weren't making the movies they loved discussing.

The main Crow edit suite was an 'online' suite where a programme would be conformed to decisions made over a much longer period in a much smaller and simpler suite. These offline suites utilised VHS copies of their master tapes and Crow offered a service to transfer these masters to VHS, a process that happened in real time, albeit using several machines at once. When the shoot vans returned in the evening, I would receive bags of shot master tapes that would require converting to VHS and I was expected to stay through the night doing this. It meant that on at least a couple of nights a week I'd stay at work overnight. For the half an hour that the tapes were transferring I'd have nothing to do, so I began to try and decipher how the suite worked.

One of the editors was a man called Mike Buday who bore more than a passing resemblance to Groucho Marx, but might have been funnier. Mike had an encyclopaedic knowledge of film and was clearly way over-qualified to be editing the fodder set in front of him at Crow. He could see how much I was struggling initially and, even though my mistakes were a frustration to him personally, took it upon himself to offer me patient guidance. I was constantly asking him how things worked in the suite and he stupidly said that, rather than sitting in a theoretical cul-de-sac half the night, I should call him – whatever time it was. Mike had a young family, two boys under the age of three, but I quickly supplanted them both as the reason Mike and his wife were lacking sleep.

When I think about how I actually felt in this period, several things come to mind. Firstly, that I had a sense of seeing something that I maybe wasn't supposed to. It was as if there was a crack in a wall, an opening that I was able to squeeze myself into. It was impossibly difficult to keep pushing, but not impenetrable. I'm aware that likely makes no sense. My upbringing had not encompassed the possibility of the world I was getting glimpses of. Again, as I write this, it seems ridiculous. It was a video company in Shepherd's Bush, not the Garden of Eden, so why are my recollections so strong that I was unworthy of this opportunity?

I was four years distant from the actual abuse I'd suffered from Bananas and had taken my first major step away from a family structure that had enabled so much of that to take place. It was the beginning of what I can only describe as a fracturing from my family and a process by which I replaced that faulty structure with a framework made up of equipment and technical processes. I felt the warmth and acceptance of Katie's family, but struggled wretchedly with any significant relationships beyond that. I think, in part, this was because there was at my core, a truth I couldn't share. Maybe the equipment and technical processes were a form of emergency insulation, like the concrete encasements used to entomb a charred and burnt-out reactor. Whatever, I was walking purposefully away from a family and a past that hurt in a manner that it wasn't safe to even *try* and describe consciously.

What I feel now, when I think about being in the edit suite, making coffee in the production office, driving the van to Hammersmith on a sandwich run, changing endless VHS tapes over and hand-writing labels – is *panic*. I was in a semi-permanent state of anxiety and that can only be partly explained by the fact that I was struggling to adapt to a complex and demanding work environment. It was a similar feeling to walking across Katie's living room, expecting at any minute to hear a klaxon, for a searchlight to illuminate my surroundings and for an amplified shriek to declare to anyone and everyone: 'HE SHOULDN'T BE HERE! HE DOESN'T BELONG!'

And he didn't believe that he should be and he did his best to fuck things up for himself and to make sure that everything would go wrong. Except he didn't realise that it wasn't him doing it, but the nauseating emotional cannibal who had corrupted a good part of his young life.

The catalogue of disasters that befell me (or 'things I fucked up') was lengthy, varied and comprehensive. In the first three months I managed the following:

Crashed two transit vans

Crashed (editor) Ralph's Alfa Romeo

Cut through middle of client's one master tape at halfway point

Multiple tape transfer errors

Enough client faux pas to furnish a book on *What Not To Do Or Say In Front Of Clients*

All of this led to my receiving two verbal warnings. I was hanging by a thread and at the mercy of the emperor's wavering thumb. The owner, Paul Kingsley, had something of an imperial management style that included multiple daytime bottles of Sancerre and a tendency for self-aggrandisement in front of clients. He would frequently walk in on an edit to introduce himself with a booming: 'Paul Kingsley – I own this place,' and humiliate me with hilarious lines such as: 'Jonathan, do you know I earn as much in one day as you do in a month?' (Which, on my salary, was quite the self-own.)

Although it wasn't of any financial consequence to the company, my most memorable error occurred in the week leading up to 13 July 1985, the day of Live Aid.

When rolls of magnetic sound and celluloid picture had been synchronised, it was necessary to run them through a machine that simultaneously stamped them every few feet with numbers that established a sync relationship. Although the process was referred to as 'rubber numbering', the codes were stamped using a hot foil and the machine stank. It was also a bastard.

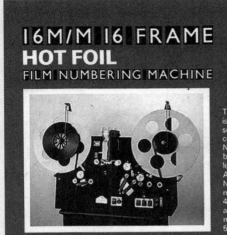

16 M/M 16 FRAME HOT FOIL
FILM NUMBERING MACHINE

LONDON

'MOY NUMBERING'

The latest 'Moy' Hot Foil Edge Numbering Machine is quick, clean, safe and economical to operate, with superb quality permanent numbering in a choice of colours on all types of film including polyester. Numbering on 16mm film is at 16 frame intervals between perforations, with four manually operated letter wheels and four automatic numbering wheels. A slow start device can be fitted as an optional extra. Numbering takes place approximately 200 times per minute. Maximum spool capacity is 2000 ft. and a 400 ft. reel of tape is sufficient to number approximately 20,000 ft. of film. The standard machine is portable, works off a 240V (single phase) 50 Hz supply and is fully guarded.

Having run 1200 feet of picture and sound through the clanking, clattering, not very distant relative of Stephenson's Rocket, I would look to the last numbers and count the sprockets to the end sync-mark. If this wasn't exactly the same number of sprockets, something had slid out of sync (the bastard would frequently tear sprocket holes, I'm pretty sure on purpose) and the process would have to be done again in a different colour. If this also went awry you had one more try with another colour and if that was also wrong (and it often was) all of the edge numbers would have to be wiped clean by hand using Inhibisol (solvent spray) and Selvyt cloths. It took forever.

On Friday 12 (the date, like the rubber numbering machine, had slipped out of sync) I had managed to have three abortive attempts at three different rolls of picture and sound, 7200 feet of 16mm picture and sound that all needed to be cleaned by hand. I was fairly certain that if Paul Kingsley got wind of this latest escapade, my status would change from 'floating assistant' to 'drowned assistant'. So it was that I came to be sat at a flat-bed film editing table all of Saturday through the entirety of Live Aid, the whole of Sunday and quite a lot of both nights.

As Bob Geldof opened proceedings and implored 'give us yer fockin' money', I sprayed Inhibisol on a Selvyt and wiped away some edge numbers.

As Status Quo took to the Wembley stage and started sawing their way through some chunky blues or other, I sprayed Inhibisol on a Selvyt and wiped away some edge numbers. As Phil Collins did drumming in London then hopped on Concorde and did further drumming in Philadelphia, I sprayed Inhibisol on a Selvyt and wiped away some edge numbers. And when Freddie Mercury muttered the words 'Ay Oh!' so many times it made me cringe to the core of my soul, I sprayed Inhibisol on a Selvyt and wiped away some edge numbers.

I sprayed so much solvent into the atmosphere in the name of *One Man and His Dog*, the ozone layer above Shepherd's Bush was permanently compromised. This task was so extraordinarily mind-numbing, so utterly soul-destroying, a thought gradually seeped into me as the days became nights: *Stop. Fucking. Up.* At least I think it was the thought seeping, but it could have been the Inhibisol.

From that weekend on, something clicked and I began to get my shit together. I think it may have been coincidental and Mike's steady influence was beginning to take effect. Every day, his patience and guidance were infinite and the fact that someone was bothering to take that time with me presented a fundamental shift. It was the antithesis of much of my experience growing up and, at first, I genuinely felt confused by it. I still know Mike (he's been back in California for twenty-five years) and he maintains now that he saw something in my creativity that he wanted to support. Maybe he'd just never come across someone who could turn fucking up into an artform?

Meanwhile, I was continuing to write. The songs of this period are heavily influenced by R.E.M. and my vocals began to mimic the sheep-like ululation of Michael Stipe. The poetry? Not so much. I was doing a huge amount of overtime which meant I was almost doubling my wages. My working hours were such that I had no social life and so I was saving money. Which meant I had to spend *all of it* on newer and better recording equipment – to make newer recordings.

I'm Looking for a Japanese Mother

After six months at Crow I'd begun to, if not understand what I was doing, at least not look like a prototype robot-dog, gone spectacularly wrong during its demonstration run in a china shop. A little confidence had gone a long way and the imminent dread of the next fuck-up had been gradually washed away by Mike's tireless mentoring.

The songs I was writing around this period were fairly scrutable *angst notes* wherein 'sin' gets more than its fair share of mentions and there are still people 'falling down'.

I'd forgotten 'Japanese Mother' and on first (re)listen I thought it was likely a reaction to something I'd seen or read at the time. There's a reference in verse two to 'five long hours in juku' which seems a bit on the nose, but with thirty-five years of class-A hindsight it seems a more elliptical cry for something. A mother, perhaps?

In and out of town again – again, no time to finish washing
Washing dishes, washing clothes and washing babies' faces – growing races
Mother smiles through tear-soaked eyes, cries out and in and out of town
'Japanese Mother', 1986

It also seems like a rejected demo from The Cure's *Pornography* sung by a pub singer in the style of Michael Stipe. Heady stuff indeed. What was noticeable was a discernible upgrade in the recording quality. I'd moved on from the cassette-based 4 track Portastudio to a ¼-inch 8-track recorder and a dedicated 12-channel mixing desk.

This was still impersonating great architecture with Stickle Bricks, but was another step towards my being able to record songs where at least the instruments sounded half decent.

If the gradual and insidious change that I referred to previously was manifesting through a desire to create a platform to express unacknowledged events, then the acquisition of skills and equipment *could* be seen as marshalling my forces for the battle that lay ahead.

Or I might have just bought an 8-track.

The Virus

Family had receded (or had *been* receded) and work had become life. It wasn't unusual to spend at least two weeknights at Crow; I'd developed a sleep pattern that allowed me to do tape transfers and catnap at thirty-minute intervals. There was frequent weekend assisting and any 'spare' time I was now devoting to learning more about the edit suite and recording. If I did have a weekend free then it was mostly spent with Katie in London or at her parents. Bananas had all but disappeared, at least in terms of a physical presence, but I think it was around this time that I first began to have a specific kind of nightmare.

Now it's long gone, but it's wretched, outrageous and wrong – it's a virus and you don't think, you just shake and shiver and shrink – from the virus.
'The Virus', 2010

It may have been prompted by the feeling of another body near me in the night. (This has only just occurred to me and as I've typed this I've shivered. So, I'm pretty sure that's a 'yes'.) These would invariably start with my being in an alien environment with a strong *sense* that I should feel secure – but I don't. Gradually the scenario (which is always indistinct in terms of geography or physical detail) becomes more threatening. Sometimes a wall or physical boundary will move away in a manner that becomes immediately terrifying, not unlike I'm witnessing the actions of a poltergeist. What's happening makes no sense, but the threat becomes absolutely distinct. As this dawning horror arrives it manifests in a terrible pain in my bollocks. This physical pain becomes much more intense and as it does the terror rises as if there's someone – *something* – screaming right behind me. Then I'm awake, most likely with goosebumps all over my torso, arms and legs and more often than not an erection. But not a happy one.

And the wounds sting at the memory of every damn thing - it's a virus.
And it won't mend, 'til this terror has come to an end - it's a virus.
'The Virus', 2010

All of this was inextricable in my mind with my family and the environment they had fostered. Little wonder it had become a habit to keep them at arms' length.

Take a Chance on Me

As an assistant I'd started to get on top of things. I hadn't got the knack of socialising particularly well with other staff at Crow, hampered by a perennial inability to say things that didn't seem just a bit weird, but with clients it was a different story. I seemed to instinctively know how to behave to put them at their ease. This was a stark contrast to my exploits with the likes of Brian the Soft-Top Restorer, the difference being I had a degree of insight into what (supposedly) creative people needed to be told.

> Basically a persuasive style, but could well give the impression of being a 'con man'.

> Tries to go along with what others want unless he wants something else strongly.

I did want something strongly. I wanted to sit in the editor's chair, because I was:

> Keen to enjoy power and authority and seeks recognition.

But I knew that the best way to achieve this (alongside spending every waking hour making every conceivable mistake at least once) was to develop relationships with some clients who might be prepared to take a chance on me in the chair.

The thing about a technically complex job (and being an online editor was technically *very* complex) is that there's only so much you can learn on your own. A boxer can be extraordinarily fit, technically proficient with footwork *and* on the bag and even really adept at sparring, but nothing can prepare them to fight (where someone else is motivated by the same potent mixture of desire, aggression and fear) as effectively as an *actual* fight.

I was spending countless weekends and nights making my own music videos, cutting odd films for friends and generally becoming pretty capable at driving the online suite. But there was no opponent. There was no one that would ever present a request that I couldn't carry out. I'd sit alongside Mike and Ralph and unlike the first few months when their hand movements across the equipment were a meaningless flurry of flicks, twists and pushes, I now understood the function of all the switches, dials and knobs and the order they were flicking, twisting and pushing them in. Mike began to feel like Dr Frankenstein, as the chirruping Gollum-like monster that sat *too close to him* all day would pre-emptively commentate on his every move or point out an alternative course of action.

'You could do that with an external key layer...'
'I don't think you've selected Audio 1...'
'The matte roll is a frame out...'

Mike took all of this with the same good-natured patience that he'd absorbed the nocturnal phone calls and endless mistakes. He knew that the sorcerer's apprentice was keen to be given a chance to show off his ability and that the sorcerer's apprentice wasn't awfully bright when it came to considering the needs of others in any given situation.

Very creative in an aesthetic sense and highly individualistic.

Can be less concerned than average about the wellbeing of his fellow man.

What the sorcerer's apprentice needed was an accomplice who might offer him direction and impose some imperatives on his burgeoning but untethered abilities.

Christopher James Barclay was, and remains, the brightest and most extraordinarily sparkling diamond of a man I've ever met. I never got to share any of the secrets of this book with him, but if I had I don't think he'd have been in the least surprised. Nothing surprised Chris. He was a tall, skinny fella – as cool as cool can be, yet warm and engaging with the cheekiest smile, most often seen following his muttering some appalling obscenity. He looked like a cross between Anthony Perkins and Joe Strummer and always sported (in his words) 'a proper London haircut'.

We met in the edit suite. He was a production assistant to a corporate producer and had recently graduated with a film degree from Goldsmiths. Chris knew a lot about film and yet never once made me feel like I didn't. As the producer and Mike set about crafting a corporate 'film' (a launch for Nescafé's new square jar that amounted to flipping pack-shots around the screen to Huey Lewis's 'Hip To Be Square'), Chris and I sat on a sofa at the back of the suite, getting to know each other. The conversation started with music but quickly became a convolution of our dreams and ambitions. I told him (with a *degree* of truth) that I was ready to edit, having taught myself over the preceding ten months. His beady eyes lit up as they scanned the illuminated banks at the front, immediately calculating what could be achieved in this room with a willing conspirator.

Chris was already making music videos but on primitive equipment, sneaking back into Goldsmiths in downtime. I immediately offered myself and the suite the coming weekend, which is how I began the journey into trying to carry out the wishes of someone other than myself. I also found myself, for the first time ever, in possession of lots of shots and no clear directive as to what should go where. I was being asked to make decisions – to edit – and it quickly became apparent that Chris liked the decisions I made and that I seemed to have something of a talent for it. The more work Chris and I did, the more I grew in confidence and the more unbearable I became; as the sorcerer's apprentice began to fancy himself as a sorcerer in his own right and to get on the *actual* sorcerer's tits.

Godstar

Genesis P-Orridge had a metal bar through the head of his penis. I know, because he showed me. That wasn't the most remarkable thing about the night I spent in the edit suite with him, members of his band Psychic TV and their entourage. That would have to be the fact that I did my first-ever edit for an *actual* client. If this hadn't happened, I'm not sure I'd have become an editor as quickly, but it did – so I did.

The music video was booked in as a night-time session between 6pm and 8am the following morning. Although Mike was a really talented editor, I could see straight away that he wasn't entirely comfortable. Various people were in variously altered states and there was a committee of different people directing. These included Genesis, John Maybury and his partner Trojan and numerous other hangers-on. And there was footage of a goat.

As soon as the edit started, I was buzzing about – listening to the myriad suggestions being thrown around and throwing a few of my own in for good measure. Mike was really struggling and, after a while, took me aside to the machine room where he informed me that this was the deep end and I was about to be thrown in. He'd see me in the morning and, with that, he picked up his car keys and left. I wandered back into the developing carnage of the edit suite and set about listening and turning what I heard into the video for 'Godstar'.

The following morning Mike came in to find me sitting amongst the wreckage and we watched the film which featured some pretty outré effects for the time (and certainly for the Crow edit suite). Mike laughed a lot and shook his head. 'You're an editor, man...' I really wasn't, but I'd been offered the chance to do something that I certainly had a flair for and it felt really good. Unbeknownst to me, Mike had been looking around for other jobs and had been offered a great opportunity in town. Later that week he handed in his notice and recommended to Paul Kingsley that I be given the chance to step up. I was summoned to Paul's office and told that in a fortnight I'd be one of Crow's two editors. My probational salary was to be £12,000 and I'd be given Mike's company car. I did what anyone under these circumstances would have done and started viewing flats in West London. That money wasn't going to spend itself.

Katie had already bought a two-bed flat in West Ealing. She'd graduated from the BBC trainee course and was now a camera assistant, shooting TV drama and away a lot on location (and earning a great deal of overtime – hence the flat). My mum, who I hadn't spoken to for months, got wind of the fact that I was staying there a lot. She phoned to let me know I was committing a mortal sin, that I was damned to Hell and that she and my dad had no intention of visiting our den of iniquity. I told her that sounded fine and we had no intention of inviting her. She wasn't happy but it felt good to let her know that her sanctions were useless.

I continued to keep my family apart from my life in London. At the time I felt embarrassed by them, but actually I think it was shame – and not at them but what I associated them with. Family was Opus Dei, family was weird Catholic obsessions, family was Boys' Club and family was very definitely Bananas who by now had a third child on the way. I had a really strong sense that I was carving out a new life for myself, but what I was actually doing was closer to carving out a new self for myself. Much of the development and character that had been stunted and perverted between ten and sixteen felt like it had permission to exert itself, although it became bound up with notions of status and financial wellbeing. I was on my way to becoming a bit of a dick, albeit without a metal bar through my head.

Under Pressure

On 1 September 1986, I started as one of Crow Films online editors, having been a runner/assistant for thirteen months. The equivalent journey today would be highly unlikely in under four years and that would probably be on top of a three-year degree. I was twenty-one and most of my contemporaries had just graduated. I was handed the keys to Mike's Honda Prelude and despite it being one of the worst designed cars of the twentieth century with an interior that looked like a bad child's drawing of a car interior, I drove around West London on my week off like Ferris Bueller did on his day off.

The weekend before I started as editor, I went down to Swanage for the weekend as Katie was there shooting the TV drama *Happy Valley* (which was set in Kenya, thus requiring quite a suspension of disbelief). On the Saturday, the legendarily good crazy golf course at Bournemouth's Winter Gardens beckoned and following this beckoning, I found myself waiting outside the ladies' changing rooms in Marks & Spencer for Katie to emerge. As I waited, I overheard a male shop assistant in conversation with an older female assistant. He was about my age, tall and looked like a young Paul Newman – almost. He'd just finished his degree and was very excited that he was about to go to work for a video company in West London. I was about to say hello and enquire as to where, when Katie came out of the changing room and we were off.

My first scheduled day on the Monday was unusually light and around 10:30 I was doing what I often did in the suite, spooling through commercials frame by frame examining the dynamics of the cuts, trying to understand how actions and movements could be connected so seamlessly. The suite door opened and Fiona, the bookings manager, came in with a young man who looked a bit like a young Paul Newman but also a bit like Russ Abbott. 'Jonathan, I'd like you to meet your new assistant. This is Spencer.' I extended my hand and said to Spencer, 'You work in Marks & Spencer in Bournemouth and I claim my five pounds.' Spencer Hill who is, thirty-five years later, my longest-standing and best friend, laughed. And we've never really stopped.

Actually, that's not completely true because the following month contained very little laughter. It's hard to laugh when you're under so much pressure you can feel your skin breaking out in blotches. When your mind is utterly blank as you desperately try to remember why the sequence of key strokes you've just performed has caused – absolutely nothing at all to happen. When you've been asked to do something by a client that you have no idea how to do and all of your impulses and instincts are screaming at you to stand up and walk out.

I had form in this regard. Before my three-month stint at the *Oxford Journal* I'd responded to an ad in the local paper from a decorating company. I'd always been quite 'handy' and naively thought my rudimentary skills with paintbrush and filling knife would allow me to compete in the brilliant-white heat of the Oxford property refurbishment arena.

I was picked up by the company van and as I settled in the back alongside four other tradesmen, immediately noticed that my three brushes in a bag were dwarfed by their paint-spattered buckets crammed with rollers, brushes, knives and (in one of them) a jar of pickled onions. On arrival at St Hilda's college, I followed the lads through to a large refectory hall that was covered

CROW FILM & TELEVISION SERVICES LTD
12 WENDELL ROAD · LONDON W12 9RT
Tel: 01 749 6071 · Telex: 9314 58 · Answerback: CROW TV G

Our Ref: PK/JW
12 August 1986

Jonathan Daukes Esq
c/o Crow Films

Dear Jonathan

I am delighted that you have chosen to accept the position of Video Editor to replace Michael when he leaves.

You will start in this position on the 1st September. Your salary will be £12,000.00 per annum based on the shift system which Fiona will familiarise you with. You will also have use of a company motor car, possibly the one Michael had if he no longer requires it.

in dust sheets and surrounded by working platforms. The foreman wandered over to me, pointed at a nearby pasting table, gestured to the vast walls around us and said, 'Get these lined then, there's rolls over there. By lunchtime.' And as he wandered off, I'm pretty sure he winked to a couple of the lads who sniggered. I looked at the box of lining paper; there were at least twenty rolls. I looked at my watch, before lunchtime there was around three hours.

I'd recently papered my bedroom (which was around one-tenth the size of this hall) in about two days. I didn't bother to do the maths. Instead I made a very different calculation and walked straight out of the college, down the high street and onto a 302 bus to Didcot. I'd faced a demon, realised it was far too demonic for me (or didn't offer any kind of worthwhile reward) and run away.

In September 1986 I had a feeling that the potential rewards of facing my demon (in this case a cigar-chomping corporate client who expected me to fly a store gift-card around the screen like it had wings – '*freedom*', see?) were considerably greater than that offered by wallpapering a dining hall in a college in Oxford. So I stared hard at the demon, kept trying and, eventually, the store-card flew.

Who Knew?

I met Katie when I was eighteen and was now, in 1986, nearly twenty-two. She knew nothing of what Bananas had done, not because I made any attempt to conceal it, but because I was still many years from acknowledging it myself. She did, however, have an instinctive mistrust and dislike of him and would avoid him wherever possible. Any family gathering would mean having to avoid the inevitable lunge for a kiss on the lips. I discussed all of this with her recently and she recalled his generally oleaginous and obsequious demeanour.

At Crow, my assistant Spencer was fast becoming a friend. As well as working alongside each other, we laughed at, listened to, watched and read the same stuff. Spence maintains that he knew nothing about Bananas and my early life until I brought it up around 2003. Spence met him several times at various family gatherings and his reflections are similar to Katie's: that he was something of an amiable fool. It seems inconceivable that from 1986, for seventeen years, this remained completely unacknowledged between Spencer and I – but it did. I could hardly tell Spencer or Katie what I didn't know myself.

I would meet Bananas occasionally at family events and we got on fine. As far as I was aware, at the time, there was no reason not to. My enemy, such as it was, dwelled internally and was yet to surface. There were allusions creeping into songs from around this period, but at this stage they were very subtle and elliptical.

What began to happen around this time is that the first vestiges of an anger stirred inside me. At various points (and usually when I'd drunk too much, which was becoming more often) I'd become irascible and self-righteously indignant. This swelling started to displace me into actions and reactions that leave me endless reasons to regret.

Model Worker

In December 1986, three months after being put on probation as editor with a second-hand Honda and £12k a year, I had begun to assert myself with clients, not only taking on existing work but also attracting new work through word of mouth. It turned out that having a musical ability, a propensity to learn technical equipment and being a reasonably amenable character to sit alongside for twelve hours a day amounted to a skill-set that made me at least adequate for the job and I was promoted to full editor status, elevated to £20k a year and given an almost new Golf GTI. I was about to turn twenty-two and, at least as far as work was concerned, life was looking much better. Albeit that batholith of anger and resentment was slowly beginning to push upward.

From December to May I became more and more confident in the suite, the pushing of buttons and sliding of faders becoming more assertive, and I began to use all the equipment instinctively in tandem with creative thought processes. Admittedly most of the time it was in the process of making corporate videos and sales informationals. There were occasional highlights such as documentary edits and the very occasional music video. I worked a week-on, week-off rota system with Ralph who was older and more experienced. Weeks on could be brutal in terms of hours; it wasn't uncommon to work all seven days with a night-shift thrown in too.

In the 80s, facility houses that were generally running between 08:30 and midnight six days a week realised that they were criminally underutilised at all other times (i.e. Sunday and through the night, every single night). To entice more business at these times, a lower rate card was introduced and the suite would occasionally be booked through the night. Incredibly, the editor who was booked on for that week would be expected to work right through.

In May 1986 I was coming to the end of a particularly exhausting week-on, in which I'd edited for approximately 130 hours. It had involved two night-edits, meaning two stints of day-night-day. It seems extraordinary in retrospect. After one of these had ended around 06:00 I drove back to my flat in Hanwell to shower and change and my vision was intermittently blurring. As I drove through the fluorescent morning darkness of the Uxbridge Rd, my peripheral vision seemed to be 'tearing' and I had a near-permanent, low-level headache. I'm pretty sure a pair of glasses would have helped, but a desperate lack of sleep and upwards of ten cups of strong coffee a day were taking their toll.

On the Sunday afternoon I was editing something or other whilst fighting to stay awake at the controls. A phone call came from Ralph to say that he had decided to stay away a further week. I'd need to cover for him, then do my rostered week to follow. Ralph was a company director (I'd been his assistant for a year) and it was assumed that I'd comply. This is the first time I ever reacted to a situation in a manner that was to become quite characteristic. Rather than say to Ralph that I was on my last legs and try to reach some kind of compromise, I assented and then proceeded to boil and seethe with indignation for the rest of the evening.

I've subsequently learned that victims of childhood abuse can react very violently against external control. It was to be another thirty-four years until I located the source of this anger, and in terms of how it manifested, this wasn't particularly spectacular (and, on this occasion, was reasonably justified). My

CROW FILM & TELEVISION SERVICES LTD
12 WENDELL ROAD · LONDON W12 9RT
Tel·01·749 6071·Telex·931458·Answerback·CROW TV G

Our Ref: PK/JW

11 December 1986

Jonathan Daukes Esq
c/o Crow Films

Dear Jonathan

Further to our conversation of a couple of weeks ago this is to confirm the new conditions of your employment as a Video Editor with this company.

(1)   Your salary will be increased to £20,000 per annum from December. You will continue to operate the shift system but no overtime will be paid.

internal voice became utterly affronted: *How fucking dare they? They're taking the fucking piss...* It was as if my interior monologue was voiced by Ralph Fiennes 'Harry' from *In Bruges*. At times like these (and over the next thirty years these times would become more frequent) I could simultaneously believe that someone was conspiring against me, that I was utterly superior to them (most often intellectually) and that no amount of escalation on my part was anything but entirely justified.

On occasions when these 'controlled rages' coincided with the consumption of alcohol (especially beer or vodka) I would burn with an outraged rectitude and frequently say or do things I'd regret. On this occasion, when the client had left around 10pm, I went upstairs to Paul Kingsley's office and left a note on his desk along the lines of: 'I'm almost dead through lack of sleep, I CANNOT work tomorrow morning and we need to talk about whether it's reasonable that I work the next two weeks straight.'

CROW FILM & TELEVISION SERVICES LTD
12 WENDELL ROAD · LONDON W12 9RT
Tel: 01 749 6071 · Telex: 931458 · Answerback: CROW TV G

Our Ref: PK/JW

13 July 1987

Jonathan Daukes Esq
50 Church Road
HANWELL
W7

Dear Jonathan

Thank you for coming to see me this morning.

I do not feel that your continued employment is advantageous to us or to you.

I regret very much that I have had to take this action but I do feel that you and Crow are not compatible and that your attitude has become intolerable.

Yours sincerely

CROW FILM & TELEVISION SERVICES LTD
12 WENDELL ROAD · LONDON W12 9RT
Tel: 01 749 6071 Telex: 931458 Answerback: CROW TV G

Our Ref: PK/JW

17 July 1987

Jonathan Daukes Esq
50 Church Road
HANWELL
W7

Thanks for your letter. I appreciate very much the fact that
you do see my point of view and I think that in acknowledging
the mistake you made you show yourself to be at least as big
a person as I always thought.

However, we cannot in the circumstances reconsider our position.
Having said that I would not in any way wish to hinder your
career and you may assume that if you put me forward as a
referee that the reference will be a good one.

I was woken the following morning by my doorbell, which had been rung by a cab driver bearing a letter from Paul Kingsley informing me that my *attitude had become intolerable* and that I was dismissed forthwith. And I was to drop the GTI back immediately. Whatever the rights and wrongs of the situation (and I could certainly have handled it in a manner that gave Paul some 'wiggle room'), I was pretty much shitting myself. I'd been in my post as an editor for six months, had just bought my own flat and was now redundant at twenty-two. I did what any reasonably intelligent person would when staring down the barrel of a gun and wrote a grovelling letter of apology.

Paul replied that at least I'd shown myself to be as big an individual as he'd always believed but, no, I couldn't have my job back.

In the intervening few days I'd researched any other suites in town that had a similar technical set-up. I hadn't learned how to *edit*, I'd learned how to operate a very specific few pieces of equipment and was about five years shy of being able to go freelance. There were two edit suites with the same edit controller/vision mixer combination and so I contacted them both. Within a week I'd done a day at Component Video and a day at Ravensdale Film & TV, both in Soho. I also got a phone call from Crow where, to allow Ralph his desired week off, I was employed for a week as a freelance. Paul Kingsley kept a low profile and I invoiced at twice my previous rate. Kerr-fucking-ching.

The following week Ravensdale asked me to come in and do some preliminary edits for a new TV channel that was about to come on-stream. I did a day with a lanky, incredibly enthusiastic Kiwi producer called Brent for the soon-to-be launched MTV.

Brent's musical knowledge was vast and he responded really positively to the way I cut. Over the next couple of weeks, I was re-booked by request and soon offered a permanent job at Ravensdale in Dean St.

RAVENSDALE FILM & TELEVISION LIMITED

J Daukes
50 Church Road
Hanwell
LONDON W7

1st September 1987

Dear Jonathan,

Following our recent discussion, I am pleased to offer you the position of Editor at Ravensdale and Television Ltd, from September 1st 1987.

The salary will be £20,000 inclusive of any overtime that may be worked and will be paid subject to PAYE and other deductions.

A company car (Peugeot 205 1.9) will be provided.

We Need a Montage

In June 1987 I was a young man with a certain amount of natural creative flair who'd learned to drive an online edit suite and discovered that my musical sensibilities were attributes when cutting sound and vision. Right now, in 2022, having spent several years learning about dramatic structure through writing and having accidentally become a film editor who's cut some commercial hits, I can reasonably describe myself as 'an editor', i.e. someone who can be presented with a mound of picture and sound and assemble it into a story in a manner that will elicit certain emotions. I've got considerably less experience than most of my peers, who have all spent between twenty and forty years cutting TV and film. However, my years spent writing songs, comedy and film and the assorted technical skills I've picked up en route, give me a slightly more unusual approach than most of them. So, go me! What I *have* developed is a strong instinct for when a story needs to be moved along – when the pace needs to pick up and events be compressed in order to reach the next critical juncture – pronto.

One of the primary skills of an editor is time compression. We do it so that you don't have to watch people doing things in real-time that don't justify being seen in real-time, like getting in or out of cars, taking long rides in elevators or unscrewing tricky jar lids. We also do it in a more concerted way to show development of a situation or individual over an extended period. It's called a montage and it's a technique that's become a movie staple and is frequently used to great effect (my own favourites are the yearbook montage from Wes Anderson's *Rushmore*, the baptism from *The Godfather*, Carl & Ellie's married life in *Up* and the training montage from *Rocky*). This last example is its own sub-genre, made explicit by the brilliant Trey Parker and Matt Stone, firstly in their *South Park* episode 'Asspen', which was so brilliant they justifiably re-used it in *Team America: World Police*.

In my story now, we're going to montage between June 1987 and September 1992, a leap of approximately five years. Why, as an editor, are my impulses telling me that we need to montage at this stage? Fundamentally, because the central component of this book – the abuse I suffered, how it shaped my development and how I then came to unconsciously deal with those experiences through writing – rather took a back seat through this period. When I started editing, and more specifically when I started editing a lot using music, I found myself (for the first time in my life) doing something well, being recognised for that and rewarded. This boost in my confidence and financial wellbeing applied a very effective sticking plaster over the wounds I'd been labouring under until then.

What happened over this period was, if anything, a further submergence of what had been misshapen, disguised by an outward layer of industry and prosperity. What happened towards the end of this period was that the diversion of career/money/consumption could no longer suppress a feeling that had begun to surge upwards. During these years I continued to learn to write and record and I think that when those skills began to get to the point where I believed I could actually attempt to express myself more publicly, the feelings and emotions I'd harboured for years began to find their way to the surface in lyrics.

So, without further ado, we need a montage.

SHADOWMAN

Title SHADOWMAN animates on

Photo of young JD taken by Bananas

Hi-tech edit suite in operation

Home studio becoming more elaborate

Work taking place in Soho enabling the pursuit of a hobby that is in pursuit of being more than a hobby.

RECORDING STUDIO IN USE

- ♦ JD and Katie partying with friends

- ♦ Colin and Tess look on in bemusement

- ♦ Late nights in Soho cutting for MTV

- ♦ Chris Barclay bringing bigger budget promos

- ♦ Recording when time permits, songs become less derivative

Visitors to JD's flat include Nick, Mike Taylor and Rex West

Work very demanding, any spare time spent writing/recording

Tendency to second-guess friends becomes more pronounced, results in frequent detachment

Socialising with colleagues feels uncomfortable beyond confines of work relationship

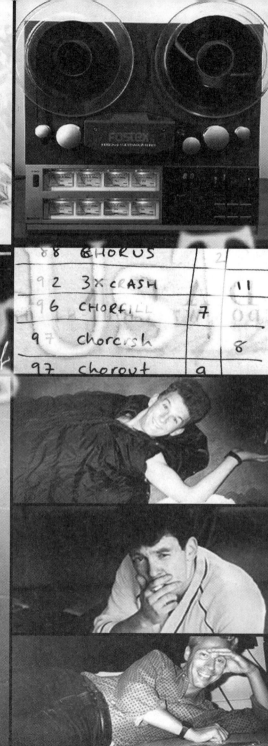

Open B – Ab – A – E
B – Ab – A – E
B – C – G – D – B

88	CHORUS	2
92	3x CRASH	11
96	CHORFILL	7	00
97	chorcrsh	8
97	chorout	9

SLIPS INTO AN
ACT FOR YOU
AS EASY AS
YOU PLEASE...
PUNCTUALLY LATE
AND THEN
ARRIVES AND
THEN HE LEAVES

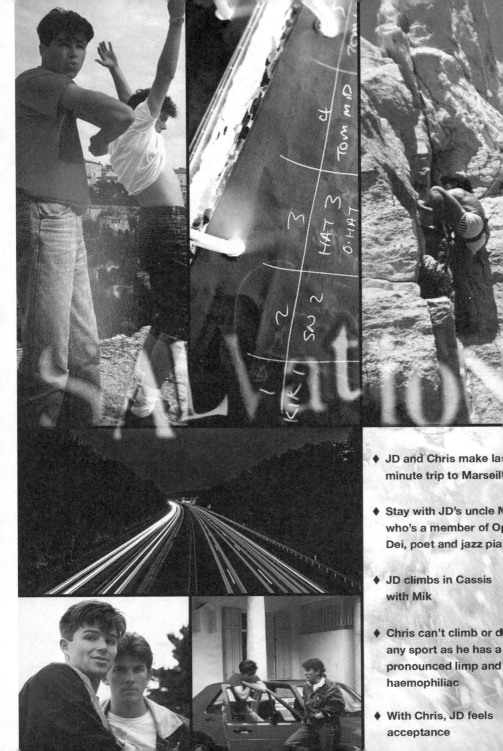

SALVATION

- ◆ JD and Chris make last minute trip to Marseille

- ◆ Stay with JD's uncle M[...] who's a member of Op[us] Dei, poet and jazz pia[nist]

- ◆ JD climbs in Cassis with Mik

- ◆ Chris can't climb or d[o] any sport as he has a pronounced limp and [is] haemophiliac

- ◆ With Chris, JD feels acceptance

- ◆ JD and Katie skiing whenever possible

- ◆ Sell their flats and buy a house in Ladbroke Grove

- ◆ JD's studio where he'll write over 200 songs, some terrible, some not

- ◆ Documentary work for Uden Associates on Horizon and Equinox

- ◆ Writes first piece of MTV title music

- Writes title music for Rapido, MTV and various ad. agencies

- JD and Katie get married and drive round Europe

- Bananas now has four children. Occasional contact with JD at family gatherings

- More reliant on booze in social situations, often ends in argument

fOrgivE

...& fORGeT?

- ♦ JD directs commercial for Converse All Stars

- ♦ Shoot in London and NYC with Katie and Chris

- ♦ Profiles in Campaign, Direction and Broadcast

- ♦ Directs further spot for Schwarzkopf and is approached by several commercials companies

- ♦ Shoots MTV promo and features Colin in first of many roles

3rd August '92

Christopher I'm proud to say I've been your friend
And now Its clearly near The end
There~~'s something I want~~ the wather
I'm lost for Things to say
Do you know my love has never been in doubt
I want to cry I want to shout
Beg ~~you for another~~ I'm asking for just one more day

♦ Chris became severely
and was admitted to S
Thomas' Hospital.
A haemophiliac, he ha
been receiving the
clotting agent Factor 8
which used HIV infecte
plasma from the US.
He died of Aids on
September 27th 1992

Swimming ou
in deep warm wate
clear and blue
I never coul
keep up with yo
You're swimmin
from me now.

Chris had been very, very sick from the summer onwards. Shortly after my last visit to St Thomas' he was allowed to return home with his girlfriend Michele and, with the aid of palliative care, descended over a few weeks to the end of his life. I visited once more to say goodbye. I sat gently on his bedside, unable to take in the unbearable lightness of his being, and he raised a skeletal hand to touch my face. His voice was a weirdly hoarse, cracked whisper. 'I'll never leave you…' I knew what he was trying to say, that our shared moments and memories would stay with me, but it scared me. I leaned over and kissed his sallow cheek, my skin alive with pins and needles as I fought myself not to cry or run. I felt fear, shame and rising nausea. Why didn't I know what to say or do? I left and as I drove across London, I sobbed uncontrollably.

In one of my early visits to St Thomas' I'd told him I was starting a band, but it seemed like a terrible betrayal. Chris would have photographed us and filmed us, he'd likely have come on tour and would certainly have had some strong advice that we lacked through our early existence. He sort of grunted as if to say 'good luck with that'. It should have been a journey we shared.

Earlier in the year, Katie and I had been out having something to eat when a conversation spiralled. Following the Converse ad and a couple of other spots I'd acquired via MTV, I visited a few commercials production houses with a view to being represented as a director. I'd had second meetings with two of them who were both keen for me to jump ship from editing and join them full time. Katie was increasingly shooting music videos and commercials and thought this sounded great, but I was hesitant. Eventually, as I ran out of excuses not to say what was on my mind, I said what was on my mind, 'I want to start a band, like – a real band.'

To her eternal credit (but arguably at huge cost to the British listening public) she responded, 'Then you'd better start a band!'

Johnny Strikes Up the Band

Starting a band is easy, or it was in 1992. You placed an ad in the back of *Melody Maker* listing your influences and declaring your intention to conquer the world – 'no time-wasters'. Sadly, your definition of a time-waster and a time-waster's view of the same rarely tallied. I fielded phone calls from countless time-wasters (your ad had to contain either your postal address, landline number or a PO Box), musicians that were at once hope*ful* and hope*less*. The occasional applicant sounded keen enough yet cool enough to warrant my posting out a demo. The field further narrowed as the demo recipients listened to my songs and spotted little or no similarity between them and the purported influences who clearly hadn't been influential enough.

An early positive reaction came from a bass player called Al and we arranged for him to come over to mine. As the door opened there was an immediate and crucial appraisal by both parties, because it's never *just* about the music. Tea made and small-talk progressing well, we retired to my studio, which was by now quite well accessorised with the recent addition of a 16-track recorder and a mixing desk that was far from Premier League but was at least Vauxhall Conference.

I played Al some further demos and he smiled approvingly. I noted his unusual surname, McAteer, the same as a kid in my primary school class. Gordon McAteer – who threw up the boiled fish. He was Al's older brother and we had attended the same Oxfordshire primary school. Kismet! The fact that Al looked good, had a sense of humour and played a Fender Jazz bass very well didn't hurt either.

A series of drummers joined us at an Acton rehearsal studio. Drummers who always wanted to do too much. 'Rehearsing the drummers' is another scene crying out for a montage, but now's not the time (and you can easily imagine it). Instead, Al mentioned the drummer from his Norwich hometown band who now also lived in London. Two nights later we lined up with Richard Childs who not only played the drums minimally and with power, but was also possessed of the spirit of Eric Morecambe.

We were three. We still needed a lead guitarist and we still needed a name, so set about the time-honoured technique of searching through albums for song titles. It yielded Radiohead (Talking Heads song), Powderfinger (Neil Young song) and Death Cab For Cutie (Bonzo Dog Doo Da Band song) and it wasn't long before our leafing led to The Monochrome Set album *Fin*. In retrospect we'd have been better off calling ourselves 'Love Zombies' or 'Strange Boutique'.

From placing the first ad to starting to rehearse to finding a name took a few months, during which I'd been writing furiously and one of the recent demos was called 'Shadowman'. It was a progression from any of the songs I'd been offering so far and it was, I believed, an attempt to put myself in the mind of a third party, to intellectualise abuse. It was also the first song I played to Andy Faulkner, a slight, shy young guitarist with a Brian May-like mop of curls and a Gibson 335 that he could play with a distinctly Jimmy Page-like influence. Andy and I sat down in my studio, I was enchanted by his ability and he loved the songs. He listened to 'Shadowman' and, several months later, was quoted in an interview:

'Johnny writes things that are very personal to him,' points out Andy.
'Yeah, I don't mind singing them in front of 300 people, but there are certain songs that are quite embarrassing because they're quite confessional, I suppose.' Johnny pauses for a moment as if wondering how best to explain. 'Put it this way, my mum was at the last gig and it was quite odd singing certain things.'

'Certain things like what?' I ask, trying my best to appear sympathetic rather than enthusiastic for some juicy goss, but Andy jumps to the rescue at this point .

'We don't push him too much on his lyrics. They mean what they mean to us, and we let them mean what they mean to him.'

With that, the matter is closed.

And the matter was closed, for about twenty years. The song I'm referencing in regard to my mum was 'Headstrong', our first single that, in the words of the *NME*, 'takes Catholicism out the back for a good kicking' – so 'confessional', yes. It never occurred to me that singing 'Shadowman' (which I did at our first fifty gigs or so) was in any way insightful to my background or character, or I'm not sure I could have sung it. Andy's response suggested that maybe he wasn't as convinced by my 'third party' projection as I was.

The four of us began rehearsing twice weekly in a smelly, woodchip-lined box in Acton's Survival Studios, wherein we not only survived but began to start sounding something like a band. Demo tapes were pushed into the wider world and one found its way to Adrian Lillywhite, formerly drummer with The Members and King and wannabe band manager. Adrian recorded us, adding a decent drum sound courtesy of his mum's garage and a semi-decent mix at his brother (producer Steve Lillywhite's) home studio and began to distribute the tapes to various A&R departments.

In the last few days I've listened to these recordings and compared them to my contemporary home demos. There was a definite improvement in the bass and drums sound, but the production approach was lumpen. The demos (clearly the result of my imitating recordings of The Smiths, early Bowie and recent Suede demos) fizzed and sparkled with crackling guitars, multiple vocal layers and all manner of falsetto/double tracking etc. In short, they were really over the top (but, crucially, exciting). The demos Adrian recorded had a distinctly more belt 'n' braces quality, yet still stimulated an early curiosity in London's record companies, albeit prematurely.

Around this time, I was introduced to a photographer called Andy Catlin who'd spent most of the 80s photographing R.E.M., Patti Smith, Sinead O'Connor and Echo & The Bunnymen, among others. Andy listened to some of the demos and was quite taken with a song called 'Sweet Obsession', which I'd later describe in a *Melody Maker interview* as being:

'…about the nature of fear – it was triggered by one of those nights when you have a dream that you just can't get out of. Also, the idea that all the people you've ever liked might actually hate you.'

> Fear - liven up my life, 'til I can't walk away from you
> Say I'm always right, when I do what I do for you.
> Me - waking up at night, when a grey blur haze walks through
> Liven up my life - Oh no no no no…
> Sweet Obsession for a one-time friend that
> laughs at the memory of your face
> 'Sweet Obsession', 1992

What I should have added in the interview was: '…in the dream that you just can't get out of because someone's got your balls in a vice-like grip'.

The identity of that someone is hinted at in verse two:

'Mister mean-serene, is your conscience so clean?'

Andy Catlin had aspirations to be a music video director and suggested he shoot a promo for the track. Soon we were performing in a white photographic studio being shot by an 8mm film camera on a swinging trapeze mount.

Meanwhile, Adrian was impatient for us to start playing live and secured us a spot at the cavernous Powerhaus in Islington, supporting Swervedriver. It was the first time of many that I experienced a very familiar feeling.

THURSDAY 22nd OCTOBER 1992
on stage at 9.30

FIN

[pow'er:ha(u)s]

1 LIVERPOOL RD ISLINGTON N1

Rather than walking out onto the stage with my three bandmates and playing the seven songs we'd rehearsed, songs that in the studio or rehearsal room I was happy with, even quite proud of, I immediately felt pressure. I was no longer *in the moment* on the stage but scanning the room; who was here? By 'who' I meant music business etc. People who 'mattered'. Never mind that a good forty or fifty of the crowd were family and friends of the band who'd schlepped across London or further to offer support.

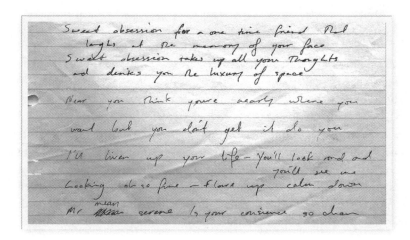

This anxiety put a wall between me and the rest of the band. I'd frequently become agitated with Richard, at his tempos. He was playing too fast – too slow – (he wasn't) and I'd shoot him glances that would do everything but instil confidence. I'd overcompensate and try to create 'intensity' by over-projecting. What was it that people did in these circumstances? Jump around? I'd sometimes try but my playing was quite rudimentary which would lead to clanging mistakes that I'd then fixate on and make more.

'altering relationships by taxing them with fear
Changing my emotions to what you want to hear.'
'I've Been Lying', 1994

A friend of Katie's was working on Roddie Doyle's *The Snapper* and there was a scene where the family are watching a band on TV. I offered our clip of 'Sweet Obsession'. In the final film you can hear the song for around twenty seconds but the clip features for approximately two seconds and twelve frames. Approximately.

Give Me the Gun

Spring sprung early in 1993 and there was much emerging in our garden. There was also some pruning going on as we parted company with Adrian Lillywhite. Andy Catlin had introduced me to a press agent called Chris Carr who'd worked with The Who, The Rolling Stones, Depeche Mode, Nick Cave and had discovered The Cure. Chris was a white Kenyan with straight, shoulder-length light-brown hair and facial features that leaned toward the Cherokee. His speech patterns were, to me, often meandering and at times inscrutable, though in retrospect, I just couldn't hear the sense in what he was saying. The more pints we all downed, the more Buddah-like he became, quoting Marley and Dylan as if imparting the teachings of Confucius. His passport declared his occupation as 'Pestcatcher' as he'd spent his young life in Kenya catching snakes for a living.

I travelled up to meet him at his 'office', The Bath House on Dean Street in Soho, and foolishly took the car. You never got to meet Chris on his own, but became part of a rambling circus of guests, dropping or collecting tapes, records, photos and other paraphernalia as Chris held court at his table. The day I met Chris *I think* I was introduced to John Cale's manager and a girl called Ali who went out with Arthur Baker. *I know* they ended up shortly afterwards at my house for a late-night spaghetti Bolognese. With Chris, there was never that 'what can I do for you / what do you want?' moment which most business relationships inevitably encompass; it would have seemed too vulgar.

About four hours and several pints after I got there, the following things had possibly happened:

Chris had accepted an envelope containing some of our demos and some 8 x 10 photos Andy had taken of us. I'd called Katie and begged her to come and get the car (and me). I'd discovered that Chris was a rabid West Ham fan and knew a lot about football. We'd discussed our common love of The Who, red wine and distance running. We'd laughed a lot. Over the next

FIN

SPLASH CLUB, LONDON

Debut

SOMETHING special this way swims; something that sounds a little familiar, but more than a little thrilling.

Utterly thrilling, in fact. There's a chronic global shortage of the qualities Fin possess in abundance: lyrical eloquence, melodies that can melt or menace, guitar pop that's alternately swaggering and shamelessly sensitive.

Frontman Johnny Dawkes' visual presence is still at the tentative stage, but his voice has the power to make his words connect, to be both heard *and* felt. The lovely "Trust" has the corniest of sentiments, really – something about how you don't appreciate love 'til its gone – but its melancholic melody is enough to make grown sceptics swoon. But the witheringly, gloriously scornful "The Man In The Fabulous Chair" shows that Fin have a set of sharp teeth under the surface.

Dawkes is a tall, dark and handsome man with a rakish fringe and an open white shirt. It's therefore pretty obvious who he's going to be compared to at regular intervals, but Fin's few Suedelike songs are offset by lots more too wayward or too tender to smell of animal nitrate. Guitar man Andy Faulkner knows how to drive dangerously, and how to cruise smoothly.

Fin's finest three minutes to date is probably "Give Me The Gun", wherein Johnny confronts the most terrifying of existential traumas: *"What about tomorrow?/Who you gonna be?/Terry Scott or Barry Norman?/Brief moments in hell . . ."* Kind of puts all those death metal horror songs in perspective.

Tired of generic, tongue-tied and witless mediocrity? The fresh and refreshing solution is the one that comes at the end of all the best French films. Fin.

You really should see them.

DAVE JENNINGS

week it became as clear as things ever became with Chris, that he was going to handle our PR and from then on, things rather sped up.

I'd begun to write a certain type of song with a certain type of sound, partly trying to mimic the production of Tony Visconti (Bowie/T. Rex), driven by strummed acoustics, honking electric guitars and lots of delays and reverb. In fact they were more heavily indebted to the very recent recordings of Suede and the production of Ed Buller, which I'd do comparative listens to whilst mixing. In fact, nearly all of our early reviews referenced Suede, who I was quite clearly drawing a heavy 'influence' from. Our first live review was in the *Melody Maker* in March '93 and having been tipped off by Chris that it was running, I drove to Rococo News on Elgin Crescent W11 who always got the music papers in first. As I walked into the shop, a bale of papers lay on the floor, the binding only just cut. I picked up the top copy and leafed straight for the live review section, and there we were, with the orange lozenge denoting this was our debut.

Reading someone else's deconstruction of your music is quite disconcerting and aside from being slightly miffed at my surname being misspelled, I thought it was all a bit over the top: 'thrilling', 'eloquence', 'swaggering', 'melancholic', 'witheringly, gloriously scornful'. Calm down, mate! I also felt like I was bursting with joy, but, deep down, there was a voice shouting, 'Just you wait, you bastards.' What? Who? Bastards?

I probably read it three times before the owner reminded me that they were a shop not a library, then I picked up ten copies and went and read them in the car. All of them. I can't remember what happened the rest of the day, but there was definitely a pub involved.

Brief moments in hell then an easy way...
So give me the gun, I'm pleading, I'm bleeding
Shut out the sun that's drying my crying
I'm off to see the man with the masterplan
So give me the gun, give me the gun
'Give Me The Gun', 1992

Our 'finest three minutes' mentioned in the review, 'Give Me The Gun', was definitely becoming a crowd favourite. We sent it to Gary Crowley's *Demo Clash* on GLR (BBC London) and won four weeks running, becoming the Champion of Champions. But it was never my favourite. Although people attributed much to its elliptical lyrics 'the most terrifying of existential traumas', the truth is it was about suicide and I had never felt remotely close. This was a song where I *was* placing myself in an imagined state of mind.

As such, any praise of the song made very little impression because, to paraphrase Midge Ure, it meant nothing to me. In May 1993, I wrote a song that meant a lot to me and, as previously noted, my mum really didn't like.

This Feeling Keeps Repeating

This feeling keeps repeating
Christ's children all entreating
'Headstrong', 1993

Having allowed the BBC to use the 'Sweet Obsession' video in *The Snapper*, their rights management team called me to offer a £200 buyout. The post production on the film was complete; it had been edited, graded and sound-mixed. I knew that our video was inextricable from the scene unless they wanted to go to enormous expense, so I suggested to the man on the phone that I'd be happy to grant the rights for the song to be used for £4,000. He choked, but quickly realised this wasn't a negotiation that he had any leverage in and after blowing off some steam and possibly describing me as 'headstrong', agreed. With no record deal on the horizon, I used the money to record and manufacture what was to be our debut ten-inch single.

'Headstrong' was correctly identified as something of an anti-religious rant but there was more to it than that. The feeling that kept repeating was inside me and had its roots in those early teenage years. There's a mix of people being addressed, not least Father Joseph Gabbiola back in confession at Grandpont House as I asked him, 'Would you try to explain why there's another world?' The second verse alternates accusation between Bananas and my mum: 'He says you're to blame and she says just the same.'

I was Headstrong, in the face of all the above, but at the same time as resisting, took all of the blame and guilt inside: 'now you've made them all your own'. So far, so self-aware – to a point. The kicker, that only I'd be aware of, is in the video that I shot on a Hi8 video camera on Paddington Basin.

The ejaculate as the egg bursts repeatedly and the wine bottle pours fluid across the torso. The captions made from a hand-cut lino stencil set 'dISgUsT', 'shAmE', 'sAliVaTioN'.

It wasn't just Catholicism that was getting a good kicking.

We packaged *Headstrong* as a four-track EP on ten-inch vinyl, adding to its allure by individually numbering all of the 1000 copies. The track-listing was:

Side A: 'Headstrong', 'Trust'
Side B: 'Lolita', 'Sweet Obsession'

Trust was a heartfelt and emotionally direct love song and Lolita was your average, run-of-the-mill glam-rock confection about a paedophile. Clearly identifiable as a commentary on the novel by Vladimir Nabokov that details the sexual obsession of an adult professor, Humbert Humbert, who grooms and rapes the twelve-year-old Dolores Haze, known by him as Lolita. The song contains the lyric:

> but for the slide that your fortune supplied,
> the child would have surfaced alone
> 'Lolita', 1993

As close to a plea on behalf of my young self as one could imagine. Whenever we played this live, I always attacked it with a ferocity lacking in other songs, I think it's quite obvious why. As Sting (who skirted similar territory in 'Don't Stand So Close To Me') would have had it, I was 'sending out an SOS', but not one that would attract the attention of the police – not for a while anyway.

Tourer, Tourer, Tourer

Could I plead misfortune? And tell you the story of how close it comes.
Could I reappoint you? The knighthood for running where cowardice runs.
'Radio', 2003

We were about to come very close, but the 'misfortune' that would befall us owed very little to chance or outside influences.

In late September '93 we recorded the four tracks for the *Headstrong* EP with producer Phil Vinall, who'd recently worked with Suede and The Auteurs. Phil found me 'a bit full-on' and did his best to remove some of my worst affectations and over-indulgences. On the demo I'd sung in an overwrought falsetto and Phil suggested I drop it an octave, only leaping up for the final chorus. It was a huge improvement. The recordings were reasonably lo-fi, spitting with aggressive, middley guitar tones. They sounded ballsy, basic and exciting – pretty much perfect for a debut. Andy Catlin had taken some pictures in which we looked like we sounded and Chris Carr took cassettes and shots to the music papers.

The exact order of what happened next is somewhat fuzzy, but we were about to find ourselves in a situation where we would have benefited from some management. We'd been approached a few times after gigs, but I had already begun to exhibit a habit of rejecting any attempts at advice or invitations to discussion. We started defaulting to Chris in most matters. Chris was a skilled and intuitive PR – if not always the most organised or strategic of people and in the circumstances that were to follow, a little strategy would have gone a long way.

Having recorded and mastered the EP, we sent it off, with the Andy Catlin designed artwork for the 1000 copies to be pressed and printed. We imagined this would be the right number for a debut that might at best be a calling card for the music press. I received four test-pressings from the factory, in order to check the vinyl before they went ahead, and pressed the

OBVIOUS

FIN
HEADSTRONG EP (Red)

ANNOUNCING the arrival of something truly, madly, deeply special.

On this evidence, Fin's snappy name should soon be mentioned alongside the likes of Suede, Radiohead and The Auteurs when tasteful folk get together to discuss the way that songwriting is becoming a vital, vibrant art form once again.

Fin are all about guitars that surge, sparkle and spring surprises, and words that set scenes that you feel irresistibly intrigued by.

There are four fine examples of their cultured craft on this debut release – the dramatic title track, the impossibly romantic "Trust", the totally wired lust-story, "Lolita", and the brisk, bruising "Sweet Obsession". There are even better songs on display in this London band's live shows, but plenty of the most glorious things in life – sex, love, faith and fascinating strangeness – are right here on this EP.

Discover Fin now and avoid being trampled in the coming stampede.

main volume. Placing the ten-inch disc on my turntable and dropping the needle, then hearing the 'barnstorming crush' of a track that I'd written upstairs a few weeks before was thrilling. Phil had done a great job and 'Headstrong' sounded so good, I decided I'd take two of the test-pressings into Radio 1 the next day.

That wasn't really how things were supposed to work. There was a network of professional promotions companies called 'pluggers' who bands or labels would pay to carefully coordinate and target certain stations and producers. These people had relationships built on mutual trust and respect and maintained an impenetrable ring of gatekeepers. I wandered into Broadcasting House and placed the two discs on the desk with a handwritten note for Jeff Smith, the producer of *The Evening Session* (Lamacq & Wiley, weeknights from 6–8). The following morning, I answered our home phone.

'Hello, is Johnny there?'
'Speaking.'
'Hi, Johnny, this is Jeff Smith from *The Evening Session*.'
'Oh – hello…'
    'Thanks for dropping "Headstrong" in, we've just been playing it in the office and we love it. We'd like to get you in to do a session for the show at Maida Vale…'

The session was booked for a few weeks away and the significance of Radio 1's patronage hadn't really hit home. There were print problems with the sleeve and production was delayed, we'd also not considered distribution – how the records would find their way to the shops. Chris had recently introduced us to Mick Griffiths, a live agent with the booking agency Asgard. Mick saw us live and offered to represent us for bookings. We were gradually assembling a team around us, a team with great individual players but no coherent management (as a Manchester United supporter in early 2022, this is a woefully familiar situation). We still had no physical EPs to distribute, but based on review cassettes we were made Single Of The Week in *Melody Maker*, who continued to throw enough superlatives at us that the *NME* felt duty-bound to hate us (or at least begin throwing a series of very back-handed compliments).

We celebrated the *Melody Maker* accolade at several pubs around Portobello Rd and the following morning I was lying in bed with a very sore head. The bedside phone rang and I dislodged it from its cradle.

'Hello, Johnny?'
'Uggghhh...'
'It's Mick Griffiths here from Asgard.'
'Ugh?'
'How do you fancy going on tour?'
'When?'
'Today...'

As I sat on the edge of the bed, crusted in drool with red-rimmed eyes, drooping in spirit and elsewhere, Mick explained that Drugstore were supposed to be supporting Tindersticks on a two-week tour of the UK but had succumbed to illness, would we be able to take over? Having put the phone down (reflecting on the irony of Drugstore cancelling a tour through illness) I then picked the phone straight up again. I re-enacted every 'we're putting the band back together' scene ever – except we hadn't split up.

Richard's boss was a huge fan of the band, Andy was unemployed and Al worked in admin for the NHS, so no one had any hesitation in taking a fortnight off. There was no time to rent a splitter van and we shoved a wicker sofa in amongst the gear* in the back of a transit panel van and set off for the first night in Nottingham – Tindersticks' home town.

There's a reason why 'dreampop' band Drugstore had been chosen to tour with Tindersticks: a musical sympathy between them and consequently their fanbases. As we were introduced pre-soundcheck, I couldn't help noticing their preference for thick woollen clothing, as if they were preparing for a bracing moorland walk through thick gorse. A walk on which they'd remove the well-thumbed copy of whatever Penguin Classic protruded from their overcoat pocket and thoughtfully read passages as their brows furrowed to a soundtrack of lumbering bass, keening violin and mournful vocal.

---

* This is as idiotic and woefully unsafe as it sounds. I've subsequently become aware of two bands who followed a similar course of action with tragic consequences. We were very stupid and very lucky.

Oh no, hang on! They were sound-checking!

Full disclosure (which is, after all, the point of this): I absolutely fell in love with their music and still listen to them today. In autumn 1993, I responded to the feeling that I liked them as an eleven-year-old boy responds to the feeling that he likes an eleven-year-old girl – and behaved like a dickhead. We weren't so much chalk and cheese (which are *actually* physically quite similar) as chalk and chimps. We were certainly cheeky monkeys. That first night was pretty awful; our glam-pop racket sending curious Tindersticks fans to rush for the safety of the bar.

The next day something weird happened. As we were driving along in the van, 'Headstrong' was played on Radio 1. I think it was the Jakki Brambles show. The following day it was played on the Simon Mayo show and he announced it was his Record Of The Week. As the week progressed, it was played increasingly frequently and every time it was played, more people would turn up at the evening's gig to hear us.

If you wanted to make a positive impression on the headline band you were touring with, a list of things to do would be very unlikely to include 'a cover version/impersonation of headline band in your soundcheck'. Our impersonation of Tindersticks' song 'Jism' was notable for its brevity (30 seconds rather than 6m 30s), but also its accuracy. I'd identified that in order to capture the essence of their singer Stuart Staples, it was necessary to throttle my diction in the manner of having a large spoonful of peanut butter in my mouth. What I hadn't identified and wouldn't for far too long, is why I felt it was a good idea to take the piss out of a group of decent people who might otherwise have been well disposed toward me.

The penultimate night of the tour was 12 November and the reception we were getting was improving every night, as were we. The venue was Manchester University Student Union and we had visitors from London.

Chris Carr had an American friend called John Coon who I'd met briefly at The Bath House back in July. John was a very loud, very abrasive, very smart and very funny man who would be approached frequently by people convinced he was Billy Connolly. Even his East Coast drawl, thickened by sixty Marlboro a day, failed to convince them otherwise. John had taken one of our demos in the summer and quite liked it, but the recent 'Headstrong' recordings had piqued his interest sufficiently to divert to the UK on a trip to France and now

to Manchester to see us live. He'd arrived in London in time to read a gushing live review of a show of ours the week previously, to see our Single of The Week in the *Melody Maker*, then heard us on Radio 1 on the drive to Manchester.

The gig that night was not only our best of the tour but one of our best ever and John, a rock 'n' roll veteran of thirty-five years in the business, was blown away. He was so impressed that when he took us for Chinese that night and Al threw a lager-soaked pork bun at him, he still paid the bill. We were dickheads.

That night over many beers and games of pool we formed a rapprochement of sorts with the members of Tindersticks, which we then rather spoiled the following day by playing football in their soundcheck at the Sheffield Leadmill. But we met Ray Davies on the way home and had egg and chips with him at Watford Gap services. Which was nice.

At some point that week, Simon Mayo noted rather pointedly that despite lots of positive feedback for 'Headstrong', no one seemed to be able to get hold of it in the shops. The track had been placed on Radio 1's B List, guaranteeing it around thirty plays a week. The station expected this to be reflected in some kind of chart position. Not only had we pressed a meagre 1000 copies, but they had barely made it to the shops before selling out. We'd unwittingly committed a cardinal sin by creating a demand for something we couldn't supply. A management team would have been aware of the imminent airplay boost and immediately manufactured more and likely put an ad campaign in to support it.

TRUE STORIES
The column that knows where Jacko's other glove is

SPARKS FLY

WE were sorry to hear of on-the-road discord between the much-acclaimed **TINDERSTICKS** and spitting support band **FIN** during their recent week together on the road. Tindersticks, it seems, really *do* live up their ultra-sombre image, reading heavy-duty novels and discussing Kafka where most bands would happily concentrate on consuming their rider, and found Fin unforgivably frivolous.

Fin first incurred their wrath by covering a 'Sticks song in their soundcheck (their displays of air violin went down particularly badly with the long-faced ones). The final flash point came when Fin played football in one venue while Tindersticks were running through their own solemn soundcheck. A misdirected volley rattled the lighting rig in mid-song. Fin are not taking part in the second half of the tour.

But never mind. They enjoyed one surreal scene at Watford Gap service station where they, **RAY DAVIES** and **THE SEA** were the only customers, and then had **LUKE HAINES** turn up at their Splash Club gig last week to see how stylish songwriting should *really* be done . . .

Shortly after 'Headstrong', we were introduced to the legendary and enigmatic radio promoter Scott Piering. Scott, who'd managed The Smiths and been responsible for the success of Pulp, KLF, The Prodigy and many more, always maintained that he could never promote us as well as I'd accidentally done with 'Headstrong'. Sadly, it was to remain true.

Narcissus

Immediately we got back from the tour, I wrote 'Narcissus' and recorded the demo. One of Bananas' early lines of attack with me had been to tell me I was too egotistical. Starting with the 'your brother's a bighead' it was then 'don't be like your brother', 'don't be boastful' etc. At the same time as he was telling me not to fancy *myself*, his behaviour and actions were of a man who obviously did fancy me. Confusing?

I played the demo to Scott Piering. His office was quite small and was all hard, clean surfaces. I'd mixed the demo pretty harshly and it sounded really aggressive – Scott liked it. The New Wave of New Wave was spreading through the Indie scene and bands like S*M*A*S*H and These Animal Men were taking over the music papers. To me they seemed like embarrassing pastiches of bands I'd loved as a teenager – Buzzcocks, early Magazine – but without the tunes. Scott liked their attitude and I think was trying to steer me away from some of our more straightforward rock inclinations.

'Narcissus' was a spiky, trashy riff and although neither of us knew what it was about, it sounded quite sleazy. There are two distinct voices in the song and it's almost as if there's an argument taking place. At its heart I can see with distance that it's a fight taking place, trying to reconcile the hypocrisy of what Bananas was saying and doing. The lyric alternates between my voice and his, but my voice is inherently narcissistic.

> You are gorgeous, I've seen you long enough to know that
> You more than rate a mention.
> Conversation, your eyes have more of me than I do
> A delicate collection.
> 'Narcissus', 1993

The aggression in the bridge as it's almost spat out:

> You are love. You destroy. Me and One.
> So impressive, rich and sweetly coy.
> 'Narcissus', 1993

One of my favourite sounding records was Echo & The Bunnymen's 'Heaven Up Here' which had been produced by Hugh Jones. Chris knew Hugh and we went for a beer. Hugh had a lovely way about him, very old-school rock 'n' roll with a slightly foppish edge. Camp, like Jagger. We had a couple of pints during which Hugh smoked all the cigarettes in Britain and laid out his 'vision' for the track. It was going to require four days to record and mix, which seemed *forever*. There was a recording studio in South London called Orinoco that was also a film studio and Katie knew people there. We got a great deal for a lockout in early December.

> When you're sleeping, the sordid seconds slide to hours
> They should have cost a fortune.
> 'Narcissus', 1993

As I delivered the vocals at the studio there was a barrier between the meaning and what I allowed myself to think they were about, a constant fog. I'd 'try' to inject something and when I listen now, I can hear the difference between the affected emotion and the odd moments where the truth sneaks out. The middle eight of 'Narcissus' is a cacophony of tom-toms with a mewling, filtered lead line that has a really fast modulation on it. The lyrics that I sort of yelled/cried are as close as I ever got to impersonating Howard Devoto from Magazine; they're sensibly buried in the mix.

So you ride out. Second sight out. Slowly slide out.
That's all you want.
'Narcissus', 1993

Fuck knows.

My dad had a copy of Dennis Wheatley's *The Devil Rides Out* and the cover terrified me. Maybe it's an allusion to that? I sound pretty scared so it would make sense.

Doctor Jimmy and Mister Jim

John Coon had flown back to the US after seeing us in Manchester, knowing that he could find us a deal. John had read the press and it felt right; he'd seen the band and we sounded right, he'd met the band and we were not one hundred per cent dickheads – maybe eighty-five per cent. He felt he knew exactly where to place us and, on Christmas Eve, had his 'traditional seafood dinner' to which he invited old friend and trusted recording engineer Karl Derfler and Columbia Records A&R Jim Dunbar. Karl had been working with Jerry Harrison and was about to get the call to spend the next twenty years working with Tom Waits; he was a brilliant engineer and knew his music. Jim was about to move to Geffen Records following a gushing profile of him in the *New York Times*.

In the midst of a marathon of scallops, oysters, abalone, gallons of white Burgundy and a bale of grass, John happened to place the *Headstrong* EP on the turntable. As the lead-line snaked through the opening riff, Jim's ears pricked up as he asked, 'Who the fuck is this?' John matter-of-factly told him the story. *Being in London, reading the reviews, making the journey to Manchester, the stunning gig and hanging out playing pool etc. etc.* Karl leaned back in his chair, nodding along as the chorus chimed in again, the ultimate accolade from an engineer of his experience – this was *the real deal* and Jim saw it all.

In the past month we'd been seen at multiple gigs by Korda Marshall, the ex A&R head of RCA, who was about to launch his own label, Infectious, with the backing of Australian media company Mushroom. Korda was keen to sign us and visited twice whilst we were recording *Narcissus* at Orinoco, feeling sure that he knew how to develop us. It would have been a smart move and Korda was a really decent guy. I can vaguely recall being a dickhead. Korda signed Ash and they did very well.

In early January, John flew to the UK with Jim who'd now joined Geffen and was keen to make his first signing. We'd become a regular fixture at The Splash Club, an Indie night that took place in the old Water Rats Theatre on Grays Inn Rd. It was a really great room, capacity of about 120 so easy to fill, decent lights and the best (small) PA system in London. The club was rammed and we went on around nine. Even at short notice we'd pulled forty or fifty and our press was such that the crowd for the headline band – Catatonia – came through from the bar.

FIN are a four-piece from West London. They formed a couple of years ago and since then have created a stir in the capital with their vibrant live shows and passionate songs. In their early days, they recorded a set for Radio One's 'Evening Session' and appeared on MTV's '120 Minutes', but it wasn't until last year's release of their debut EP, 'Headstrong' on Red Records, that things really took off. It became an MM Single Of The Week, prompting our reviewer to claim, 'Discover Fin now and avoid being trampled in the coming stampede'. It now changes hands for up to £20. Comparisons range from Radiohead to The Auteurs to Blur, mainly due to the band's belief in strong songwriting.
They have a new single, 'Narcissus', out now and support on tonight's show comes from Bubbleman.

John stood by the sound desk on a raised area and watched Jim, who'd shuffled to the mid-ground. We played a short set of about seven songs, all of which Jim had heard either on the EP or demos. It felt more like our headline and as we finished 'Flow Over Me' in a wail of delayed feedback, the room was shouting for more. In rehearsals we'd been covering Magazine's 'Shot By Both Sides' and came back on with it as an encore. I had no idea that Jim was a huge fan of Magazine and as we tore into the opening riff, Jim turned to John Coon and flipped him the finger as if to say 'OK, you've got me…'

I've no idea how our gear got home, but that night we ended up in John's suite at The Pembridge Court in Notting Hill with Jim. There was champagne, cocaine and John and Jim spent quite a while scribbling numbers in a notebook.

Jim went back to the US, then returned a fortnight later with two other Geffen A&R men, Tom Zutaut and Mark Kates, who also wanted to see us. They came to meet us at our rehearsal room in Acton; the three of them shuffled into the shabby box looking more like a band than we did, all dirty boots and great coats. Zutaut had signed Mötley Crüe and Guns N' Roses and spent every song head bowed and eyes shut, nodding along in a trance-like state. He obviously approved. Kates was responsible for Sonic Youth and Nirvana being on Geffen and was also visibly into it.

We'd scheduled another Splash Club show and once again pretty much took the roof off. John Coon caught up with Zutaut in the bar before the Geffen trio had to go for a dinner. Zutaut's passing comment was: 'I've told him, *Jim, sign the fucking band…*' Jim went back to the US and a few days later John called me to say that Jim was coming back in early February and bringing Ed Rosenblatt, the head of the label. This was encouraging, but something didn't feel right to me; if he wanted to sign the band so badly, why hadn't he just done so? John was back in San Francisco and couldn't return immediately as he had other business. He told me to relax, that these things could sometimes 'be a bit wiggly'; Jim loved the band and wouldn't be returning with Rosenblatt otherwise.

The next three weeks in London, alone without management, were frustrating and my worst impulses rose to the surface. The last Splash gig had received a shitty review from the *NME*, and even the *Melody Maker* had interpreted our covering Magazine as somehow us being bitter. I'd adored them for ten years for fuck's sake!

I went to see Scott Piering, who darkened my mood further by playing me the latest S*M*A*S*H single, 'Lady Love Your Cunt'. By the time we released *Narcissus* on 14 February, I'd begun to exhibit a bunker mentality and was interpreting the forthcoming visit of Jim and Ed from Geffen as the precursor to a disaster. With the benefit of (a lot of hindsight) I was clearly allowing the pressure of what was likely great success to get to me and catastrophising. I'd done it before and would continue to do it. We now had the might of Scott and his promotions team at Appearing behind us, so our hopes were high for *Narcissus*, which we'd taken the precaution of pressing an initial 2,500 CDs as well as numbered vinyl.

We'd shot a video in an all-white studio with plaster columns featuring vases of daffodils and bowls of goldfish. Under the studio lights the water warmed up and the fish all became drowsy, languishing in the bottoms of the bowls. I knew how they felt. MTV had played our previous video on the Indie show *120 Minutes* and there was positive feedback to the new one. Compared to the haphazard release of *Headstrong*, we were much better prepared. What we weren't prepared for was Scott's news that Radio 1 'didn't quite love' *Narcissus* and it was going on the C list.

Our third Splash Club gig in four weeks had a weird feeling to it; we should have played somewhere else – anywhere else. The crowd was depleted following our two very recent shows and I was a bundle of negative energy. I made the schoolboy error of 'playing for the A&R man'. We had drinks with Jim afterwards, but the enthusiasm of the first Splash show had dissipated somewhat; he clearly didn't quite love us as much and that wasn't a great trajectory. The following night we played Coventry University Students' Union.

Don't play a students' union on a Saturday night – unless you're a covers band. If you do play a students' union on a Saturday night, don't drive the American A&R man to Coventry in your car without his American buddy to act as wing-man and keep things frothy. I was already in a mental tailspin and because John Coon was stateside and Chris Carr didn't drive, I ended up with Jim in my passenger seat for two hours up the M40. I did what any singer-songwriter who was paranoid their record deal was evaporating would do and, in the numerous tense and awkward silences that developed, I vomited into the void. It was like 'pass the mustard, Brian' without the benefit of the mustard.

By the time we arrived for the soundcheck there was a psychological gulf between me and the rest of the band who'd gone up with our soundman and roadie. Over the past few months we'd acquired our own soundman called Phil, who now managed our live mix at every gig. This meant we sounded significantly better than we used to. And a roadie/guitar tech called 'Spud', previously with The Pogues and Buzzcocks. This meant we got to the stage with all guitars in tune, with fluorescent tape marking trip-hazards and were protected from angry audience members that I'd abused in a fit of nervous anger.

The gig wasn't disastrous. Disastrous would have meant a pissed bunch of students wanting to dance and getting stroppy at the deluge of clanging glam-pop blasting from the stage. Disastrous would have been a rising tide of pissed-up yelling from the students, not remotely interested in our music, all shouting to make their conversations heard on a Saturday night out with their mates.

That would have been disastrous.

What made it something else – something even worse than disastrous – was my attempting to quell that yelling and stroppiness with a stream of sarcasm turning to outright contempt at them, their clothes, their lifestyles, their existence.

What made it catastrophic was a bottle of beer that landed on the stage, that I booted straight back out into the crowd. The lad it landed near ran to the front of the hall and pushed my mic stand, which whacked the mic into my bottom lip. I called him something that sounded like 'fucking cunt', on account of it being 'fucking cunt' and he then tried to visit our dressing room and only the significant presence of Spud kept him the other side of the door.

I cowered within, surrounded by a beer-soaked band and a very perplexed A&R man from the US who attempted to reassure me that the show really wasn't all *that* bad.

We barely spoke on the long drive home.

Our first significant write-up in the *NME* was riddled with clues as to our internal stresses and how they were being perceived from the outside.

GENITAL GIANTS

"I DON'T know why people keep making these fish references. Our name is derived from the French for 'The End'..."

Meet Johnny Daukes, lead singer and guitarist with **FIN** (not pronounced "fan", despite the above comment) and a good, solid, old-fashioned rock star. Slightly pretentious, a bit of a showman, but a true believer in traditional musical values like Honesty, Hard Work and Quality Songwriting.

In a scene invaded by the amphetamine logic of the NWONW and the fiery postures of the rap/rock collision, it's ironic that it's Fin, with their conventional line-up (Johnny, guitarist Andy Faulkner, bassist Allan McAteer, drummer Richard Childs and not a little ranty bloke in sight) and their robustly classic indie rock sound, that stick out like a badger in a belfry.

This is not the stuff of instant tabloid horror stories, but of the time-honoured route to success. Since forming in the summer of 1992, they've clocked up over 100 gigs and bunged out two indie singles – the barn-storming crush of 'Headstrong' and the sturdy idolatry of 'Narcissus' – prompting mass drooling amongst the American A&R fraternity, and fuelling

rumours that their first EP now changes hands for £20 a throw.

"If that's true, I'm a rich man," grins Johnny. "I've still got a load under my bed! But I'm not at all surprised at the interest in us in the States. They just recognise us for what we are: a unique band."

And a potential big earner, presumably. But, seeing as we're speaking in the wake of Kurt Cobain's death, and Fin are being chased by – amongst others – Nirvana paymasters Geffen, it's a day for sober reflection rather than wild anticipation.

"We're kind of the opposite of the New Wave Of New Wave," continues Andy. "That seems to be all about an attitude and, while it's a good one, it's not an attitude we have. We'd never go out of our way to be deliberately controversial..."

Well, there is the naked bloke on the 'Narcissus' sleeve.

"If we'd wanted to shock we'd have gone a lot lower with the shot and put the guy's cock on the sleeve. That would have been bollocks."

Quite literally. But the truth is, Fin have no need of such gimmicks. Their brash melodies, epic guitar sound, wordy lyrics and all-round veneer of CLASS has already won them an unlikely admirer in the form of Fab FM Golden Hour jock Simon Mayo. Success, albeit in the sneak-up-on-you style of musical cousins Radiohead, should follow. And, if Fin do join the ranks of rock heavyweights, we can at least rely on them to stir things up a bit.

Mark Sutherland

● **The 'Narcissus' EP is out now on Red records. Fin play around at Kensington Orange (June 2) and Camden Falcon (4) before heading out of town for a string of regional dates.**

Squid Pulls Away

In March 1994 I was looking back at a year that had started with our first live review and ended with a deal at Geffen Records that was, at least according to John Coon and Chris Carr, still very much alive. Also very much alive, or at least beginning to awaken, was a feeling inside me that I couldn't put my finger on. Since Chris Barclay's death I'd developed a worsening eczema; I'd suffered with it as a kid, but it seemed to get bored with me once I hit puberty – quite different to Bananas in that respect. Following a visit to see Chris in St Thomas', I'd become irrationally anxious that I too might have HIV. There was absolutely no reason for it and nothing in my lifestyle that would have made it possible – far less, likely. But I became fixated, culminating a few weeks after his death in my taking an AIDS test. It was negative, but the anxiety and attendant stress brought my elbows out in an itchy, flaky rash. I then developed a near-constant irritation around my cheekbones, eyes and forehead.

> I bite and scratch that lights a match that burns around my eyes
> The desperate search for honesty increases the disguise.
> 'Why We Are', 1994

Throughout 1993/94 this worsened as the feeling wakening within me strengthened. A song appeared in early '94 unlike anything else I'd written (although its waltz time and string-heavy backing was decidedly Tindersticky). It was called 'Squid', and addressed someone:

> The darkest ever eyes, are they black 'cause they're deep
> Or has something you held down inside - slowly died.
> Does it worsen it to think, are you shrouded in mystery
> Blinded or cloaked by the ink - you slowly sink
> 'Squid', 1994

At the time I felt I was writing about a feeling of alienation, the struggle to fit in. The last verse was not unfamiliar lyrical territory, in fact it was becoming more familiar with every song.

> **Sometimes you smile, but it's strictly a facial sensation**
> **All part of your style, pulled from your file.**
> **Could you be real, don't be hard drop your guard**
> **For once in your life say what you feel,**
> **not what you think that you should feel**
> 'Squid', 1994

I told the band that it had been inspired by Phil our soundman who had dark, black, dead eyes not unlike a shark – or a doll. It was an odd explanation, odd because it made no sense other than Phil had dark eyes – but it was something, enough for me to justify it to myself.

> **Squid pulls away when I reach out my hand**
> **Squid's been abused and his mind is confused**
> **In a way that he can't understand**
> **Squid pulls away when I reach out my hand**
> 'Squid', 1994

I seem to be addressing my young self, trying to reach out to that scared boy. We played the song once or twice live and the effect of singing the final chorus should have been enough to make me question what I was saying.

But Squid was confused in a way that he couldn't understand. That's what'll happen when you've been abused.

179

Geffen Dumb

On 14 April 1994, FIN peaked. Not in terms of writing; I'd say that was one of the last songs I wrote for FIN in early summer of 1995, 'Parade'. But our performance at the Astoria in support of The Cranberries was pretty much as good as we got. Not that you'd have known it if you'd read the *NME*'s review. News had spread around London about Geffen's interest, so even after writing us off as: 'unremarkable, such bands are two a penny over here', their writer qualified himself by predicting we'd be 'whisked off to the States where they're as rare as communism'. Little did he know.

That night we played a live version of 'Junk Male', the third track off the *Narcissus* EP and one of the four tracks we recorded for our live BBC session. The song is a reflection on being dumped, receiving postcards from an ex and facing weekends alone watching films and drinking beer. It's quite 'stately' and has a vaguely Smiths-like quality until the chorus where the stoic resignation is torn away by the brutal chorus:

I need to jump on your face, to put you back in your place.
Give me five more minutes and I'll make you believe
that you really can't leave.
'Junk Male', 1994

Over the past fifteen years, I had found myself becoming more argumentative and prone to anger in my relationships and friendships. Though there was never violence or the threat of it, I could at times be brutally harsh. Low-key disagreements could escalate when I felt that someone else was wrong, disrespectful or even expressing themselves clumsily. It really didn't take much. These outbursts were, I think, attempts to wrestle control and most of the time they negated anything I was saying that made sense. Once I had reached the tipping point, I couldn't resist piling on for what felt like sweet relief. It was one of these outbursts that ultimately blew apart the Geffen situation.

Jim Dunbar returned for his fourth visit to see us and was clearly agonising over his decision. He wasn't to last much more than a year at Geffen, failing to sign anyone – so maybe it wasn't us, it was him after all? We were playing the Garage and had recently taken on the lawyer Kaz Gill of the firm Statham Gill Davies, who were representing pretty much every decent band of the time. Kaz had gained a reputation as a deal-maker and in the absence of a coherent management structure, I felt represented a likely route to a record label. I suppose to an outsider, especially one used to closing deals, our brief yet complex dalliance with Geffen must have appeared quite frustrating. I know it did to an insider.

As we took to the stage in the packed venue, several things were immediately apparent to Jim. In the month since he'd seen us, my frustration at the press coverage being afforded to the NWONW bands, the acres of *NME* articles, the fascination of certain radio DJs who'd got fingers in labels and were promoting their own acts, the whole London-centric scene that was celebrating itself (but not us) boiled over and I took the only course of action I felt I could. I cut my hair short and bought some plastic trousers.

These weren't huge strides (W31, L32) but alongside me, Richard had cut his hair short and dyed it blonde. As Jim was recalibrating to this strange (and obviously knee-jerk) visual transformation, Kaz wandered over and introduced himself, enquiring as to whether Jim was going to 'shit or get off the pot?' This witty Brit-banter never goes down well with other half of the Special Relationship and when our entourage repaired to the usual post-gig haunt, *Angelo's* greek restaurant in W2, Jim was in a very strange and defensive mood.

Which probably explains why I went on the attack.

I can't remember much of the detail, but I do remember that months of feeling I was at the mercy of his whim may have got the better of me. It had started with some playful taunting, but soon developed and I tipped. I knew that Jim was from a fairly wealthy media family and I may have resorted to some kind of 'it's alright for you born-with-a-silver-spoon pricks' type of content. I may have done.

However many nails were already in the coffin of the FIN/Geffen alliance, this was the final one.

Beneath My Skin

There was another nail in a coffin shortly afterwards, a knee-jerk reaction from me that altered the make-up of the band and that we never recovered from. Al McAteer and I had something of a love/hate relationship. Most of the time we got on really well, but there were times when he irritated me and no doubt that antagonism was prompted in him by something in my behaviour – though I honestly can't think what would possibly annoy a bass player in a singer/guitarist/writer who micro-managed every aspect of the band's music and creative output.

The straw that broke the camel's back wasn't an actual straw – pints of beer don't have straws in – but it did find its way down Katie's back, and it was Al's pint. In truth, I made Al a scapegoat for the terrible disappointment of the past few months and the sense of failure that engendered in me. I know people who, when faced with a career setback or personal problem, can gird themselves and resolutely set about turning the ship. I elected to chop the bow off the ship, then weld a new one on whilst it was still moving.

I even wrote a song about it afterwards, the execrable 'Decision', sticking the knife in even deeper with the line:

> In my ideal of the future, I'd replace you by computer
> That says nothing for your actions or your charm.
> 'Decision', 1995

My flesh crawls to write this, as if it wasn't enough to eject him from the band I had to double-down so as to reassure myself that my actions were justified. If I saw Al now, I'd love to buy him a pint, as long as he promised not to pour it down my wife's back.

My reaction to the existential crisis the band were in was a survival strategy I'd used before and would again. I wrote and recorded my way out of it with what became the *Skin* EP.

The lead track, 'Beneath My Skin', trawled my last days with Chris Barclay, the consequent anxiety and fear I was infected with and the eczema it spawned. I offered it to Kylie Minogue, but her management never got back to me. Although on the surface the song is fairly clear, beneath its…err…skin, there are undercurrents of a malaise that was, once again, trying to escape.

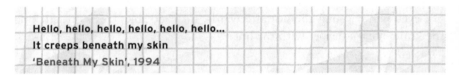

> Hello, hello, hello, hello, hello, hello…
> It creeps beneath my skin
> 'Beneath My Skin', 1994

The second verse broke unique lyrical ground by really getting to grips with the whole eczema thing:

> I make me feel, like I'm the only one
> I push the tide, but I just get soaked again
> And the salted water breaks the crusted shell,
> the bag that holds my bones
> And the cracks and doubt conspiringly swell,
> 'cause I'm so damned alone
> 'Beneath My Skin', 1994

Were it not for the salt water, this would have been refreshingly direct. What *was* direct was another track on the EP, 'Fade'.

Fade – Into my shame
You sit back and watch me fade – Fade away
'Fade', 1994

These tracks were recorded at a grubby studio in Chiswick, which seems apt as they were, in retrospect, fairly grubby tracks. Jim Dunbar may have given up on us, but John Coon hadn't and had returned from the US with his engineer buddy Karl Derfler who, at six foot four and with more hair than the average king-size mattress, had a presence that was at once commanding and yet incredibly calming. So basically, a great engineer. It was the first time I'd worked with Karl and I've continued to do so on various projects for twenty-seven years. He's a guru, a mensch, a Pro Tools genius, and every time I speak to him on the phone, I feel better about everything. That's practically a superpower.

What had also been a superpower in hindsight was Al's bass playing. Our guitarist Andy's girlfriend, Stella, had been drafted in *and that always works well, right?* That's not to cast aspersions on Stella, who was more than adequate, but when I look back at live videos of the time, Al played with a real authority; adding stops and passing notes that only a natural bass player can. It probably didn't help Stella that, in the session, I immediately stepped in to play bass on the first track we recorded, which must have been a real knock to her confidence. The first track was called 'Moisturizer', which posits genuine existential trauma.

You can spend as much as you like, to stop yourself from ageing
And in your dreams apply the creams that halt the signs of
Ageing into something that's a deeper kind of beauty
'Moisturizer', 1994

With the song's references to moisturising ageing skin and 'Beneath My Skin's *actual* references to *actual* eczema, *Select* dubbed me 'the Dennis Potter of indie rock' (Potter suffered terribly from psoriasis, which he notably addressed in *The Singing Detective*). It's a description I'm still proud of, even if it wasn't *meant* as a reference to my literary ability. Although 'Moisturizer' and 'Beneath My Skin' were singled out for reviews and airplay (Radio 1's D list; we were on the slide) it was the other two tracks on the EP, 'Love Me' and 'Fade', that contained the fragments of the bomb that had gone off twenty years ago.

The verses of 'Love Me' contain two lines each:

Remember you are dust – and everything you do
You never earn my trust, although you think you do'
'Your constant self-denial, makes you a stupid fool
You think you're self-possessed, you're someone else's tool
'Love Me', 1994

In both, the first line could apply to any Catholic or, more specifically, member of Opus Dei, but each time the second line homes in on an individual, the chorus identifies that individual.

'You say "love me"…'

The conflict in 'Love Me' and the shame referred to in 'Fade' were real and ever-present and they fuelled the constant self-examination I subjected myself to. 'Fade' became the song John Coon would love most from the FIN catalogue and he'd refer to it often over the next two decades.

Looking back, the 'clues' in the songs seem fairly relentless, but in every case, at the time, there was no hint in my mind that I was alluding to Bananas. And it wasn't just me that couldn't see it; at the time, neither could John – nor anyone else around me. Whether it was my compensatory behaviour or an exterior projection that I'd evolved, there were few indicators of what was taking place beneath my skin.

FIN

FIN limped on for another year. There were a load more gigs and we continued to be quite impressive live, but there was (at least to me) a sense of diminishing momentum. As Britpop caught light we sat damply by, not even on the periphery. There were odd mentions as 'ones to watch' etc. and we continued to be 'heavily tipped' by industry publications, but I knew we'd had our chance and blown it. It's possible that my fatalistic attitude was self-fulfilling, but there was also a tension appearing in the band. Andy and Stella were pushing to go in a more 'power-pop' direction and felt that Andy's writing should be given more consideration.

Our next single was released with the financial backing of 3MV, a distributor whose staff were committed fans of the band. At this point, we should have been one album in and I'd have been writing our second. The songs I was writing were more expansive and complex, there are a few that I still listen to now. My favourite is a song that was only ever recorded live (I don't know how or where). The chorus is a confusion of thoughts and images I'd voiced over the previous few years. It's a song I feel immensely proud of and it would sit happily on a good *R.E.M.* album.

```
I -I - I - The people's sanction, I - I - I - The pleading mantra
I - I - I - And one for all, for all I do or see
I - I - I - A self-obsession, I - I - I - A cheap confession
I - I - I - Parade the thoughts that you release to me
I- Am - Your - Desire
Set you out, then set you up, then set you on fire
'Parade', 1995
```

With the internal pressure from the band and the belief that we needed another radio-friendly single, I set about writing one. The result, 'Jetstream', is just that: a blatant attempt to write a radio-friendly piece of power-pop. Except it sounds like a pub rock band covering a Billy Bragg song. I find it almost unlistenable now, but the lyrics (which are mostly doggerel) have their moments.

> We are bright star, speed like fast car, running for the same horizon
> Snowflakes, sun's rays, raindrops, shared days
> Running for the Jetstream of your mind
> 'Jetstream', 1995

It's all ephemera. Vanishing. I think I was saying: 'The Game's Up'.

The best thing about it was the picture of Chris Barclay on the cover.

Our next live performance was the Sound City event in Bristol that was broadcast on Radio 1. The whole experience of the gig was a clear illustration to me of why we hadn't and wouldn't make it. Headliners Elastica swept into the venue to soundcheck, swathed in ratty fur coats and dark glasses. They walked past us (we were hunched on the floor amongst our amps like schoolkids) without a glance. In their own minds; glamorous, essential, film-stars, heroines.

Middle band Gene were possessed of a little star quality, even if most of it existed in the imagination of their charismatic singer. They had a couple of good tunes and, to their credit, were always in the Britpop roll-call.

Maybe the truth about us was the conclusion that our last reviews spelled out: we were good, just not different enough.

We released a compilation of all four EPs as a mini-album, *Positive*.

While peers happily imitated Morrissey's flamboyance, though, nobody came close to emulating his muse until West London's FIN released their third EP, 'Skin', last December. Sadly overlooked, the beautifully wrought 'Beneath My Skin' added a mournful cello to a formula indebted to The Smiths and the result verged on the poignancy of 'How Soon Is Now'.
Shaun Phillips, *Q*

Too sombre for Britpop accreditation, too well balanced for full-on PJ Harvey-dom, they sit awkwardly between the two. For every Suede-esque riff there's also a hint of R.E.M. at their most bucolically understated. Despite application of such rock-psychodramatic standbys as 'stigmata' and a song that deftly communicates the awful poignancy of being diagnosed fatally ill. Fin have much solid songwriting backbone, but no unique selling point.
Roy Wilkinson, *Select*

FIN's last gig was at the Reading After Dark Club. It wasn't after dark for me though, not by a long way. For Richard, Andy and Stella there must have been some relief; I don't think I was much fun to be around in those last few months.

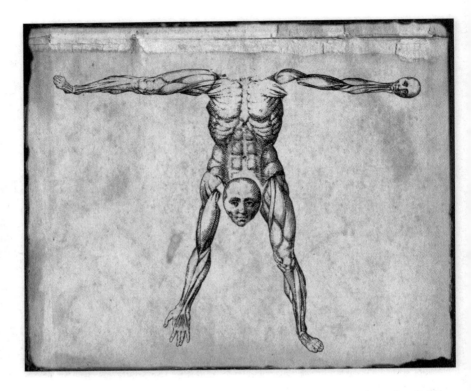

I thought this section was complete, but on a run my thoughts led me somewhere unexpected. I was thinking about how I would visually illustrate my experiences as a child and how it had affected me from that point onwards. I imagined something like this, albeit much more freakish and horrific.

And then I remembered a line from a song I wrote in 1992 that described being 'wrongly assembled'. It was just before I started FIN and was called 'Living My Life'. The song was, in my mind, an attempt to put myself in the position of someone with a physical disability:

Have you ever been strange? Felt like you had been wrongly assembled
So you think you need change, talk to me tell me what I resemble.
'Living My Life', 1992

This is what I meant when I wrote in the prologue about 'the twisted remnants *of a crashed* airliner'. This disfigurement is what I'm attempting to dissect and reassemble in its undistorted form, *'to find a route back to the uncorrupted me'*.

The three years of writing, recording and performing with FIN had included countless messages from my subconscious, either aimed at the outside world, myself – or both.

In Between Days

Don't say you're alone – and don't say you're afraid
Don't tell me that once, you had it made.
'Cause I know that's not so – I know it's all lies
I don't hear a pain or fear in your sighs
'Ripple', 1995

As soon as I split FIN, I was freed to write whatever, however, and quickly assembled a clutch of songs with a more intimate sound. Songs that sounded like what they were: home recorded and introverted.

I'd heard two albums at the time that had alerted me to a different path of writing and recording. Ron Sexsmith's eponymous second album and Sparklehorse's *Vivadixiesubmarinetransmissionplot*.

Ron Sexsmith had a naively confessional lyrical approach combined with softly shimmering guitars, warm percussion and glockenspiel. It was unaffected, unaffected and lacked any histrionics. Sparklehorse was pretty much the work of one man: the motorcycle-riding, stetson-wearing Virginian, Mark Linkous. The album sounded like nothing I'd ever heard: wheezing, clanging, scratching and possessed of a rawness that suggested no adherence to any studio convention. One of the first songs I wrote was, unsurprisingly, an attempt to make sense of the frustrations of the previous years. 'Waiting For The Lights To Change' featured a distorted vocal, beatbox and duffed-up guitar sound clearly influenced by Sparklehorse.

Tomorrow the trees will all be green and the streets will all be clean
You'll be right back in control again.
And all that you wish for will come true, there'll be mail and calls for you
Everyone will know your name.
'Waiting For The Lights To Change', 1996

So – a song about my band *not* making it in the style of a band who *had* made it.

'Everyone's Favourite Ingredient' had 'a naively confessional lyrical approach combined with softly shimmering guitars, warm percussion and glockenspiel'. The lyric paraphrased a Sainsbury's commercial of the time wherein the voiceover described making a meal: 'Take a few chicken thighs, add a scoop of oil, leave to simmer for twenty minutes then serve on a plate… Sainsbury's – everyone's favourite ingredient.' My twist (again) was to make it a song about my band *not* making it in the style of a band who *had* made it, in this case Ron Sexsmith.

'Take a man who believes he's failed, when his hopes and his dreams are stale
Take the salt from his red-rimmed eyes, beat with air from his deep dry sighs
Add a drop of his favourite drink, leave to simmer and seethe and sink
Watch the others around him rise and when he falls down don't be surprised'
'Everyone's Favourite Ingredient', 1996

At some point in spring 1996 I approached a number of publishers with tapes of the dozen or so songs I'd written post-FIN. One of them was Chrysalis Music who quickly became my favoured option. Firstly, they were around the corner from my house and, secondly, they were the only people who replied. I was initially offered a small development deal of £5,000. The day they made the offer I went home and wrote a song called 'Come Out' which was interesting for two reasons. Firstly, it encouraged Chrysalis to increase the offer to £10,000 and, secondly, it was the appearance of my referring to a 'virus'. In 2010, long after I'd acknowledged the abuse, I wrote a song about the process of the previous seven years called 'The Virus', but in 1996 that knowledge or realisation was still a long way off.

Surging on at lethal speeds, confusing wants – confusing needs
Refuting sense, creating bad desire
The virus growing thick and strong that suffocates the right and wrong
Erase yourself – goodbye.
'Come Out', 1996

Over the following few weeks, aided and abetted by Kaz Gill and by my knocking out new songs faster than Bananas and my sister were knocking out children, we managed to entice Chrysalis into an advance of £20,000 and one Friday afternoon I put pen to paper in their offices and became a published artist. Someone had shown enough belief in my songs to pay for them. My A&R man was called Rich King and, temporarily, I felt just that.

Actually, as un-rock 'n' roll as it is to say it, money wasn't really an issue. Aside from being married to a very busy camerawoman, in early 1995 I'd picked up a gig that over the next twenty years would become (as Arthur Daley would have it) 'a nice little earner'.

Before I'd given up editing, I'd worked a lot with an MTV producer called Mark Ford who'd then gone on to Rapido TV and the music show *Rapido*. I'd done a few bits for them and, at some point, in '94, I got a call from Mark with an odd request. Over our years working together, he'd got used to my habit of mimicking whoever we were cutting. I could do pretty much any accent, no doubt thanks to my mum's tuition at the breakfast table. Mark explained that Rapido were making a new series called *Eurotrash* and the idea was to re-voice interviews with various continental misfits using British regional accents. I think they'd done series one already with Johnny Vaughan who (in spite of being a very funny man) wasn't really versatile enough with voices. Mark asked

if I'd do a voice test, I did and was asked to do the series. *Eurotrash* became Channel 4's longest-running commission and I voiced series two to sixteen and further specials.

The Belgian goose farmer who shot home-made pornos? That was me. The Dutch artist who painted with his own shit? That was me, too. The adult German in the nappy suckling on his octogenarian wet-nurse? Yup, you guessed it. The first few series were definitely more free-form and anarchic as we strayed from the scripts and gave free rein, not just to the accents we used but also the character's speech impediments and foibles. As a result of *Eurotrash*, I got a voice agent and found myself staggering into the world of radio and TV voice work. Every week would bring commercials, cartoons, documentary narration and channel promos. For a long time, I was the voice you'd hear on Virgin mobile phones and have likely helped sell you VW cars, Head & Shoulders and told you that *you've been Tango'd*.

This characteristic, of getting a half chance and turning it into something, had become a habit and was to repeat itself throughout my creative life. There's very little I won't try and it never occurs to me that I shouldn't do it just as well as people who've received years of training. It's either a gift or a curse, as the other side of it is a permanent restlessness to move on, which often means I don't do something for long enough to break through inevitable barriers. I don't think this has got anything to do with Bananas and the abuse, I think it's more likely I was born a cocky little git who gets bored easily. Over the years I've taught myself to be able to do the following and have earned a living doing them at various points:

1. Recording engineer
2. Film editor
3. Director
4. Songwriter
5. Graphic designer
6. Voice artist
7. Comedy writer

I've received no formal training in any of these disciplines and consequently lack a depth and understanding of the history, techniques and principals involved in most of them. The result is that I'm frequently doing impersonations. As a songwriter, there were always hints and suggestions of other artists in my music, but arguably nothing definably original. Of all these occupations, the one I've gravitated back to (or in truth, *been gravitated back to*) is film editing because originality is not the primary skill required. You're cutting someone else's script and acting in the service of a director. What it does require you to have is superb political skills and vast reserves of patience – so I guess my days are numbered there too.

I suppose it's possible that those years between ten and sixteen, where I learned to be mistrustful of myself (or, more accurately, was taught to trust the self I was shaped into) have impeded my ability to make decisions that are based in what should have been my intuition. I'm accepting that might be a possibility, because as I've discovered in the process of writing this, those years have worked their way into everything ever since.

Surging On at Lethal Speed

The tunes that I'd written since splitting FIN were now begging to be taken in a far less intimate and introverted direction as the lure of playing live returned. Richard and I had stayed friends and it was a given that he'd play drums. A *Melody Maker* ad brought Shirley, a six foot three eighteen-year-old (who made the mistake of telling us her nickname was 'Big Bird') on bass and a very talented multi-instrumentalist called Janey on cello and keyboards.

I've got a heart, a muscle filled with fat and blood
I've got a soul, a boiling gas of fear and love
And in that soul, I store the memories of the pain
That broke my heart - to stop them happening again
But the memories fade, so I smile and say
Inside my heart is full, Inside my soul is still
Inside. Inside.
'Heart & Soul', 1996

And inside it remained. If things were bad for me, for my hero – the racing driver Ayrton Senna – things were considerably worse, as he'd died on 1 May 1994 and was therefore dead. In mid-May '94 FIN had done an interview with the *NME* who were keen to know how I felt about the recent death of Kurt Cobain. I said it was a shame but I was far more upset about Senna's even more recent death.

I think if you asked Richard, Shirley and Janey what it was like to be in the newly formed Senna with me, their responses wouldn't have been that different from Al, Andy or Stella. I was just as autocratic; maybe erring towards being a benevolent dictator. Either way, musical collaboration wasn't on the menu. The four of us rehearsed to the point where we were pretty

the paradise bar . 19 kilburn lane W10
monday 2nd june . on-stage 8:00
admission by invitation only

together and Chrysalis arranged for us to play a low-key gig in room above The Paradise, a pub in Kensal Green.

The low-key gig was actually what's called a 'showcase', a word that brings me out in hives and calls to mind bands from a rock school or performing arts college. It was our fault (my fault); I'd allowed myself to believe that our quality of songs and interesting visual line-up (AND A CELLO!) would render us irresistible. There were several A&R in the audience, not least the legendary Chris Briggs who'd signed all the bands ever and had reacted very positively to our recordings. This would be a shoo-in!

'To be fair,' John Coon remarked afterwards, 'if you don't get signed from that, Elton fucking John wouldn't have got signed either.' Needless to say, we didn't get signed. It was a good gig, but I guess the X-Factor just wasn't there, neither was Chris Briggs by the end.

I've just read Alan McGee's *Creation Stories* and, in comparison, my 'descent into cocaine hell' is going to come across a bit 'Peter and Jane Go Snorting', but I had a phone number for a man named 'Vince' and was calling it more and more regularly. For me, with my psychological make-up, this was a bad idea. Cocaine temporarily masks certain character traits – inadequacy, nervousness, self-doubt – replacing them (momentarily) with a confidence and bravado bordering (at least in my case) on recklessness. Oh – and paranoia!

Following the showcase my frustration (and consequent drug consumption) got the better of me and so Janey had to go. It couldn't be my songs or 'stage presence' that were the problem after all. I actually think Janey was relieved as she was a talented songwriter who didn't quite fit into the tight social group that Richard, Shirley and I had formed.

There was a harder edge creeping into my songs and as a three-piece it was necessary to make some changes to ensure our dynamics worked. I'd never been a particularly proficient guitarist, my playing (like every other skill I accrued) was short-circuited to get me to an operational base-point. I knew 'all the chords', which was enough for me to write songs. But for the first time I began to have to push myself further. Rich King was a very good guitarist (way better than me) and versed in a world of bands I'd not really listened to. Through Rich I was exposed to Dinosaur Jr, Sebadoh and Mogwai. He encouraged me to sort out the equipment I was playing through and to invest in some decent vintage effects pedals and amp.

I re-equipped my studio, upgrading to a 24-track tape machine, an automated mixing desk and lots of decent effects units. This accounted for the entire £20k advance. In retrospect, the person who lost out most here was Katie, who was entitled to at least half of that for her extraordinary support throughout the FIN years. I'm fairly sure some resentment crept in around this time that would ultimately contribute to our demise.

That studio in our back bedroom at Oxford Gardens W10 was a really powerful creative tool and a space where I felt absolutely at peace. In my own way, and without any real outside help, I'd created something that wasn't a million miles from the recording studio at Genetic that I'd been in awe of as a teenager.

The studio looked straight out at the elevated section of the A40 and looming over that were Grenfell Tower and its sister. The recordings I made in the house could easily have been album masters. We should probably have

gone ahead and released an album around that time as the songs had a real coherence, but having tried to go it alone with FIN, I felt we needed the validation of a label.

In terms of subject matter, the whole Catholicism/Opus Dei axis was still front and centre and the lines that, at the time, I felt were slightly enigmatic imagery are now as clear as day:

> And I'm not so far out that I can't see
> The people on the cliff-top looking down on me
> With a beacon they refuse to burn
> And I have waited all my life for this
> And swum for miles through seas so black and deep
> Where a dove sets out but won't return.
> 'Swimmer', 1996

What's striking from many songs of this period (among others) are the number of references to breathing. I'd been abused by a man with severe asthma and on countless occasions – nights when he'd use being 'cold' as an excuse to get into my bed – I'd be on red-alert to the sound of his wheezing, to ascertain if he was awake and that an attack on me was imminent. I'm quite certain that Bananas would bridle at the suggestion that he'd 'attacked' me as there was never any...

I've paused here. This goes to the heart of so much that makes this (and has historically made this) so extraordinarily difficult to understand and explain.

I was going to write: 'there was never any physical violence', but what do you call being overpowered by someone twice your size…

At the risk of this becoming a Russian Doll of a chapter, something else has just occurred to me. I wrote a song in 1992 (around the same time I wrote 'Shadowman') called 'Twice My Size' that was, on the face of it, about domestic abuse. As I wrote the words, 'twice my size', I flinched reflexively as the underlying meaning of (and motivation for) this song has literally just bobbed to the surface and become apparent to me.

> You're cold - unremittingly cold, Impartial in the second degree
> You've told - told me again, the big man with the battering ram
> 'Twice My Size', 1992

And there *was* physical violence. What else do you call waking to find someone's hands squeezing your genitals?

But back to the breathing.

> As the pain subsides and the lungs inflate
> In the youngest born of the Empire state.
> Adjusting low to medium, breathing in pure oxygen
> 'Oxygen', 1997

> Breathing to enervate your airspace
> Breathing to deflate your aspirations.
> 'Moths', 1997

> Do I taste to help you taste?
> Do I breathe to help you breathe?
> If I place your fist inside me will it help you to believe?
> 'Blind', 1998

Hmmm. It was becoming quite relentless.

Throughout 1997 the recording, writing and cavorting continued, then an opportunity arrived to 'tap into America'.

Sowing the
Seeds of Love

Saturday, 30 August 1997 and early on Sunday morning, Senna were flying to New York to play the legendary club CBGB as part of the CMJ festival. The invitation, which bemuses me to this day, had nothing to do with our potential and/or popularity, but was the result of John Coon calling in a favour with an American publishing organisation, the BMI.

The resulting flights, taxis and peripheral activity must rank as one of the great ecological disasters of the last century when measured on the energy output vs gratification scale. The immigration letter Chrysalis wrote (below) proving highly prescient: 'they will not be receiving any sort of payment'. However, none of that was on our minds that Saturday evening as we prepared to travel. That preparation involved drinking a lot of vodka, snorting a lot of gak, watching CNN mute to a soundtrack of Sparklehorse, Smashing Pumpkins and Mogwai, and seeing the news break that: LADY DIANA HAS DIED IN A CRASH IN PARIS!!

As night became day, upstairs the snoring form of John Coon was disturbed by a racket from downstairs as, for some reason (too much vodka and gak*) I was wandering around in my pants singing along to 'The Queen Is Dead' whilst whacking a colander with a wooden spoon.

* (How much vodka and gak is enough vodka and gak? A question that I researched on too many occasions, but, sadly, as the experiment reached what might be termed its 'revelatory peak', it frantically accelerated through creeping paranoia before hurtling headlong into accusatory mayhem that could only be assuaged by what was then, very definitely, too much vodka and gak.)

We somehow made it to Heathrow and I was now wearing a wraparound skirt over my pants and had a guitar case in my hand rather than a colander. The flight began eventfully, fuelled as we still were and full of excitement, expectation and more vodka. But like a toddler who's been jacked-up at a family wedding on nothing but cake and fizzy pop, eventually we passed out.

I don't like waking up at the best of times, and with a headache that would have fucked a lobotomised robot, a mouth that someone seemed to have filled with sandy excrement, and debilitating pins and needles in all my extremities, this was not the best of times. We were landing at JFK (which seemed odd as we'd not long taken off) and for a moment I wondered if this was some kind of hoax. As the moment progressed, I realised the hoax would have to include the participation of all the passengers, the staff, the groundcrew *and the sun* and quickly accepted that it was more likely we were landing – which meant I'd been asleep for over five hours – which also meant – gah! I was absolutely desperate for a piss. As I lurched from my seat, the nearby stewardess attempted polite discouragement...

'Sir!'

I lurched onward...

'Sir, you have to sit down!'

It was out of the question for me to sit down, because I hadn't done a wee for five hours and if we landed, then taxied, then waited to disembark – then I'd wet my pants *and* the seat and then they'd regret not letting me go to the loo and I'd have wet trousers and pants. So, on I lurched – into the loo, where I weed. When I emerged, I was confronted by the stewardess who told me (whilst preventing me from sitting down) that *under no circumstances must I ever use a toilet when the seatbelt sign is illuminated.* I assured her that there was very little chance of that happening again on this particular flight, but she was weirdly insistent that I agree I'd never do it on any flight and I told her politely that I just couldn't promise that. She rolled her eyes to all the listening passengers, then marched off. I was embarrassed, but my trousers and pants were dry and we had a gig to play!

Spencer had moved to the States about four years previously and we were staying with him in Manhattan. He lived in the West Village in a tiny but tastefully decorated flat with his wife, toddler and newborn baby. As we shuffled down his narrow corridor, guitar cases gouging lumps from his tastefully painted dado rails and our heinously fetid breath presenting a real Health & Safety hazard to the nervously-backing-away toddler, I could feel a tiny sense of trepidation from Spencer and his wife (who had already opened every window in the tiny but tastefully decorated flat). In rock 'n' roll folklore, bands always live with other bands in shabby, sprawling properties where dealers drop by unremarked-on and unsuitable things happen with unsuitable hangers-on in a boozy, greasy fug of iniquity. They don't live with a couple and their toddler and newborn baby in a tiny but tastefully decorated flat with magazines published that month, five different varieties of ground coffee and vases containing actual flowers which knock over easily.

We were to sleep on the living room floor with a combination of pull-out mattress, sofa cushions and a yoga mat – thus rendering the living room/ kitchen unnavigable. Over the course of three days and nights, the fact that we didn't come home before 4am and the newborn baby was feeding regularly at night, ensured that no one got any sleep and tempers on all sides were stretched very thinly. It's difficult to pinpoint the worst incident as it's akin to being shown an ant colony and asked to pick out your favourite ant, but the morning where Spencer's wife (who was holding down a very high-powered job in publishing and having to express milk at night for daytime feeds) was exasperated as to why the plastic bottle of breast milk had gone from the fridge, mere hours after we'd got back from a pub crawl and Richard had guzzled a huge bowl of Rice Krispies is, on reflection, my favourite ant.

On our second day it was the gig. Jetlag, nocturnal feeds and days of alcohol abuse ensured that we were in less than tip-top condition, but we made it to CBGB for the 4pm soundcheck. Rich King was staying in palatial luxury at the Soho Grand and filling in for us on second guitar. We'd recently subjected ourselves to 'a makeover', which had led to several changes:

- I'd taken to wearing skirts and dresses. Tonight's would be a pink chiffon, drop-waisted number.
- Our musical direction had toughened up somewhat and we'd developed a harsher and more direct guitar sound.
- Richard seemed to have developed a taste for breast milk.

CBGB was a shithole held together with stickers and the gloopy residue of a hundred-million spilled pints. The sound system was fairly primitive and (as it always does in a soundcheck) bounced around the harsh, empty interior. We were reassured by the soundman (as you always are in a soundcheck) that 'it'll sound great with a few bodies in'. We were unknown in America, so this didn't bode well, but buoyed at having blasted out songs from the stage that established The Ramones, Television and Talking Heads, we headed for the Soho Grand for a cocktail or two at the pleasure of our trusted (and very good at the guitar) King.

Our stage time was 10pm, which allowed for us to have a couple of drinks, walk to the flat, shower and change (inc. obligatory 'which dress' quandry) then walk to CBGB to stick it to our crowd (or at least Spencer, John Coon and the soundman). So instead, we were still at the bar at 8pm, having drunk more than two cocktails and, it appeared, having lost Shirley our bass player – who was six foot three and not normally that easy to lose. After a frantic five minutes searching the hotel bar, we found Shirley and found out why we hadn't been able to find her despite her being six foot three. She was comatose across a sofa, having consumed what we had to assume was more cocktails than Shirley could drink and remain standing, or even awake. As we had a gig in under two hours which would require her to be, at the very least, awake, we had a problem. With Richard and I under each of her arms, we propelled Big Bird outside, into a cab and back to the flat.

The next hour is best imagined as a short film soundtracked by the Benny Hill theme tune and involves Shirley being dumped in the bathtub fully clothed, drenched with a cold shower whilst simultaneously force-fed several triple espressos (I can't remember which of the five varieties), encouraged to get undressed/dressed through a closed door (great opportunity here for jump-cut montage – two feet in one trouser leg – face peering through arm-hole – any and every garment back to front – Shirley knocking over a vase of flowers) then propelled back out into a cab that deposits us at the club with ten minutes to spare before our stage time. The short film ends as we arrive at the venue to see crowds still queueing to enter, then go inside the venue (which is very healthily stuffed with more than a few bodies) as the support band finish their set.

The previous night in Greenwich Village and SOHO we'd come across numerous candlelit vigils in memory of Diana Spencer and I'd been taken aback by the depth of emotion and sincere sadness of many New Yorkers for someone they had almost certainly never met. We stopped and talked and were asked several times to sign books of condolence, which we did with a gradually melting cynicism. I remarked on this during the gig and it provoked an immediate and heartfelt burst of applause. This warming wave of empathy, this affectionate and cordial response to my observation, provoked a reaction in me that I'd shown so many times before and would do so many times again. Unable to reciprocate in a way that didn't make me feel insincere, I took the next best option. As the waves of warmth were still radiating, my relentless 'brain' had already embarked on its next voyage to the outreaches of needless alienation. Before I was really aware of what my mouth was saying, I could hear something bouncing (in spite of the bodies in the room) from the back wall via the PA system, that sounded a lot like I was apologising for not having a book of condolence ('sorry') but nonetheless inviting anyone that would like to, to come backstage after the gig and sign my 'shorts of condolence' ('not sorry'). I'd been heckled a few times earlier as, every time I squatted to adjust any effects pedals, my pink chiffon dress rode up to display my white Calvin Klein shorts in all their mundane glory. So, I'd put two and two together, added a sprinkling of self-defence and inadvertently gone on the attack, to the general bemusement of the majority of the crowd.

We played out the rest of our set, which seemed to go down well; our closing song 'Dressing Down' was something I'd written in the last days of FIN but which had been repurposed in our new stripped-back line-up, and it worked. The song builds from a stark opening that, in retrospect, evokes Radiohead, but, at the time, was born of my having similar influences to Radiohead. It actually sounds to me like the bastard child of Pink Floyd and the Pixies. Sort of 'Pinksies'. The song builds to a crescendo of self-evisceration around the phrase 'why can't you just be you?' then cuts brutally to a dead silence. We sidled off in that odd state where you've created an atmosphere of intensity that everyone in the room wants to continue, and you want to continue to sustain, and yet you have to fade to black, to allow the flickering of what you've just done burn itself into the consciousness of everyone who saw it. You have to go to your dressing room, suck hungrily on cold beer and await the praise of those that have absorbed the flickering.

There was a gentle knock at the door and we beckoned the knocker to enter, *let the praise begin!*

A slight, pale girl shuffled in, having likely just shuffled out of a film by Michel Gondry. She was wrapped in chunky knitwear, sockless feet in brown Birkenstocks (hence the shuffling) and a Greek fisherman's cap atop her small head. If we shuffle back into the film then she's played by Rooney Mara or Saiorse Ronan and if what happened next happens next, then I'm played by a hybrid of Alan Partridge and Ronald McDonald.

The girl, who had watched us play for the previous hour and been touched enough by our performance to summon the courage to approach us backstage, asked to sign the 'shorts of condolence'. I wish I were making this up – and I wish I was therefore making up that I burst out laughing and the girl, cheeks reddening, confusedly turned and fled the room. I also wish that we'd flown home the following day, because that would have meant that what happened the following day didn't happen. But it did, and it happened because of who knocked on the door next. Ironically, as my behaviour was the antithesis of 'Sowing The Seeds Of Love', our second visitor was Curt Smith, once the boyishly handsome and fresh-faced lead singer of Tears For Fears, now the boyishly handsome and fresh-faced New York property developer and founder of Zerodisc, his own independent record label. Alongside Curt and practically barging past to shake hands first was (and here's where this started to resemble the dressing room from an early 80s *Top Of The Pops*) Hugo Burnham, once the drummer with visceral post-punk polemicists Gang Of Four and now a cigar-chomping A&R with Warner Bros. Backs were slapped, gush was gushed and Curt enquired as to how long we were in town and would we like to visit his recording space in Brooklyn?

The next day, nursing the inevitable hangovers that resulted from a night out in New York stoked by interest from two (very) different labels, the three of us were stood in the live room of Curt's rehearsal/recording space. On the other side of the glass in the control room were Curt and his engineer, Charlton, who had an open, friendly nature and the unflappable, slightly goofy nerdiness common to most recording engineers. We were there because Curt was impressed by what he'd heard at the gig and wanted to hear some more. We played two new songs, 'Narco' and 'Oxygen', both of which built from tiny, spectral openings to pretty ferocious climaxes and, for a three-piece, were quite impressive arrangements. What was also impressive (from a purely anthropological point of view) was that whilst I'd negotiated this exercise and its attendant combination of foot pedal dexterity, my brain had been occupied by 'Charlton' and the comic possibilities this presented in order to impress my bandmates.

RECORDING/REHEARSAL SPACE – INT DAY

The droning feedback cuts abruptly as JOHNNY (a slim, spiky-haired and young-looking thirty-three-year-old man in a wraparound skirt) stomps on one of the myriad pedals in front of him. In the control room, the boyishly handsome and fresh-faced CURT and his engineer CHARLTON nod in appreciation of the 'Floyd-stroke-Pixies' racket that's just subsided.
Charlton looks across to Curt and mutters under his breath

CHARLTON

Pinksies…?

Curt nods as Johnny, who appears to be on the verge of saying something, flashes a glance at RICHARD and SHIRLEY as if to say: 'Watch this'.

JOHNNY

Have you been to the UK at all, Charlton?

Charlton is warm and engaging, a puppyish appreciation showing at the attention from the artfully dishevelled British wordsmith.

CHARLTON

Oh yeah! I love London, man, such a cool city.

JOHNNY

Really! Pretty different from New York, eh?

CHARLTON

So different…so different…

Johnny looks again to his bandmates as if to say, 'Here it comes'.

JOHNNY

You know what I can't get over is the cops here…they're so aggressive. Totally different to the English bobby, Charlton.

CHARLTON

Oh yeah…sure!

Richard and Shirley fight to suppress a smile as Curt stares down at the floor, unsure what just happened. Or why. Charlton has a slightly uneasy feeling at the change in atmosphere but can't put his finger on what's going on. Johnny hasn't noticed any of this as his brain has been occupied in its next contrivance. He clicks on his tremolo peddle and strums a couple of shimmering chords as an unconscious amuse bouche to the imminent zinger. Again, the glance to Richard and Shirley…

JOHNNY

How do you keep in shape, Curt, you a runner?

CURT

Sure, when I can. It can be tough in the city.

JOHNNY

How about you, Charlton?

As Johnny drops the bait, he spots the imperceptible flicker of recognition from Richard.

CHARLTON

I have my moments!

JOHNNY

Fairweather fitness, eh?
(laughs)
So how would you describe yourself, Charlton, athletic?

Curt's English and a football fan, so he can tell what's going on, if not why. Richard and Shirley know Johnny is being an arse, but are still giggling. Charlton's unease is growing and there's a suspicion that the guitarist he's engaging with might be doing that English thing that Americans really hate, partly because they're too sincere to really do it.

Johnny's not started writing comedy (it's debatable whether he ever will) but already has an instinctive awareness for the 'rule of three', and continues...remorselessly.

> JOHNNY

Where do you come into London from...Heathrow?

> CHARLTON (slightly nonplussed)

Er...yuh, normally it's...'Heathrow'/...that's the airport, right?

> JOHNNY

That's it. So, what do you do to get into town? Tube? Cab? Limo!?

> CHARLTON (laughs nervously)

Oh sure! No, but I'm pretty lazy so I usually jump in a black cab.

> JOHNNY

Aahh! The delights of the M4!
Three thousand miles and what's the first
sight that greets you, Charlton? Heston!

The 'joke' has gone too far. Even Richard and Shirley have begun to recoil from what's straying from mischief into cruelty. Curt tries to move things on.

> CURT

What about something from last night?

Without looking up, Johnny begins to strum the opening chords to 'Dressing Down', steps up to the mic and starts the first verse

JOHNNY (singing)

The posters on your wall
Say you haven't grown at all
And you're dancing to the tune
From another person's room

As we track away from the band, back through the control room and
out of the door, the ambient sound of the rehearsal room mixes through
to the full, more polished and present sound of the produced track. As
the song progresses, we see a visual montage. The band in the back of a
yellow cab on the FDR expressway, the 747 climbing into the sky, the
day transitioning into night.

SONG continues:

Your chance has disappeared
Just like you always feared
And you sit and stare through space
With a blank unchanging face

We see the band in their LAWYER's office, KAZ GILL. He holds out
a faxed offer from Zerodisc and shakes his head in disappointment.
Johnny looks at the offer, raises his eyebrows, and we see the fax tossed
into the bin.

SONG continues:

Like the paper that you waste
And the piles of food you taste
To the friends you never made
'cause you couldn't think what to say

We see a sixteen-year-old Johnny walk across the school playground.
There are GROUPS OF BOYS either side, studiously ignoring him. He
leans against a wall and turns his collar up, pretending to concentrate on
something in the middle distance.

SONG continues:

So you had another drink
But it didn't help you think
And your actions false and wild
Only make you more reviled.

We see sixteen-year-old Johnny sing these last two lines back in the
Brooklyn rehearsal space but instead of Curt and Charlton, BANANAS
is sat behind the desk in the control room. Holding Johnny's gaze with a
half-smile.

SONG continues:

Why can't you just be you....

SONG reverberates out.

When we arrived back in London, it was early: 7am-ish. We all got in a
cab, dropped our gear back at mine in North Kensington, then walked up
to Kensington Gardens. I think it was Shirley's idea. The flowers had been
building up for five days and the smell was beginning to turn from perfume to
a slightly iffy, funky perfume. The paths and grass were carpeted with bouquets
for hundreds of yards in every direction and we gingerly picked our way through
to the gates, which were also covered entirely. From my jacket pocket I pulled a
demo CD of ours. It was a clear plastic wallet containing a white piece of paper
with seven tracks listed, contact details and SENNA in bold type. I slid the
paper slip covering the disc from the sleeve and we all stared at it. Richard took
the pen and wrote a single word, then we put it back in the wallet and placed
it into the open wrapper of a bouquet hanging on the gates. It said 'Bollocks',
because it was bollocks, that someone who had struggled to find happiness and
looked to be on that path had died so needlessly.

Hugo Burnham got in touch. He'd fallen in love with our demos and been
blown away by the gig but his A&R director had been at CBGB and felt there
was something 'a bit off' about us. We split up soon afterwards.

'I can't eat that now, Buddy'

After two failed attempts to 'hit the big time' in the music business, I rather surprisingly made the decision not to make it three. Whatever it was that I was doing, it seemed the cosmos didn't want me to do it. I did wonder though, if the cosmos could be fooled into thinking it was someone else doing it, whether it might relax its criteria somewhat? I'd been introduced to Christian Ulf-Hansen who, as well as being the head of the publishing organisation BMI, was also a doggedly enthusiastic husky racer. He once explained to me that when you're in the sled and strapped behind a pack of huskies in full flight, you are frequently spattered in their excrement. 'That's nothing,' I laughed, 'you should try being in one of my bands.'

Christian was a fan of my songs and felt I'd be a good fit to write for the American singer/songwriter Andrew Dorff (though as I was being introduced to write for him, I suggested he should really be described as a singer/songsinger). My feeling was that if the cosmos was more disposed to Andrew, it might not realise I was involved and allow him to enjoy success with my songs that I could then enjoy the publishing income from. As experiments go, it was an interesting one. For a bit.

Andrew was the son of a famous country music writer Steve Dorff and brother of the actor Stephen Dorff. He had the peculiarities common to kids who've enjoyed a privileged upbringing, like not having much of a clue about how real life worked. Andrew was staying for weeks in a crazily expensive suite on Park Lane, then at an equally crazily expensive flat in Belsize Park. I tried to spend time writing with him but it required days of cajoling and negotiation as he'd be preoccupied by having to track down some 'really great broccoli' or attend a tasting of fine Burgundy at Berry Brothers. Cigars were a huge distraction and he could discuss the merits and demerits of various humidors for hours.

Andrew also had the affectation common to many rich kids of dressing like a tramp. He had a big fuzzy beard, wore dark glasses 24/7 and was so often enveloped by a knitted beanie and a hood, I wondered if he was in Witness Protection. He'd ask really intense questions with lengthy and complex constructions that would end up being 'Do you think it's possible to eat too many nuts?' Food and its preparation was all-consuming (though often stopped short of *actual* consuming) and this reached its nadir in a recording studio where I offered him a floret of my broccoli (that he'd been quizzing me about for over fifteen minutes) and forked a piece onto the side of his plate. He immediately pushed away the plate of untouched and expensively prepared salad: 'I can't eat that now, buddy.'

I eventually got three tracks onto his forthcoming album and recorded guitars and backing vocals with him at Air Studios in St John's Wood. Sadly, the cosmos must have worked out that I was concealed within this musical Trojan horse and Andrew was dropped by his label before the album could be released. He was a complete oddball and I have only affectionate thoughts about the time we spent together.

As I've written this, I've googled Andrew and been dismayed to find that he died in a jacuzzi accident whilst on vacation in Turks and Caicos in 2017, aged forty. He died on 19 December, my birthday.

RIP Andrew, I hope I was kind to you. Fuck off, cosmos.

By late 1997, the first clue emerged that I was beginning to suspect (or at least my hippocampus was beginning to send out dispatches about) the trauma of my childhood. In a song called 'Not The Only One' I talk directly about *memories* and *recollections*, rather than disguising past events from myself by camouflaging them in another issue.

> He picks himself up to full size, as memories flood in his eyes
> Says 'la - di - da - di - da'
> Then slowly thoughts begin to drip, as recollection takes a grip
> Says 'la - di - da - di - da'
> 'Not the Only One', 1997

The refrain is odd, like I'm putting my fingers in my ears so as to pretend that I can't hear.

> He dangles from these lessons learned, and pegged out to dry up and burn
> Says 'la - di - da - di - da'
> I strain to hear hope riding in, but the air is static now and thin
> Says 'la - di - da - di - da'
> 'Not the Only One', 1997

I remember writing and recording this and having absolutely no idea what I even *thought* I was writing about; there was no 'shell-concept' it was smuggled in, just one of those opening lines that sounded good. My mind was on the move.

Arguably weirder is a song from the same time, although the title 'With God On Our Side' wouldn't have turned any heads from anyone who'd been following my output of the previous seven years.

> * NARRATOR'S VOICE *
> 'THERE WAS NO SUCH PERSON'

But you, who have resolutely endured the previous 213 pages, will be intrigued to hear that I wrote a song *from the point of view of Bananas*. At least, that's the only explanation I can find.

> You take this kiss, onto your lips. Swallow my fever.
> You take a bow, forget here and now. This all precedes you.
> Stock, still - boxing with shadows we shoot, kill.
> Preying on marrow-deep feelings, we're appealing.
> Striding on manfully - upright
> shoulder-to-shoulder we stand - fight
> With God on our side we entreat you. We defeat you.
> 'With God On Our Side', 1998

There's definitely an 'Onward Christian Soldiers' thing at work, but it all gets more personal in verse two.

You take the blame, I'm jumping your train. Blowing you smoke rings.
Tell me the time, I'll make it all mine. Lie still think sweet things.
Eyes wide - playing with fireflies inside
Plucking the leaves from your index, we're a reflex
Smothering wilfully - Don't think
eyeball-to-eyeball we don't blink
With God on our side we define you. Undermine you.

It's conflating the thrill that (one must assume) the abuser feels, with an almost Crusader-like, apostolic religious fervor. I know that there was frequently a glint in his eye and a weird sense of heady mischief as his hands would impulsively grab, then almost simultaneously smack his own face in reproach.

I suppose there could be a perfectly innocent explanation for references to being *pegged out*, *preyed on*, *smothered* and *undermined*. But if you tried to make it, I'd likely push my plate away and tell you: 'I can't swallow that now, buddy.'

'I'm funny, how? I mean, funny like I'm a clown?'

I first met Paul Evans in 1992; he'd started going out with one of Katie's best friends and we got on really well. Paul was a copywriter, football fan and loved Bowie *and* The Monochrome Set. We couldn't *not* get on. He was also really funny, so it's not like we had everything in common. Initially the four of us socialised together but gradually Paul and I became closer and would regularly meet for a few pints. In 1994 Harry Enfield and Paul Whitehouse made a one-off mock documentary with their DJ characters *Smashie and Nicey* called 'The End of an Era'. Aside from its gag-mungous script and unintended toppling of Radio 1's DJ hierarchy, it caused Paul and I to adopt speech patterns that we still employ today. I'm sure we're not the only fifty-something men who referred to each other as 'Great Mate' for years, but we might be the only men who shortened it to 'GM' and, even now, refer to each other's wives as 'Mrs GM'.

See? Hilarious.

What weren't hilarious but seemed to be (at times) quite funny, were some of the conversations in the pub around early 1999. I'm sure we weren't the only thirty-something men who thought their pub bantz worthy of actually writing down, but write it down we did, until we had a notebook with around forty characters and scenarios we began to think of as a potential sketch show. Katie and I had employed a local painter and decorator called Jack Murray, whose homespun wisdom and nasal delivery demanded I privately mimic them. Mel and Paul then got Jack round to decorate and Paul and I began riffing on things we'd call 'Jack's World'. Jack was perplexed by modern life and would ponder on aspects of it, such as the change in kids' names:

'Brooklyn, Rocco, Tiger Lily? What's wrong with some of the good old names? The names from the bible like Matthew – Mark – Luke...

...Judas.'

Around this time, I was at a friend's house for dinner and sat next to a lady called Sandy. She knew I'd been in a band and was asking what had happened to us. I lied and said I'd got too busy doing voiceovers and that led on to us talking about *Eurotrash*. Sandy explained she was a comedy producer and had been working on a pilot for the comedian Peter Kay.

* OPPORTUNITY KLAXON!!! *

With customary modesty and reticence, I explained I'd been working on some sketches and had an outline for a show. Quickly realising she'd poked a nest full of probably very unfunny hornets, Sandy gave me her address and invited me to send her some of the material. This was duly posted the following morning. The day after, my Nokia 5110 rang and it was Sandy.

> SANDY

Hi, Johnny, it's Sandy.

> JOHNNY

(Johnny *thinks* 'Sandy?')
Hello – how are you?

> SANDY

I'm great, thanks.
I got the Jack Murray stuff.

> JOHNNY

Oh…good. Did you…err…?

With the benefit of the ensuing twenty-three years, I now know that if you hear back this quickly, it's always good news.

> SANDY

They're really funny!

JOHNNY (Incredulous)

Oh – thanks.

SANDY

I think you should go and see Jo Sargent at the BBC.

I was going to see Jo Sargent at the BBC! I didn't know who *she* was, though I did know what *it* was. But first I had to go to see a lady called Nicola at London Management. I'd now done four series of *Eurotrash* and Maria McErlane, who was the cheekily perky narrator, had recommended I should get myself a voice agent. There was gold in them thar hills!

London Management was primarily an agency for actors and writers, but had a voice department to promote the actors in the burgeoning and lucrative market. I played Nicola some extracts from *Eurotrash* I'd brought on a cassette and she loved them. We talked about other things and I mentioned my imminent meeting with the Jo Sargent. She was intrigued (a versatile voice artist with comic potential!) and I produced a folder with the sketch material, which she scanned, chortling frequently. She stood up and asked if I minded her showing them to someone, left the room and came back a few minutes later, smiling. 'Pop next door, someone wants to see you,' she said, indicating an office across the corridor. I popped across the corridor into the office and there behind a desk holding my sketch pages with a broad grin across his face was someone who looked like a six-year-old boy, but was a man.

Duncan Hayes was, at the time, a relatively junior agent at London Management with a few edgy but relatively unknown clients – Johnny Candon, Katherine Jakeways, Ricky Gervais. I sat down opposite him and he carried on reading – and chuckling.

'Did you write all this?' he asked, a broad smile across his chops.

'With my mate, Paul – yes,' I replied, feeling 'my Great Mate Paul' might have been a bit much. He asked me who'd seen them and I explained that we were a blank canvas but hoping to be daubed a bit by the Jo Sargent next week. He pricked up his ears, which protruded from his slightly shaggy, Beatlesque haircut and asked me if I'd like an agent.

In the early days of FIN, a bunch of my cousins used to come to gigs and would bring a wheelchair-using school mate called Ash. We had a song (about a serial-killer who was inspired by the words of Jimmy Savile) called 'The Man In The Fabulous Chair' and it became a sort of anthem that we'd dedicate to Ash who was always right at the front. I hadn't seen Ash for a good six years so I was surprised, as I sat opposite The Jo Sargent, when he barged into the room, pulled up beside me and said, 'Daukesy, you old bastard, what are you doing here?' Given that I was attending a pre-arranged meeting with The Jo Sargent in her office and he'd come in uninvited, I felt it would have been more appropriate to ask him the same question, but he was now *Ash Atalla – Producer* and would soon become *The Man In The Fabulous Chair Who Produced The Office* and had huge reserves of self-confidence and belief, so pretty much the opposite of me. Ash had suffered with polio as a child and his daily struggles must have been immense. I've rarely met anyone with his positivity and drive, but at the time I just thought: 'What the fuck are you doing, you mouthy twat? I'm pitching to The Jo Sargent!' I needn't have worried as someone else then walked into the office.

This was in the old Television Centre, before the BBC embraced the concept of Open-Plan-Hot-Desk that decimated anyone's ability to actually concentrate. But in spite of that, the meeting was becoming about as personal and intimate as a sponsored busker playing the trumpet at Waterloo Station.

'Hello, who's this then?' said the man who'd just come in with a slightly befuddled air like he'd just got out of bed. The man saw my motorbike helmet and yanked up his trouser leg to reveal a horribly disfigured calf muscle. 'Watch out or you'll end up like this.' Things were getting surreal. One moment I was pitching some sketches to The Jo Sargent, then I'd been ambushed by The Man In The Fabulous Chair, now Jon Plowman, the Head of BBC Comedy, was trying to convince me not to ride a motorbike because he'd once been bad at it.

The Jo Sargent explained to Jon (and to Ash) that I'd come in with some sketches on the recommendation of Sandy. Jon Plowman picked up the sheets of paper and started reading – then he smiled – then he chuckled. He spoke to The Jo Sargent as if I wasn't there. 'These would be a good fit for the Green Light Awards.'

The Green Light Awards was a new comedy writers' initiative and the prize was a half-hour pilot on BBC Two. It turned out that of the eight shortlisted shows, one had just been picked up by Channel 4, so there was a last-minute vacancy. Jon said if I could put a proposal together and pitch it to a panel the next day, we'd be in with a chance.

I can't recall everyone who I pitched to, but I know Peter Bazalgette (chairman of Endemol) and Addison Cresswell (agent to Jonathan Ross and Jack Dee) were there. I'd written and recorded some title music which I played on a boom box then acted out some of the sketches as if it was a live show. There was quite a bit of laughter and a few days later we were told that we were on the shortlist and were invited to the National Comedy Awards where they'd announce the winner.

When Love Breaks Down

My recollections of interaction with Bananas around this time are sketchy. Katie and I continued to have very little to do with my family and our lives were much more centred around hers. She'd been a director of photography for a while now and was shooting a lot of commercials and music videos. Our lives were becoming rather separate and I think I was allowing the sudden change in my fortunes to go to my head.

Voiceovers were slowly increasing and I was prematurely becoming comfortable with the idea that I might be some kind of writer (I know, right?!). We were both straying beyond the confines of our marriage and becoming different people to the kids who'd met at Habitat sixteen years before. The last two years of our marriage were actually horribly painful for us both; there was doubt, dishonesty and mistrust on both sides. I can't blame any of this on my past and it would be disingenuous to do so. I think that my tendency to want to prove myself sexually may have had its roots in a deeper sense of inadequacy but it could have been countless other things, either innate or learned – so fuck knows. Like a lot of couples who are no longer communicating with any honesty we sought relationships with people who either would, or that we could realistically convince ourselves were. *'He/She understands me'.* Yeah – I bet.

I knew it was over when Katie was shooting a commercial in our house and I saw a glance between her and her focus-puller. It was awful at the time but they're still together and have two teenage girls the same age as mine, which tells you everything. I'm really happy for them. At the time I wasn't quite as happy and wrote a song called 'Replay'.

You're crying out – for a replay, a baby's fist of heat on a cold day.
You hand me a gun and it's loaded, the safety catch is bent and corroded.
From years of rain and it's cold and pain and you.
'Replay', 1999

Someone else whose safety catch was bent and corroded, or indeed non-existent, was Bananas who (along with my sister) had just welcomed their eighth child into the world. And they weren't finished. Still, credit to them for staying married. I suppose that in the light of his only known victim being male and his wife (and the mother of his children) being female, one can at least credit him with versatility.

It didn't help Katie and I that in the later years of our marriage, I was doing coke quite regularly and it led to a culture of secrecy as I tried to disguise the extent of it.

> In the cold light of day, you could sleep for a week
> And the poison's rise in a million dead sighs from the thrills that you seek.
> This body enlivened, this spirit stone dead
> Your wire-framed jaw spits what's best left unsaid.
> 'Vitamins', 1999

In late 1999, faced with the imminent collapse of my relationship with the woman who'd been an intrinsic part of my salvation since my late childhood, I did what any sensible person would do and started boxing.

Biff Bang Pow!

I was in a fluorescent-lit garage with sweat dripping off the roof, desperate for breath as the stench of the caged bulldog's fart tore into my nostrils and all the time trying to avoid being punched in the face (again) by Neneh Cherry.

Clay O'Shea's boxing gym was a focal point of West London in the late 90s, replacing Maida Vale Narcotics Anonymous as *the* networking centre. The clientele was a Who's Who of music business, fashion, magazines – and me. I may not have been the richest, most influential or notorious of Clay's clients but within a year I'd become the undisputed King of Burpees (an unofficial title I bestowed on myself – secretly).

Tucked behind the Westbourne Pub on Westbourne Park Rd, W11, the gym was actually a single car garage with a lino floor, fluorescent strip lights, a few bags strung around and a large dog cage that housed 'Bulla', Clay's flatulent bulldog. I started going in early 1999 and was soon supplementing my frequent runs with two boxing sessions a week. This wasn't 'boxercise'; Clay had fought professionally and our training involved regular sparring. The sessions were relentless and the only let-up was when you were allowed to 'rest' by running on the spot punching a bag. Newbies would frequently be driven to the point where they'd fall out of the door to the outside and throw up.

Clay could be terrifying; anyone making the mistake of easing off would be barked at: 'Michael Jackson!' (*Off The Wall*) and everyone was given a nickname. I became 'The Rug' due to my luxuriant head of hair and Neanderthal hairline, and also 'Kid Chocolate' for the frequency and ease with which my ribs would fracture. He was a fascinating and contradictory character, revealing himself to be a poet and later appearing on *Dragons' Den* with his AbsPak, just one of several inventions.

I boxed with Clay from '99 until 2008 and aside from it helping me become very fit, it gave me a physical confidence I'd always lacked. It wasn't a question of ever being aggressive, but knowing I had the ability to defend myself definitely made me less susceptible to intimidation. Having been overpowered at times as a child, the training I got from Clay helped me to hold myself differently from thereon.

A Bit of a Blur

Duncan, Paul and I sat in the back of the cab, suited and booted (it was the National Comedy Awards and bearing in mind 'the rule of three' I'd also tooted). In hindsight (and hindsight is at my door of late more frequently than the Amazon delivery man), this wasn't the smartest thing to do. The first people I saw as I walked into the venue were Blur and Miranda Sawyer. I'd bumped into Blur seven years previously on Camden High Street whilst we'd been out flyposting for a gig, so I clearly needed to have a one-way conversation with them. As I walked away, I heard Miranda Sawyer ask 'Who the fuck was that?' Quite.

We were unaware at the time that the Green Light Award for New Comedy had been decided in favour of 'Cyderdelic', a spoof doco about a group of eco-warriors, who were already represented by Addison Cresswell. However, the judges had been impressed by my pitch and decided to split the prize (a budget of £250,000 to make a half-hour pilot) so that they got £175,000 and we got £75,000. We would crucially also get a half-hour slot on BBC Two.

The next few months were progressively more terrible. I was thirty-six but behaving more like an eighteen-year-old. My expanding ego, nourished by the sniff of success and the snort of excess, made me an increasingly vacuous person to be around. I shudder to think about what I said and did and can only seek to mitigate the monstrosity with the thought that I was wrestling with what was surfacing inside me.

Hello... I'm Jack Berry

We'd proposed the show as *Hello... I'm Jack Murray* until I bumped into Jack in the street, telling him of the commission and forthcoming transmission. He was horrified. 'Oh no – I'm sorry, you can't do that 'cause the boys at the pub'd take the piss something rotten.' It became *Hello... I'm Jack Berry*, which was unfortunate as some people thought it was a (bad) pun on Chuck Berry. Which hadn't even occurred to me. The show was OK, very patchy and (with the benefit of the now permanently resident Mr Hindsight) a bit cringey in parts. But we got a great review from the *Telegraph* that concluded: 'Think *Python, Stella Street, Fast Show* – but different. It just proves what jolly japes can be squeezed from tiny budgets and big imaginations: roll on the series.'

Hello, I'm ack Berry
C2, 11.20 pm
ere's a sketch show your
rst surreal nightmares

are made of: a BBC Green Light Award winner written by Paul Evans and Johnny Daukés, it's short, sharp and clever, taking the rise out of every topic imaginable – from builders and bikers to feelbad rides with baby in the park and the Music Listening Awards. Think *Python, Stella Street, Fast Show* – but different. It just proves what jolly japes can be squeezed from tiny budgets and big imaginations: roll on, the series.

The Daily Telegraph

One of the selling points of the show was that all the sketches were linked, either by an outgoing or incoming word or image, a concept that didn't really work but was indicative of my distrust of the material and the need to frame it in a 'concept'. Something I've done repeatedly.

When we were working on another show years later, a co-writer would remark: 'You're trying to make sure the gear knob and headrests have the same logo on before you've attached the wheels' (or something close). It's similar to the feeling I had when playing live with the band; in my mind the songs weren't enough so I'd overcompensate, sometimes to an alarming extent. What was also alarming was some of the content in *Hello...I'm Jack Berry*, specifically two sketches.

They both centre around a character that we called 'Mr Inopportune' – they were my idea and this is exactly how they were written.

MR INOPPORTUNE – THE THERAPIST

Close-up of a man's whimpering features. Cut wide to reveal a THERAPIST's counselling room. He is sat in a modern leather chair at a desk, the client (MARTIN) is lying on a couch in the foetal position rocking gently and obviously in a very fragile state of mind. The client is speaking in short, whispered sentences, dragging realisations from deep within his psyche, gently being led forward and encouraged by the doctor.

THERAPIST

'Go on, Martin – you're in your bedroom...'

MARTIN

'...and I'm under the blankets with my torch where it's safe, but I can hear...'

THERAPIST (calming)

'Ssshhhh – it's alright – what can you hear, Martin – tell me what you hear...'

MARTIN

'footsteps – slow and heavy – coming up the stairs – and along the landing'

THERAPIST

'alright, Martin, slowly – slowly...'

MARTIN

'now my bedroom door is opening – and I can hear someone coming in...'

THERAPIST

'stay very, very calm, Martin – I want you to shine the torch into the face of the person. Shine the torch in their face and tell me *who* you see...'

Martin takes a deep breath on the couch, lifts his hand as if pointing the torch, opens his eyes and a sudden realisation crosses his face.

At that very moment we cut to the therapist who hits the speakerphone button on his desk:

THERAPIST

'Millie, can you give Rob Hopkins a call,we're lunching at Mediterraneo, tell him I'll be about another...'

He glances at Martin, then checks his watch.

THERAPIST (CONT)

'Say, seven or eight minutes? Thanks.'

He switches off the speakerphone and turns to Martin

THERAPIST (CONT)

Now, sorry, Martin, where were we...?'

Martin is lying in a near-comatose state of deep trauma.

Now, I'm not a psychotherapist (though I was playing one in the sketch) but, I'm sure if I was one, I'd be intrigued that I'd written that sketch. When I described it to my *actual* psychotherapist, she felt it was quite positive, given my mental state at the time. It clearly shows that, subconsciously, I was trying to make some sense (albeit using ridicule) of what I'd experienced.

As interesting and apparently logical as much of the previous might seem, the next sketch is absolutely batshit. It's Mr Inopportune again, but this time he's a teacher, talking to a school assembly about abuse. A bit 'on-the-nose'? Well, strap yourself in.

At the time, Bananas and Janet were running a school that was funded by Opus Dei. I've got no idea how this came about but I'm quite sure that if you had nine children and no plans to stop, maybe 'get a school' might edge onto your to-do list? We needed to shoot in a school and though I knew on some level this felt *very wrong,* the need for a location (and a cohort of schoolkids) won out and I was very economical with the description of what we were doing. In among the cohort of schoolkids (who are only seen from behind) were a number of my own nieces and nephews, unaware that the script I was delivering (which they likely didn't fully understand), had its roots in the abuse I'd suffered from their father. Fucked up? Undoubtedly.

MR INOPPORTUNE – THE TEACHER

An exterior shot of a school, we hear the hubbub of an assembly
gathering which quickly subsides as we cut inside. A teacher is stood on
stage behind a lectern addressing a hall of primary school children.

TEACHER

Good morning, boys and girls.

SCHOOLKIDS

Good morning, Mr Daukes.

TEACHER

This morning I want to talk to all of you about abuse. Now this can be something that you are subjected to at home, maybe by an uncle or close family friend – maybe even your own mum and dad. Or you might suffer from abuse from other children at school...or worse still from someone in authority like one of your teachers. Whatever it is and wherever it is from, it can be a terribly lonely and frightening experience.

A long pause as the teacher looks around the hall.

TEACHER

So, if anyone here is being made a victim of this most appalling cruelty...

There's silence in the hall as the teacher looks out across the children with concern.

TEACHER

Could you stand up now, please...?

The teacher looks around and, seeing no one stand up, smiles. Everything is OK!

TEACHER

No one? Good!

Hello…I'm Jack Berry didn't contain any other hidden messages, but when the reviewer (Edna Pottersman) had written: 'Here's a sketch show your worst surreal nightmares are made of…' she likely didn't know how accurate that was. At the risk of (yet again) beating the drum marked 'I had no idea', I still didn't – or at least I hadn't admitted anything to myself. But the memories that I'd suppressed were very clearly coming to the surface. It would still be a little while but a song from the time, 'To Catch The Stars', gives more than a clue as to the dialogue I was having internally and the dawning realisation that I had issues to address.

> You're going to have to come outside sometime
> You're going to need to take a drink
> Your shrink-wrapped lifestyle may protect your thoughts
> But it won't help you think.
> 'To Catch The Stars', 2001

The song diverts into social awkwardness and feelings of estrangement:

> You're going to have to take the risk tonight
> To catch the stars or face the drop
> The conversation may flow freely but
> Could just as well dry up.
> 'To Catch The Stars', 2001

The last verse comes squarely back to the impending reckoning that I must have felt was coming.

> You're going to have pull that skin away
> And let the first few touches sting
> Your shattered nerves betray, you've lost the plot
> You cannot feel a thing.
> 'To Catch The Stars', 2001

The *Telegraph* review of *Jack Berry* concluded 'roll on the series'. It didn't. The BBC declined to take the pilot any further. At the time, I'm not sure I even noticed.

Bikes, Porn
and Another Wife

I separated with Katie in late November 2000 and was immediately busy in the production of *Jack Berry*. That Christmas I went skiing with my brother's family then went off round the Alps on my own, somewhat of a loose cannon with a loose screw. On my return, making *Jack* notwithstanding, I became what the kids now refer to as 'a bit extra'. Everything was taken to excess. Boxing, boozing, biking and other things that did (and didn't) begin with a B. I'd been with Katie for eighteen years from the age of eighteen and Notting Hill in the early noughties had made hedonism as convenient as shooting fish in a barrel, except the barrel was full of vodka and drugs and there weren't any fish. Because what kind of hedonist wants fish? I was hardly Jim Morrison, but I was blowing the doors off.

There was a flurry of work-related stuff that wasn't really work:

I contacted a motorbike magazine called *Two Wheels Only* and got a monthly column and there was a documentary made about *Eurotrash* called *Unzipped*.

A friend was producing pop videos and I did some bike riding in promos he made for Blue (*Fly By*) and Westlife (*World Of Our Own*).

Rapido made a pilot for a show that was 'a light-hearted look at porn' and I was the presenter, Tommy Hjardman.

I wrote a bunch of sketches for a *Two Wheels Only* video and got to hang out with some superbike and Grand Prix riders.

On 29 November, a calendar year after I'd split with Katie, I went to my friend Johnny's birthday party. I was introduced to a cute girl who looked like Audrey Hepburn, she mistook me for Johnny the birthday boy and kissed me on the cheek, saying, 'There's your present.' Unabashed, I shot back, 'Where's my cake?' She kissed my other cheek. We got chatting; she was an actress with the Royal Shakespeare Company (classy!) and had previously been a

soloist with the Royal Ballet (cultured!). This was catnip to my sense of being something of an uncultured philistine, aside from the fact that she was very pretty and quite a laugh. Over the past year I'd become accustomed to what you might euphemistically call 'speed-dating' and was throwing out line after line. As the party wound down, a bunch of us went back to mine, including Audrey Hepburn, but despite luring her to my lair the best I could come up with was lending her Jeff Buckley's *Grace* (Hallelujah!).

Emboldened whilst calling round to get the Jeff Buckley CD, I arrived dressed as Santa doing wheelies on my scooter with a bag of mince pies (Casanova swore by it). My persistence and originality was rewarded and we were soon an item.

As the experiences of my childhood had slowly begun to dawn on me, for some reason, in the early stages of this relationship (and for the first time in my life), I nervously shared scraps of them with someone else. Maybe it was 'pillow talk'?

'How was that for you?'

'Amazing – you?'

'It was good, but at one point I had a flashback of what the bloke who ran the Boys' Club (and is now my brother-in-law) used to do...'

'Sorry, what?'

Well, not exactly, but maybe not a million miles away. I think it helped that Sarah (no longer masquerading as 'Audrey Hepburn') had experienced her unfair share of childhood trauma and didn't feel that acknowledging it was in any way a weakness.

You're going to have pull that skin away
And let the first few touches sting...
'To Catch The Stars', 2001

And sting they did, but not in a manner I would have predicted. I began to experience strong feelings of inadequacy, not based on any realities but seemingly a by-product of admitting to the abuse. It was shame, I suppose, but provoked an intense anger.

It was the first episode of anger, in the first season of anger in what was to become a long-running succession of seasons.

A Problem Shared

In the spring of 2002, my younger brother Nick came to stay for the night. Nick was a Royal Marines Officer, at that time seconded to HM Special Forces (SBS) and was taking a brief period of leave. Nick and I are visually similar (though he's *even* shorter than me) and have a lot in common. We make each other laugh easily and get pissed together easily, often simultaneously. Having had dinner with Sarah, we were proceeding to do both of these. In the light of the scraps I'd recently begun to share with her, I think she could feel where the conversation might be going, excused herself and went upstairs to bed.

I can't remember exactly how mine and Nick's conversation evolved, but there was Armagnac drunk and it sticks in my mind that we were walking to the living room when I stopped him in the corridor. I looked him in the eye and heaved out a sentence that felt like an enormous wire-framed wreck. An ugly outline that would require endless in-filling, detailing and colouring.

'I was abused by [Bananas] when I was little.'

I don't know what I was expecting: shock? anger? sympathy?

I got none of them immediately. Nick held my gaze and with eyes that were already tearing up, he replied, 'So was I.'

All the air was sucked from the room and, in an instant, so much inside both of us collapsed. There were immediate and endless tears. A terrible mixture of the relief we felt from sharing, the awful shock of each realising what our brother had experienced and a combination of the two, from the one other person on earth who truly recognised what that felt like.

If that sentence is an incomprehensible mess, then for most of the night so were we – finally able to share details, feelings and consequences that no one else could possibly have understood. Our conversation and the wildly contrasting emotions it brought was unique – yet it's one we've repeated with slightly different degrees of passion several times since. To hear that, between 1984 and 1986 when I was becoming an editor at Crow and enjoying the lifestyle that brought, my little brother was being regularly sexually assaulted was truly sickening. For Nick, to imagine what I'd endured between 1975 and 1980, when he was aged four to nine and I represented so much to him, was appalling. We were both able to contextualise what we'd individually experienced by framing our lives relative to one another. For both of us, the hours of information we exchanged, the details and depths of depravity that we shared was the end of so much and the beginning of so much else.

It may have been the next day, it may have been days later, but we discussed our shared admissions with our sister Joely (who, it transpired, Bananas had exposed himself to in 1979). With all we knew, I called and spoke to someone anonymously at The Lucy Faithfull Foundation, a child protection charity dedicated solely to preventing child sexual abuse. The woman I spoke to informed me that the history I was recounting amounted to a series of very serious crimes and that if I disclosed identities, she would have a duty to report it to the police. I asked whether, in her opinion, these were likely isolated incidents. She said it was more than likely that they were not.

The next day, we called the Police Child Protection Unit that was closest to where Bananas lived. Shortly after this, Bananas' home was raided by CID. After we'd informed the police, I contacted my parents, told them I needed to see them and drove down to Didcot.

We walked by the Thames in a nearby village and I felt a yearning for the summer afternoons we used to spend jumping from the nearby bridge, messing about in inflatable boats, or even being stung by nettles. As my parents walked alongside me, brows furrowed, I struggled to say the right things in the right order – acutely aware that I was saying the wrong things in the wrong order. They didn't want to hear any of it. It was a feeling that I've had almost every time I've ever discussed any of it with any of my siblings – like you're belching up tar over their freshly laundered clothes.

They were both quite detached and it certainly didn't seem like a shock to them. There was no sympathy to speak of and the pervading feeling seemed to be: 'Well this is going to be difficult for everyone'. My dad didn't have a clue what to say and Mum gave off an air of simmering annoyance.

In these respects both of them revealed much about themselves. Dad struggled with anything that strayed beyond logic and, I guess, having to assimilate that two of your sons had been sexually abused by your son-in-law certainly strayed beyond logic. In many ways Mum's reaction was harder to accommodate. In matters of emotion, my experience of Mum was that she defaulted to a learned position that was constrained by her religious beliefs and practice. It's possible that her emotional palette had been what made religion attractive and that she was comfortable with this set of instructions and mandated responses. Whatever problem one presented, the advice frequently included reference to 'the Lord' or the caveat that she would need to 'pray on it'. Under the present circumstances and with the breaking news that her *fellow devout practitioner and Opus Dei acolyte, to whom she'd abdicated responsibility for her own children* was a paedophile, she had (as she would have put it) 'a face like a smacked arse'.

At some point I remember my mum saying something along the lines of 'well, we're going to have to speak to [Bananas] about this' and it crossed my mind that they didn't have the slightest clue as to the gravity of what had taken place and what it was going to mean. This thought should have concerned me a great deal more.

Over the next few days, it emerged that several of our sisters also had incidents of *interference*, mostly isolated, but a further testament to the appetite of a man who had decided to feast so comprehensively on the Daukes family.

Nick and I were interviewed at length, me at home in London and Nick at home in Poole. The detective sergeant assigned to us was DS Reiss, a thick-set man who looked like he enjoyed rugby and fighting. He had that peculiarity of being a bit of a geezer who spoke in overly florid sentences. So we got on fine.

Recounting the history of my abuse was exhausting. There were frequent questions, questions of frequency and details I'd not have chosen to share with a rugby-loving geezer. I'm glad I'd already shared a lot of it with Nick and the dam had broken, so to speak. Even then it was hard not to repeatedly become upset.

It was self-pity, of course. As I recalled various scenarios and occasions from the past, I was overcome with sorrow for the little boy in the tent, for the older boy praying to be left to shower alone, for every one of my young selves on every occasion we were denigrated and debased. What I didn't tell DS Reiss, was how these occasions were then used as currency, to bribe my deformed character further out of shape, because that wasn't a crime – at least not one with a name.

Let me go ... No - no - no - no
Let me go ... Let me grow

Rhyme. No Reason

Sarah had been cast in a play at The Citizen's Theatre in Glasgow. *Britannicus* by Racine is a five-act tragedy in rhyme and when Sarah asked if I'd like to come up and see the play, I couldn't think of a reason not to quickly enough – so I had to go. The thought of sitting through three hours of medieval verse was as enticing as being slowly immersed in a vat of fermenting human waste but, actually, the reality was so much worse. I'd have understood it more if the actors had been shouting into saucepans in Korean and I'd have definitely stayed in the bar for the second half but for the fact that it was in a tiny studio and I was one of only seven people present.

I made a few trips to Glasgow. It's a fantastic city to hang around in (especially if you like booze) and we'd go for beers at The Pot Still, then on for dinner at The Ubiquitous Chip. There were lots of other places and I can't remember any of their names so they must have been good. One place I do remember the name of, because I started doing something very odd in it. It was late morning and I was sat in Costa Coffee on Sauchiehall Street. I was likely fuzzy-headed and attempting to clear the mists with a large espresso. I pulled a notebook from my bag and started writing.

Hello there, how's your day?
Swings and roundabouts? Light and shade?
The peg seems square but the hole seems round.
Life's on the up then it all falls down,
and somehow, as the hours drag past,
you slip and slither from first place – to last.

And had I left it there, the world would never have known what a rhyming verse feature film sounded or looked like. Also, Rotten Tomatoes would probably have a different 'lowest-ever-rated film of just 8%', but I didn't so it hasn't.

What I had started to do was write a poem about our lack of control from the point of view of a mischievous god. A very strange thing to emerge from my pen mere weeks after acknowledging what I had for the first time in twenty-two years. Or maybe not.

I am however getting ahead of myself as, at this stage, I was in the merest rumour of some foothills of a poem about fate and destination written by (a) god.

I carried on scribbling for a few more days, then went back to London. I'd been home a few hours when the first phone call came.

A House Divided

After the storm there will be nowhere to hide
A house divided with the blind ranged on one side
After the storm with all disguises washed away
A truth revealed, no facts concealed,
where God-as-shield has had its day
'After The Storm', 2021

Having been interviewed, Nick had been deployed to the Middle East where, in advance of the start of the Iraq invasion, he'd probably been embedded with some Marsh Arabs collecting GPS coordinates – in all likelihood whilst wearing a fireproof wetsuit. Our ability to communicate was non-existent.

The first sign that the situation at home was changing was when Joely telephoned to inform me she was withdrawing her statement. She had begun to feel pressure from various of our siblings and our parents about the likelihood of an impending trial and there were the first rumbles of disunity about this course of action. I've subsequently learned that this is very common, especially in the case of historical sexual abuse within a family. The tendency can be to minimise or explain away past offences in a manner that judicial process wouldn't. A court looks dispassionately at the offences and reaches its conclusions without regard to the perpetrator's current situation. Our family began to do the opposite. Joely's withdrawal didn't affect the likely outcome of the trial in the slightest as, without wishing to trivialise her experience, in legal terms it didn't really add to the gravity of the allegations Nick and I had made. It did, however, presage a change in the support we would receive from our family.

The first phone call from my dad started benignly enough. Asking how I was and what I'd been up to. Which was immediately odd – he never asked those things (he never rang, it was always Mum). I don't remember the exact conversation word for word, but I'll never forget this line:

DAD

Look – this business with [Bananas], don't you think it's
gone far enough?

I'm the first to admit, I can be reactionary. Dad's test had pointed it out over
twenty-two years ago.

Tends to form opinions quickly. Feels that his instincts are right and that a great
deal of investigation is not required. `

In recent years, in dealings with my siblings regarding this history, that
conclusion has been obvious – but it doesn't *always* make me wrong. If
what you're saying is true but it's making people feel uncomfortable: their
discomfort is outweighed by the necessity that you speak up. In this situation,
I was immediately on red-alert at the words 'this business'.

JOHNNY

Sorry – 'this business'?
Do you mean the sexual abuse of your sons?

He huffed and puffed at my blunt directness, as if to say *why was I making
this so difficult?*

DAD

Well…we don't *know* that.

JOHNNY

Yes we do. We absolutely do know that. I can assure you that
I was sexually abused by ———— ————— between the ages
of eleven and sixteen.

More huffing and puffing; he was irritated at my absolutism in the same way
that he was when we argued about politics. At some point in the conversation,
my mum (who'd been listening in) interjected that this was awful for my
sister and that *they had ten children.*

JOHNNY

'Are you saying that because they have a large family, we shouldn't make it known that he's committed child-sex crimes? Surely that's *more* of a reason?'

The call degenerated. The more my parents attempted to ameliorate Bananas' actions and obfuscate the truth of what had occurred, the more explicit I became as to *exactly* what he had done to me and Nick. It's a pattern that has occurred subsequently in several conversations with my siblings. They just want it to go away, failing to understand that, until they acknowledge the explicit specifics of what he did, it never will go away – for us.

When the conversation ended (either my dad or I slammed the phone down) I was charged with adrenaline and the sheer injustice of what I was being asked to accept was making my skin prickle. I couldn't call Nick and, at the time, none of my friends had the first idea what was taking place, or the history behind it.

After the storm when all's declared and all is known
This knot - this fetid rot - this viral clot swept from our homes
This exhibition - This atrocity - These bones'
'After The Storm', 2021

Comedy, Cowardice and the Letter

Although a series of *Jack Berry* had failed to come to fruition, I was propelled on the winds of comic possibility and began spaffing out ideas like one might spaff out something else if one were attempting to make other things come to fruition. Duncan's stock was rising (!) with that of Ricky Gervais and Stephen Merchant and he began to put me forward for different writing gigs. The first was *The Catherine Tate Show* ('No, thanks') but was quickly followed by *Monkey Dust* ('Yes, please!'). I wrote several sketches for the treacly-black sketch show but, surprise-surprise, didn't enjoy the collaborative process of the 'writers' room' – which seemed to entail my blurting out loads of ideas that more famous people got paid to write up. Meanwhile I was papering Duncan's desk in proposals for:

Think (new ways of looking at electricity, dolphins and cheese)

All Revved Up With Nowhere To Go (a 'transport-based' sketch show)

Stretcher (a more nightmarish development of *Jack Berry*)

Radio Free Europe (a spoof radio network that was to become *Radio9* but not quite yet)

So much funny!

Less funny (but only marginally so if you read those proposals) was the growing opposition I was facing to what was now an inevitable criminal trial for Bananas. A further phone call from my dad brought the following exchange:

DAD

'You do realise that [Bananas] employs around thirty people who will all lose their livelihoods?'

JOHNNY

'Do you actually want me to describe *exactly* what he did to me and Nick?'

DAD

'It's not that simple.'

JOHNNY

'These are crimes, not mistakes. Crimes he committed and your sons were the victims.'

DAD

'I just think we all need to take a step back.'

JOHNNY

'He'd wank over me. He'd constantly be grabbing at my cock. He made Nick suck his cock. He sucked a thirteen-year-old boy's cock...'

DAD

'Stop it, this isn't helping—'

JOHNNY

'You're a coward—'

DAD

'Will you just listen—'

JOHNNY

'You. Are. A. Fucking. Coward.'

And he was, albeit one who lacked the emotional tools to process the situation. At the time, he just wanted it all to go away. The chorus of all those who wanted it to go away, which was comprised of my entire family (apart from Nick, who was 3,500 miles away) was deafening. In truth, I was beginning to want it to go away myself.

What I did next was true cowardice and I'm ashamed of it to this day.

I was facing a situation where I was about to potentially imprison a man who had corrupted me fundamentally and twisted my character from the age of ten. I was scared of him, terrified even. With my younger brother's help, I'd found the strength to not only admit to that corruption, but to instruct and then cooperate with a prosecution that was undoubtedly going to have far-reaching consequences.

At the outset of this process I'd stated very clearly that the main purpose was to enable other potential victims to come forward and I had voiced that to my family. I now realise that not only was it a dishonest declaration, but I was laying the ground for what was to come next. It's taken me years to understand and admit that I *do* feel vindictive towards him and I *do* want the crimes he committed to be made public. Yes, I would like further victims to be able to come forward and find peace, but all the time I was suppressing the shame and consequent rage he had wrought it was impossible for me to escape the experiences I'd suffered. Having been overpowered and manipulated as a child, I was about to experience it again.

I can't remember whether a trial date had been set, but I believe it was imminent. I was in my kitchen, likely musing on yet another 'hilarious' comedy show idea, when the doorbell rang. I opened the door to find one of my siblings, holding a letter. Several years later, as part of a further attempt to bring Bananas to justice, I would write a report that contained the following statement:

> With Nick stationed in Iraq and the family increasingly opposed to the action, I was feeling more and more isolated. At this point I was presented with the last-minute intervention of a family intermediary carrying a hand-written letter from [Bananas]. In this letter, [Bananas] admits to everything Nick and I have alleged. He says that his own family was cold and loveless and that he quite literally 'fell in love' with Nick and I, confusing his expression of that love as sexual urges. He explicitly states that he has never abused another child and, further, that his own children would never present a temptation to him. He writes that he wishes me to keep the letter and, should any other victims ever present themselves, that we should take it to the police. He is in effect handing us a 'loaded gun'.

The combination of being offered an escape from the entire situation, the persuasive nature of the letter, how it was presented *and* who it was presented by – was too much – and I folded like a cheap deck-chair. It was weak, the weakest thing I've ever done, and had I been strong enough to tell the intermediary where to go and what to do with the letter ('fuck off and stick that fucking letter up your arse') this sordid saga would have been dragged into the open and I (and my entire family) would have avoided a further nineteen years of conflict and misery.

'Mr Hindsight? You again! Come on in. Yes, I'm sure I could organise you a parking permit…'

There was a further indignity, as I wasn't simply able to withdraw my statement. DS Reiss was understandably livid. His investigation had taken months and wasted probably hundreds of hours of police and now Crown Prosecution Service's time. My blood curdles at the thought of this and at the memory of the meeting at my house with an incandescent DS Reiss, who was pretty much in my face throughout. The same family intermediary then advised as to the text of a letter to the CPS to ensure they dropped the prosecution. It was only last year, when I found this letter in a computer folder, that the awful impropriety of this came home to me. I'd been coerced into stopping the prosecution of the man who'd abused me and then further coerced into convincing the CPS on his behalf. That's fucked-up with a fucked-up topping and a further order of fucked-up on the side.

Sarah and I went to Goa for a fortnight, where I set about deliberately doing what I'd done unconsciously for two decades and put it out of my mind.

I Can Just Turn the Radio On

Your punctured body-bag, those dry and empty sacks
The promise that you disowned.
And in the mortuary, you made a pass at me
Asked me to jump on your bones
And I can just turn the radio on
'Radio', 2003

In the years since '99 I'd been using a digital recording platform called Pro Tools and whilst I was in Goa, had something of a 'eureka' moment. For a while I'd been writing sketches and show ideas, doing more and more radio and TV voiceovers and becoming pretty proficient with Pro Tools. Rather than continuing to punt TV proposals, why not make a radio show?

Duncan and I had become good mates by now and were socialising a lot. Our personalities and energy levels were very different but complementary. Duncan had come to boxing and was now a regular fixture at fight club where he'd attempt to hurt me in the ring and I'd have to beat him off. He definitely found my constant reinvention a bit much and so, when I came into the office with my latest wheeze, he was bemused at best.

JOHNNY
'I'm going to make a show for Radio 4.'

DUNCAN
'Of course you are...'

Duncan was understandably frustrated that I wouldn't 'play the game'; establish a track-record writing with other people, collaborate for a while. So I did what I've done many times since – and went away to make some of it.

I've always been sceptical of commissioners being able to 'get' something off the page. What I was proposing was essentially a 'spoof radio show' which sounds (and normally is) teeth-grindingly awful. In fact, the Radio 4 commissioning guidelines at the time specifically listed it as something they *weren't* looking for.

I'd met a young stand-up comedian called Hils Barker whilst we were both doing voiceovers for a terrible animated cartoon called *Celebrity High* – a show so bad that history has forbidden it from being kept in its dustbin. Hils was really funny and I played her some pieces I'd written called *Think* (the cheese, dolphins, electricity stuff) and explained a concept I had called *Radio Free Europe* – where presentation is at the controls and content is firmly bound and gagged in the back. We started writing together and amassed a bunch of material for a radio station that combined the presentational excess of Capital with the pompous self-reverence of Radio 4. We recorded a few items and Duncan arranged for me to go and meet the Radio 4 Head of Comedy, Caroline Raphael. Caroline loved the recordings, which were sonically identical to the media we were pastiching, and commissioned a series of four half-hours. At the suggestion of the Head of Radio Entertainment, the wonderful John Pidgeon, we changed the title to *Radio9*.

The series was really popular and people wrote mostly nice things:

> Wednesday night saw the start of *Radio9* – weird, wacky, wicked and, just possibly, potentially wonderful.
> **Financial Times**

> From the first raucous jingle, you know *Radio9* is going to be a lot of laughs. Johnny Daukes must have spent his youth with a transistor radio clamped to his ear.
> **Sunday Times**

> *Radio9* arrived and its country music sketch about bestiality was a hoot – Glittery Mule's *Filthy Horse* deserves to be a hit.
> **Independent**

Fine radio comedy from the mighty Johnny Daukes.
Heat

Tasteless, puerile and lacking any discernible humour.
Sunday Express

What went unnoticed was a small but telling vignette in a sketch called 'Bob Bradman's Bed and Breakfast on a Budget (on a Bicycle)'. The sketch features a flashback as the adult Bob recalls the 'slightly disappointing walking tours' of Dorset as a child, spending nights under canvas with his father. There's a sound effect of a rhythmical rustling in the tent and young Bobby asks his father what he's doing. His father responds, 'Nothing – and don't tell your mother, she won't believe you.'

This picture was taken by Bananas on a Boys' Club camp in a tent where there was rustling. On occasions like this there were incidents I didn't tell my mother about, but if I had, I'm pretty certain she wouldn't have believed me either.

Radio9 was broadcast in October 2003 and Sarah and I were married in December. Bananas was at our wedding party.

So I was obviously fine by then. Obviously.

Smack My Pitch Up

Sarah and I spent a fortnight snowboarding in Courchevel for our honeymoon and while we were there, we created another person. When we got back, I set about creating another show. We'd been recommissioned for another series of *Radio9*, but making radio wasn't really ratio-ing on the resources vs rewards metric. I wanted to make TV and through *Jack Berry* and *Radio9* I'd come to the attention of Nicola Shindler at RED productions and Kenton Allen at Shine TV. If you google these people now, you'll see that they have made all the television, won all the awards and are two of the pillars that hold up TV's temple. They were both keen to see if we could make something together and I pitched the following ideas:

Smack My Pitch Up was an idea I wrote with David Quantick. I knew of him as an *NME* journalist and then met him at the Radio 4 Christmas party. We got on really well and still do. David has a work ethic that makes me look like a slovenly corpse and has written more shows and books than there are sheep in New Zealand. The concept was idiots pitching terrible ideas for lottery funding.

Watching The Defectives was a six-part series where we followed a character each week covertly, exposing them for living double lives. They were then brought together for a seventh episode that became a very dark game show Suck on that, *Squid Game!* (It never got made.)

We Interrupt This Programme was a loose development of *Radio9* and was a TV show where the constant stream of promos and ads swamped the much poorer drama content.

The Might Network was basically the same show transposed into a drama so we actually met the people making the shows at the station. It was a terrible idea.

Kenton took me in to pitch to the BBC; it didn't get anywhere but he started to come to boxing. He also took me to the National Comedy Awards but I got nervous-drunk and may have said something bad to an important agent. Nicola took me to see Sioned Wiliam at Channel 5 and they both agreed that I had some great ideas that really should progress. I did some follow-up work, but sadly there was no progress. Nicola was a rabid Man Utd fan and kindly gave me tickets for several matches. Kenton and Nicola both tried to help me but I think they were confused as to who I was and what I did. They weren't the only ones.

That was about as far as I got with TV companies. I just never seemed to make sense to other people and I was getting frustrated, so I did another stupid thing. It was a bit like the frustration after the Geffen debacle when I kicked Al out of the band, but much worse.

Ricky Gervais and Stephen Merchant had now made two series of *The Office* and it was hugely successful. Rather than thinking how great it was that I had an increasingly influential agent (and Duncan was flying), I decided to take Duncan to task for not giving me enough attention and blaming him for what I perceived as my lack of success. One particular night in a member's club on Shaftesbury Avenue, where I'd almost certainly got myself a little too *hyped*, I accused him of not 'shepherding' one of the projects sufficiently.

I was a class-A cunt.

I know he was pissed off, quite rightly. Rather than apologise, I left for another agent, Michael Foster, who I stayed with for about a month. Leaving Duncan was the stupidest thing I ever did; I lost a great agent, but, worse than that, I lost a good friend. I've regretted it ever since.

Broadcast

Writer/director/series producer Johnny Daukes on how he brought to life an ambitious show based on a spoof channel, involving some 30 items per episode and a cast of 240

THE MESSAGE is a comedy series that's being promoted as "the future of television". This description of unfeasibly clunky drama, hackneyed trails, inappropriate advertising and banal channel promotions could have been designed to reassure television executives that it was a nightmarish view of the future. But I prefer to describe it as taking a long hard look at TV's present.

Back in autumn 2000 I received an email saying my broadcast pilot for BBC2 wouldn't be picked up as a series. Oh. I take stock. I'm just another ex-video editor/commercials director/producer-musician/motorbike stunt rider who scrapes a living doing voice-overs for *Eurotrash*. So what now? Of course! Radio.

I spend three weeks putting together a pilot for spoof radio station Radio 9 – 'Round-the-clock radio… 24 hours a day". Luckily, I've got a Pro Tools studio in my spare bedroom and lash up a half-hour episode for BBC Radio 4. Luckily, Caroline Raphael loves the show and commissions a four-week run. And luckily, Jon Plowman hears episode one and emails me to say how much he loves it.

Meanwhile, I'm doing the rounds of indies with a TV idea called *We Interrupt This Programme*. It's a TV station where shows are constantly interrupted by a stream of promotions, ads and trails. No takers, but one experienced producer positively gushes that "Radio 9 is a glorious cul-de-sac". Doesn't he know there's no such thing as a cul-de-sac if you drive fast enough?

Plowman's hunch is strong and I'm asked for a "taster for the offers round". Sounds like canapés and for £8,000 it could well have been, but I buy Final Cut Pro, a 16:9 DV camera and get stuck in, reworking the idea as "The Message – The Channel with so much to say, but no idea how to say it". In go the inappropriate test commercials (recycle or die). The resulting 15-minute pilot prompts [former BBC3 controller] Stuart Murphy to say: "Gimme a six-part series." Oh!

Our budget is BBC3 sketch show, but to look like a channel we've got to reach spectacular highs as well as spectacular lows. Viewers have very sophisticated antennae and won't buy a spoof if it's not absolutely perfect. I decide from the outset that *The Message* must be so authentic that if someone's got the sound down they'd have no idea it was funny.

Jon P agrees to let me produce the series from my own office in W2 and to operate as a virtual indie. The generosity of Serious Pictures gives me a home as well as limitless advice and favours (and gives the BBC an extraordinary hike in production values).

I team up with Ben Quinn, an Aussie who shares my ludicrous optimism and an ability to multi-skill at the very lowest level. Ben will direct about 40% of the show and end up with a flaky knowledge of After Effects, Shake and my unpredictable temperament.

Like a military unit we are well prepared and very well disciplined. We finish shooting on schedule and with no overtime incurred. We've used Hi8, Super 8, DV, DigiBeta and 35mm and have originated with courage. In a non-linear digital world it's too easy to leave all options open and is, I believe, creative cowardice. If you want footage to look like it's been shot by the public then use a camcorder and the camera mic. Don't try to distress it afterwards, the viewer will know. This doesn't hold true for everything. We shot a hanging and a violent beating which, if you look closely enough, are actually faked.

We devise a post plan that's best summed up as not going into Soho. We save ourselves £150,000 in post costs that finance the extra shooting by buying four Mac G5s with dual screens and masses of storage, then pull in the talent to operate them. A German genius called Thorsten does every pixel of graphics, 2D and 3D, while an English idiot called Johnny cuts most of the show (and, incidentally, sings and writes the theme tune). We shoot for four months and post for five.

The response so far: "It's just like watching TV," which is good, I think. Is it funny? Well, you've got to love a good hanging and a violent beating, haven't you?
The Message airs on 20 May at 10.40pm on BBC3

Plowman's Hunch

> This bitterness can run and run and never pause for breath
> And when it catches up and squeezes, chokes you half to death
> If happiness is not like this, I'll take it with both hands
> Then force myself into its mouth and whisper my demands
> Happiness – Oh happiness, it comes on me in waves
> Then soon as I have dropped my guard – it turns around
> 'Happiness', 2005

Jon Plowman had read my proposal for *We Interupt This Programme* and was sufficiently interested to offer me £8,000 to make a taster tape for the forthcoming offers round (where submissions are offered to the channel commissioners). I made a fifteen-minute version of a show that I was now calling *The Message*. The show was commissioned as a six-part series for BBC Three and the article opposite from *Broadcast* magazine explains what we did and how.

As interesting an experience as it was to make *The Message*, there's little-to-no content in it that's relevant to this book. There was a sketch called 'God's Tiny Creatures' which was comprised of three people singing kids' songs whilst dressed as a bee, ladybird and nappy-wearing baby. The songs were all horribly inappropriate with subjects ranging from drugs to cancer to dogging. 'Don't Forget They're Only Trying To Be Friendly' was about paedophiles.

> There's a man (there's a man) up the park (up the park)
> And he's always on the swings even tho' it's nearly dark
> His glasses are tinted and his hygiene is on hold
> He's wearing an anorak although it isn't cold

I should have been the last person to reinforce the stereotype of the paedophile being the weirdo who hangs round the swings, knowing the much more common and mundane reality that they are, more often than not, known and 'friendly'.

Making *The Message* was mentally and physically exhausting. We had a newborn baby at home and I was working really long hours and most weekends. The night before we started shooting, our home was burgled and I had a fight with the burglar in the street suffering bad bruising to my face (I think I did a few of his ribs with repeated hooks to his body) and it was definitely a tricky few weeks.

Not long after we'd finished post-production, I got an email from Jon Plowman telling me that the controller of BBC Three who'd ordered the programme, Stuart Murphy, was leaving the channel. Shortly afterwards, I was summoned to TV Centre to meet the new controller of BBC Three, who was very honest about not being a fan of *The Message*. He was going to make the channel 'more primary-coloured' and felt what we'd done was 'a bit cerebral'. I can only imagine how I came across in the meeting. We were subsequently scheduled on Saturday night at 10:30 (new comedy back then needed to be a weeknight when your audience was at home) and, from then on, we were moved to a different slot every week.

The BBC decided against giving the show any backing or marketing and the silence and non-cooperation of the channel worked fatally against us. This (almost uniquely) wasn't a situation where I'd pissed someone off, it was just really bad luck. I did *then* piss someone off by writing to the Head of BBC Vision and explaining to her in a four-page letter why the BBC had failed in its duty of care and why her new channel controller had let me down.

The email I then received from the controller (who'd been handed my letter from above) expressed surprise that I wasn't happy with how I'd been treated.

I wasn't happy – and I also wasn't well.

After the first few weeks of transmission it became obvious that the programme wasn't reaching an audience and we certainly weren't going to be offered another series. This was a serious blow for me. Not only had it taken years to develop momentum and then a vehicle, but I would now be seen as 'damaged goods'. Someone who'd had a chance and blown it. This realisation, on top of being physically and mentally exhausted, brought me to a very strange physical and psychological state.

I came down with a particularly nasty cold which lasted for a couple of weeks. As I was recovering, I began to experience a tingling sensation in my fingertips, then my feet. Having been ill, the constant tiredness didn't immediately concern me, but then the tingling became a numbness and started to spread up my forearms and lower legs. I began to trip, catching my feet on kerbs and steps. It was as if my brain didn't know where my limbs were. I went to my GP who said it was likely a viral overhang from the cold. I hadn't run for weeks because of the virus, but now even walking was becoming tiring. My legs and arms were weak and getting worse, so I went to a private doctor. He inspected me, testing my strength and reactions and seemed concerned, referring me to The Cromwell Hospital for further investigation.

The tests were extensive: bloods, muscle strength, neural response, sense of humour. I had multiple electrodes attached all over my body and head to measure all sorts of stuff. Eventually I was diagnosed with Guillain-Barré syndrome, an auto-immune condition where the antibodies fighting an infection attack the myelin sheath of the nervous system. For several weeks it worsened until I was barely able to leave the house. In extreme cases it can lead to breathing on a ventilator and is fatal for one in twenty sufferers.

For the first time that I could remember, I was stuck. I couldn't move, I couldn't play the guitar (still), but I *could* sit and hold a pen. So, I dug out the poem from Glasgow, the rhyming verse thing about fate, and carried on. Four weeks later I was feeling much better and had 120 pages of scrawl that was now called *Acts of Godfrey*.

Wendell? Gee!

I don't feel cold - I don't feel strong - I don't feel much at all
And this could be hate - or just a mistake - or maybe too close to call
'cause I'm alright with this - and I'm on fire with this
But I bite down on this.
This fear comes in waves - this fear comes betrays
But it's never bright or bold
It breeds from within - and breathes through my skin
Leaves me so dried and old
'cause I can't fight with this - and I'm so tired of this
But I'm still tied to this
'This', 2007

And I was still tied to it. Throughout this period the malaise that I spoke of in 1994 creeping 'beneath my skin', was absolutely still there, even if I had now started to understand what I was writing about (at times). In 2007 we'd moved house from North Kensington into a bigger place in Harlesden NW10 with a huge garden, and as much as I wanted to feel 'fresh-starty', there was a sense of something very rotten inside me. I had once contracted sepsis via a tiny scratch on my ankle and a feeling had crept over me for a couple of days, before I noticed the multiple spots on my legs. It had felt like a slightly nauseous waking dream. Being poisoned, basically. This felt very similar.

When childhood experiences like mine are discussed or written about, the term 'buried' is often used to indicate how they are dealt with in the short term. Maybe that's an accurate definition of some people's experience, but not mine. To bury something requires thought and premeditation. To bury something you need to dig, deposit and then cover. Depending on the size of the thing (literally or metaphorically), it demands effort. I didn't bury my experiences, but rather they were encoded into me. I absorbed them unconsciously, quietly and imperceptibly. They were inextricable, as if during my physical and mental growth between ten and sixteen they were added alongside everything I learned and ate to become part of my fabric for years. For about thirty years to be precise, as I can pinpoint exactly when they were stripped out and exorcised.

In July 2007, I visited a shaman by accident. Sarah had an appointment booked with a therapist (called Wendy) who was unable to make the appointment, so her husband called Wendell (who was also a therapist) offered to see her but then she couldn't make it and asked if I'd like to go. I didn't really think I wanted to go, but for some reason I went. I locked my bicycle to the railings of the Notting Hill terrace, walked up the steps and rang the top bell. As I ascended the carpeted internal stairs, I mused on the fact that Crow had been on Wendell Road. I'd not thought about Crow for years; that was before I became a father, a comedy writer, a musician, a voice artist and developed an exterior that belied my turbulent and contradictory internal state. Crow was twenty-two years ago but this reflection caused me to shudder, like a wave passed through me or something stirred within.

> Could you be more real, come in from the sides
> Let's see these things brought into the light.
> And the fears that you freeze and all the deserts and seas
> They won't seem so wide, when you can be free
> 'Ripple', 1997

I stopped at the small top landing and sat in the chair as I'd been requested through the front door intercom. I felt nervous, anxious even, and I had a distinct sense of internal panic. The muted voices the other side of the door were now less muted and the soft footsteps indicated closure (or at least closure of that particular session). The door opened and someone left. I can't remember anything about them as my attention was elsewhere. Wendell, an Afro-Caribbean man of about forty, was staring at me in a way I didn't expect to be stared at by a welcoming therapist. He tilted his head to one side as if to say, 'What's the story?'

'Hello,' I ventured. 'Sarah couldn't come but thought it would be OK if I did...'

Wendell fixed my gaze; he appeared wary and on edge and didn't seem the type to be on edge. Gathering his composure and clearly pretending to seem inquisitive, he asked, 'Why?'

It was a good question; it was a more direct question than I'd have anticipated, but a good one nonetheless. Before I had a chance to answer, or even think of an answer, Wendell continued, 'There are two of you. There are two of you here.' My instinctive reaction was to do a comedy double-take over my shoulder, but I didn't. Something in Wendell's demeanour was marrying with the odd thoughts I'd had on the way up the stairs. And what he was saying made sense.

> The man inside is waking from his sleep and thinking things you won't believe.
> A game-plan so well made that's set to stay and won't be played
> If I can just get to my feet.
> 'Seed', 1995

What I think was happening as I ascended the stairs was that the homunculus inside me was wakening to the menace it was feeling from being in proximity to a presence that threatened its existence: Wendell. I realise that makes me sound, well, *unsound*, but I've had a long time to think about this and it seems as Occam's razor'y as it can be. Whatever, Wendell beckoned me into his room and asked me to tell him what was on my mind. So I told him everything about Bananas, or a twenty-minute precis.

'He's here, he's here with you,' said Wendell with absolute certitude and I experienced a sense of anxious elevation, as if someone had released a bag of chaffinches into a hitherto unknown cavity inside my chest. Wendell calmly explained to me that as well as being a therapist, he was also a shaman. *Did I know what a shaman was?* I said I thought so. Wendell calmly explained further that he could perform an exorcism and rid me of the presence he'd detected that was inhabiting me. By this point I was feeling at the very least 'a bit other' and it was clear that something was happening that had previously not happened – at least to me. One thing I was certain of: Wendell was on the right side of whatever battle seemed to be arranging itself in this modest yet currently very significant room.

There was a flat, padded platform in the centre like a massage table (it may have *been* a massage table as I'm not sure there'd be enough of a demand to manufacture an exorcism table) and Wendell suggested I lie on it. He asked me to trust him and not to be scared by anything I might see or hear, that some of his movements and actions might be quite unusual. Again, I felt not the slightest threat in his words or demeanour and as I lay down on my back, I felt completely relaxed.

I'd seen a couple of therapists and the odd counsellor in the past, only for a session or two, long enough to con them (or at least con-vince) them that *I was fine*. This felt nothing like any of that. There was no tinkling water feature, there was no meditative music or whale-song (some of the other things *may* have been massages), there was just a very simple, third-floor room from the windows of which I could see the upper branches of leafy plane trees and hear the sounds of passing buses.

Wendell asked me to tell him some more about Bananas. None of it came out in order, rather there was a series of unconnected sentences. It felt like the information was being proffered by Bananas, hoping each nugget would suffice to satisfy Wendell's curiosity. I was powerless as to what was being said, but the longer the litany went on, the more I felt a swelling in my chest. Wendell signalled for me to be still, not to be *quiet* – he wasn't trying to silence me but the emphatic movement of his flat hand silenced me.

And then I began to cry – and cry – and cry. Hot streams of tears that flooded over my cheeks and around my neck. I was silent but shaking as the massive swelling in my torso seemed to pump the tears endlessly. I sobbed and sobbed as the hot rivulets soaked across the chest and shoulders of my T-shirt.

'Pffffffttttt.' From pursed lips, Wendell spat a dry – sharp noise, like the sound of an arrow flying then hitting a target. There was a dry rattle from a gourd filled with seeds. Wendell moved around the table and my sobbing form – his legs bent at the knee, almost prancing.

He shook around me, he was like the wind, like a kite on the wind, like a shutter clattering – but all the time flitting around me, the bed, the room. I cried harder and harder, the swelling now feeling like it wanted me to eject it and all the time the 'Pfffffftttttt', the shaking seeds, the concentrated, maniacally forensic attention as Wendell did battle.

I left the physical sensations of the room as my chest seemed to be opening, accompanied by a roaring sound like a jet-plane on take-off. I was still lying flat on my back on the table, but my chest opened wide and light burst upward towards the ceiling then beyond. I felt an endless column of light rushing and roaring from me upwards – upwards – upwards, pulling me, yet all the time I felt Wendell ensuring I stayed. He was flying about me, his actions, sounds and will all furiously coordinated as the column gained infinite height. The roaring intensified, the light poured out of me, burning everything to white.

My strained and silent window, swings open to reveal
A boundless barren landscape I'd ignite if I could feel
A tiny spark of hope, but though I try I cannot hold
Let it go - Let it go.
Live in fear of light you don't belong
You bleach to white to right your wrongs
To right your wrongs
'Bleach To White', 1998

Silence. 'He's gone now.'

Wendell was sat on the chair near to me and I returned to the room. I was shaking with the aftershocks of the relentless crying, shuddering like a toddler. Something fundamental had shifted within me. Although it was going to be years before I was able to understand the occurrences and consequences of my abuse, the first part of the process was to be the forcible stripping out of some of that wiring. It felt painful and raw, like a clumsy initial rooting around to extract shrapnel, but it was a necessary start. Even if it had happened by accident.

When I got home, I went to my office which was still in a spare bedroom in the house (I was in the process of building a wooden cabin at the bottom of the garden that would become my studio). In my filing cabinet there was a file marked with Bananas' initials and in it were various pieces of paper pertaining to the thwarted prosecution from 2002/3. Amongst these papers was the handwritten letter in which Bananas admitted his guilt and gave assurances as to us being his 'only' two victims. I took the contents of the file to the bottom of the garden where, alongside the footings of the concrete raft that my new studio was to be built on, there was a pile of garden cuttings and bits of the old shed which I was about to burn. I set light to the bonfire and threw all of the papers into it. It felt like I was purging physical artefacts of what Wendell had just ridded me of; it felt cathartic and was a necessary part of a journey that had a long way to go.

Sarah maintains that there was something different about me from then on, that this was the beginning of the end for us. I don't see it that way, but it affected me internally and maybe she saw it differently as it changed how we related to one another. We had our second daughter three months later in August 2008 and she was conceived in love, so maybe the change Sarah felt was my being freed, maybe I lost a dependence? I do know that the songs I wrote around this period had a deep sense of sorrow and loss.

All Our Good Friends

I decided to make a record, but wary of being connected to recent comedy exploits, I used a project name of *All Our Good Friends*. The phrase came from a random sentence generator and I liked the sound of it. Some of the songs were older, post-Senna, 'God and the Aeroplanes' was from 1999. I recorded all of them on my own in the bedroom studio.

Before the album was finished, I got the urge to play live but didn't want to get a band together. I used the backing tracks I'd recorded and cut films to them using odd footage from stock libraries and bought four old TVs. The first gig was at a pub off the Harrow Rd called The Regent. It was August and the hottest day of the year. Playing songs on stage felt more comfortable than it ever had. I loved every minute and the thirty-minute set was over too soon. The best of it was my nearly three-year-old daughter, stood at the front, gazing at me wide-eyed and grinning throughout, like 'Dad! What the hell??!!'

I played another two gigs over the following few weeks which went down well. Playing with real TVs behind me instead of real people seemed to be a great move but, actually, I think playing without a homunculus inside me was the difference.

If being back on stage was good, releasing a record was about to be more good. I had no expectations whatsoever for the album that I'd decided to call *Promise*.

The front cover photo, taken of me when I was eleven by Bananas, was a way of reclaiming something of the promise I had back then. I put a photo of my mum looking salty on the back composited with a picture of me upside down. Because.

Mum had died unexpectedly, early in 2007 and I was to revisit the events of her death in a screenplay in a few years' time.

I sent CD copies of *Promise* with a brief press release to the music papers and a few broadsheet reviewers, expecting tumbleweed. I got an email from a weird address informing me I was going to be Record Of The Week in the *Sunday Times*. I thought it was a mate taking the piss and replied as such. I then got a phone call from a man called Mark Edwards asking for a picture to accompany the review they were running in the Culture section that weekend. I took a photo in the park over the road and emailed it, then on Sunday morning went out to buy the *Sunday Times* and, yes, there it was. It didn't feel like the first FIN live review at all, not that thrilling excitement. There was no frenzied boozing; I think I had a boiled egg, but it was deeply satisfying. With that and the gigs, I hadn't let myself down. Rough Trade loved the album and made it their Record Of The Week too. They sold out and asked for another hundred copies.

Promise got a mound of great reviews, easily the most of any record I've ever made and I'm pretty sure it was because I had no expectations and did it for the best of reasons – because I wanted to make some music again.

Vic Timms

Most of 2008 was spent taking a ninety-page poem about fate, turning it into a film script and then raising the money to shoot it. The effort required to find the necessary finance far outweighed the actual writing, but that likely says more about the screenplay than anything else. It took months to produce a forty-eight-page glossy brochure detailing the intricacies of the Enterprise Investment Scheme (EIS) and conforming to all the necessary legalities to make such an offer.

I spent around a fortnight learning Adobe InDesign to enable myself to work with the layouts. It was exhaustive, exhausting and basically a huge sales pitch. The script was set around a sales conference and the central character Godfrey (Simon Callow), was a mischievous but ultimately quite useless God who decides to 'help out' the hapless Vic Timms, an alarms salesman.

VIC TIMMS

I sell alarms, intruder and fire,
and far from suggesting my purpose is higher
than monetary gain, my conscience is sure
that I keep those I deal with safe and secure.

Dad had been an insurance salesman for much of our childhood and unlike the archetypal salesman, was not motivated by sales targets but by helping clients who he genuinely believed benefited from the safety net he offered. For the purposes of the film, Vic sold fire and intruder alarms which are easier to physically portray than life insurance. Dad's career was steady and unremarkable and he was frequently overtaken by colleagues who would hit higher targets and be promoted above him. His bosses must have found it frustrating.

VIC TIMMS

My boss, who suggested I come on this course,
feels that I'm lacking in guile and force.
He says that my methods are costing him dear.
I should generate trade from the climate of fear

But Dad had a strong ethical sense that he wouldn't step beyond. He was a man apart in many ways. When we were kids, other dads would be outfitted in jeans and tracksuits with trainers, Dad would stand on the sideline at football in a tweed sports jacket, cavalry twills tucked into Wellington boots, puffing away on his pipe. When I was little, I found it a bit embarrassing, now I think of it so affectionately, though the embarrassment may have stemmed from pity at his solitude.

VIC TIMMS

I happen to think that's corrupt, and despite
your assertion that profit will make it alright.
To be decent and honest is quite black and white,
and it's hard enough getting to sleep every night.

When I was writing *Acts of Godfrey*, the theme of *whether the end justifies the means* was definitely informed by aspects of my family history. My Uncle Chris was definitely of the 'everything goes' school of goal attainment and this had rubbed off heavily on my older brother who had risen to the top in magazine publishing with an ability to get any*one* to do any*thing*. The sales course at the heart of the film examines the degree to which one needs to be honest. As the sales trainer Brad puts it:

BRAD ANGEL

Today's theme is The-Appearance-Of-Truth.
Can the 'apparent state' of a situation be used
to leave a client somewhat confused.

What wasn't so clear in my mind was another aspect of Vic Timms that was a little closer to home. Vic, who we're told by Godfrey at the outset is *'unlucky at work and in games of the flesh'*, is initially at odds with the unprincipled estate agent Mary McDalen, but with Godfrey's interference via the administration of a love potion (actually a hybrid of Viagra and coke called 'Poke') the two are brought together. At a dimly lit dining table, the pair talk intimately. Mary advises Vic that he's too confrontational and quick to anger:

MARY

I know you're a decent and sensitive bloke,
but you rise too quickly to every slight...
and it makes your life a constant fight.

VIC

You're right... I sometimes act too tough...
(hesitatingly)
I guess... I don't think I'm...enough.
(very quietly)
I'm scared of being a...reject.

As much as I knew I was writing Vic as my dad, he was an amalgam of us both. I was quick to anger and would go to war at the drop of a hat, sometimes at just the sight of a hat. I knew that feeling of not being *enough*. In the film, Vic has a recurring nightmare where he's wet himself and is forced to take off his shorts and underpants in front of his class. Although my recurring nightmare was different to this (more physical pain than psychological), throughout secondary school I hated communal showers (and still do). At primary school, and in any activities pre-Boys' Club, I'd been an enthusiastic nudist. Everything had changed between ten and sixteen.

These feelings of not being 'enough' weren't confined to physical inadequacy, but to many aspects of my character and behaviour, leading me to frequently overcompensate.

At home things were becoming increasingly fractious. Our mutual attraction based on aspects of each other we felt compensated for our own myriad shortcomings weren't proving to be the glue we'd hoped. We were almost diametrically opposed in how we approached every situation and day-to-day functioning was becoming a constant series of compromises and disagreements.

> and you fight the thought that it's them and me
> As you try to look like the perfect family
> First blood to the young one.
> Then late one night in a drunken blur
> You scream the worst thing you could say to her
> First blood to the young one.
> 'First Blood to the Young One', 2008

My mobile phone rang one afternoon – it was my sister Janet, who was in the neighbourhood with Bananas. What could they want?

A False Parade

I was in my wooden cabin, the studio I'd built at the bottom of the garden. I'd been working for a while intermittently on some songs that might become a new record. So far, the tracks were falling into a few categories:

American politics post 9/11 –   'Shoot You Down', 'America Sleeps',
                                'Wrong Man (in the Wrong Place)',
                                'Vincent'

Financial collapse –   'Atmosphere'

'Domestic upset' –   'First Blood (to the Young One)'

The phone rang as I was playing a slide guitar line for the chorus of 'Shoot You Down', a song that proved thankfully well wide of the mark as it vocalised my fear that some NRA nut would take out the recently elected President Barack Obama. I was annoyed with myself for leaving my phone on. There's nothing worse when you've spent an age perfecting a guitar line than having it ruined by phone interference turning your amp into a morse-code transmitter. This was worse.

What happened next is best described in two accounts, written by Nick and myself:

Extract of letter from Johnny Daukes to siblings:

1 September 2009

[Bananas and Janet] called me in late September 2009 and requested that I meet them in 45 minutes at a local pub. I sat down and [Bananas] said 'I lied to you.' I said, 'Go on.' He said, 'I abused ▮▮▮▮▮▮▮▮▮▮▮▮▮▮▮▮▮▮▮▮▮▮▮

I prompted [Bananas] to continue. They told me that ▮▮▮▮▮▮ had been to see a psychiatrist and I quizzed them as to the identity of this psychiatrist. I was alarmed to hear that it was the same psychiatrist that [Bananas] himself had visited; [psychiatrist's name], who is a member of Opus Dei. They proffered the further information that ▇▇▇▇ had been sent to see a priest, as if it were some kind of mitigation. At this point I said, 'You live your lives according to a fairy tale'. By that, I meant that ▇▇▇▇▇▇▇▇▇▇▇▇▇▇▇▇▇▇▇▇▇ needed real practical psychiatric help, not the notion of forgiveness based in a belief system. It was not a judgement of ▇▇▇▇▇▇▇▇▇▇▇▇▇▇▇▇▇▇▇▇ It is of no consequence to me what beliefs they subscribe to (until they offer them as inextricably beneficial to ▇▇▇▇▇▇▇▇▇▇▇▇▇▇▇▇▇▇▇ Further, the fact that they felt that it was appropriate to refer ▇▇▇▇ on to Nick as: 'Nick has already dealt with this' is a quite extraordinary leap of logic and smacks of a terrible disdain for the painful journey Nick has himself undergone, in an attempt to minimise the damage caused to him by [Bananas].

Extract of letter from Nick Daukes to siblings:

12 July 2019

In the summer of 2009, I was returning from a weekend in Germany and Janet tried to contact me overnight. I ignored this until I reached Calais mid-morning and then called her. She answered ▇▇▇▇▇▇▇▇▇▇▇▇▇▇▇▇▇▇▇ over the course of the ensuing few minutes' conversation that it became apparent that what she meant, but had not said, ▇▇▇▇▇▇▇▇▇▇▇▇▇▇▇▇▇▇▇ He had done so in 2000, approximately 2½ years before signing the letter stating that he had not abused anyone else except Johnny and me. Later it became clear that [Bananas] had confessed this to Janet back in 2002. I have never asked Janet if she knew what the letter [Bananas] wrote to Johnny and I contained, but find it inconceivable that she could not have known he lied and that she therefore colluded with him.

I came back home in a daze. As I walked into the house it was obvious to Sarah something was very wrong and she asked me. I told her what I had learned. The magnitude of this was obvious. The shock gave way to upset and I broke down. It was all back again.

Time - was healing. Sewn, made good.
Memories and feelings, pain understood.
There's no right way or wrong way to live
But one thing I know is that I've got no forgiveness left to give
So, excuse me for walking away now.
'The Virus', 2010

Sarah's father Tom was a senior partner in a legal firm and Nick and I travelled to meet him and discuss our options. Tom had a friend who was a barrister with expertise in the field of child sex abuse cases and prosecuting paedophiles. The world was very different in 2009 with regard to historical cases and when the barrister examined the facts of what had taken place in 2002, our withdrawing statements and petitioning the CPS to drop the prosecution, he advised we had little to no chance with judicial process as we would be considered 'unsafe witnesses'. Through an extraordinarily tortuous, divisive and painful process, as a family we agreed to have Bananas assessed for ongoing risk in the light of this fresh revelation. We found an independent company who specialised in the assessment of sex offenders.

There were immediate interviews with Bananas, Janet and all those concerned. This process was undertaken with the best of intentions and (at least as far as Nick and I were concerned) in the belief that it would be transparent in terms of disclosure. When the interviews were complete, there was a summary report circulated that contained a series of conclusions and recommendations. These included:

- There was little likelihood of Bananas re-offending (or having done so since 2002).
- Bananas would receive ongoing psychotherapy and assessment.

This penitential fake I.D. That's undermined the best of me
Is exorcised and shot into the sky - goodbye.
Your reverence for plain untruth, your soul created wasted youth
Made all that should have seemed so right so wrong. So long.
'Anthem (for Wasted Youth)', 2010

This summary report was compiled from the results of three much more detailed assessments of Bananas, Janet and a general concluding report that we were not to see until 2019. Had we seen these reports in 2009, we would have taken a different course of action. The summary report also omitted one very important key fact that was to remain hidden until 2019.

You might read of these events and of the previously thwarted prosecution and smack your head in exasperation. How, yet again, did we mishandle things so spectacularly? It's like we're the star striker of a football team who's just blasted the ball over the bar when presented with *another* open goal. What you can't see is that the striker is disabled by invisible leg-irons and it's a miracle they're on the pitch to start with.

That's what it's like. A bit.

The album I was working on now had the working title *A False Parade*, for many and varied reasons. The most recent songs were 'The Virus' and 'Anthem (for Wasted Youth)'. The disclosure of another victim of Bananas' terrible incontinence increased the list to three (that we were currently aware of) and prompted the song 'A Roll Call'.

> This house isn't safe, this building's condemned
> Free fall, there's the last call, but still we pretend.
> 'A Roll Call', 2010

The song was inspired by the awful resurrection of the past few months, but became inextricable with my failing marriage.

> This carcass is high, this well has run dry
> Names change but all stays the same, as the screams become sighs.
> 'A Roll Call', 2010

The verses were obvious metaphor, delivered in a reasonable Roger Waters, but the middle 8 and solo were fuelled by a real sense of anger and spite. The choruses seem to address Bananas directly:

> And you wanted to walk with me, to fumble and talk with me
> But here comes the roll call - counting us down
> It's the roll call - bearing down on our souls.
> 'A Roll Call', 2010

The situation between Sarah and I had by now become critical and the last song written for the album (and the last song on the album) was 'Wrecking Ball'. It's a desperately sad song to hear, even now. It was painfully clear and honest about what I was and what I was doing:

> I stand before you - a wrecking ball just waiting to take a final swing
> And all I promise, and all I say is nothing, compared with what I bring.
> 'Wrecking Ball', 2010

The next verse was written to Sarah and our daughters. I knew that what I was doing was going to cause pain.

> I stand before you - I see you call, your anguish is falling on deaf ears
> My role is vacant, a spirit washed away by a wave of future tears.
> 'Wrecking Ball', 2010

Sarah gave me a painting for my birthday in December 2010 of a bird. I felt she had painted me – puffed-up and self-important – telling me something more eloquently than she could express in words. I used it as the album cover for *A False Parade* as it perfectly encapsulated how I felt about myself:

And what would you say, in retrospect?
You did a good impression of a man.
The finery and clothes – the rainbow
All smoke and mirrors, a peacock's fan.
Now everything I've done and will ever do
Is waiting to pass judgement again.
And you can stop this wrecking ball
By stepping up and cutting its chain.
'Wrecking Ball', 2010

Pieces of Fate

Having written *Acts of Godfrey*, a script wherein a fractured and underconfident man with adequacy issues is united with his soulmate through an act of fate, I set about trying to raise the finance for the film. The promotional document that I'd spent months making was printed and I was ready to post out around 400 to try and garner a production budget of around £300,000.

In the Korean movie *Chong-al Meikeo* (The Bulletmaker) a bitter young silversmith, Yae-joon, spends a year fashioning a single bullet from poisonous copper beryllium. He needs it to pierce the armoured breast-plate of Princess Ha-rin, who has humiliated his father at a gardening festival. He will get one shot and it will kill the princess outright.

To test the efficacy of my document (and the two accompanying scenes I'd filmed to showcase the verse) I sent the brochure to a man I'd known for a few years who was, as the expression goes, a 'high-net-worth individual'. I received a prompt email inviting me to come and meet with him with a view to his providing the entire budget.

Bang!
(Thump)
'Goodnight, Princess!'

The most significant thing that happened in the production of *Acts of Godfrey* was nothing to do with what ended up on the screen, but was the meeting between an actual fractured and underconfident man with adequacy issues and his soulmate. The act of fate in this instance being: the prospective line producer who saw the call for crew on a website, was intrigued, read the script and thought, 'This is genius, I need to meet the writer.'

I used to arrange meetings at the Royal Institute of British Architects in Portland Place; it has loads of space and light and there's never anyone there. The first floor was a vast, marble-pillared modern space with lots of isolated tables and a coffee bar with waiter service. It's where I first met Julie Clark and we return there on 8 October every year. We made the film, fell in love and were married in 2018. The third and last time for us both.

Making *Acts of Godfrey* was a lot of fun. Julie was a very experienced line producer, which was lucky because the high-net-worth individual was an inexperienced producer and seemed to take many decisions that, whilst well intentioned, ensured his investment wouldn't be recouped. I've spent the last five years editing (and co-producing) films with producers who absolutely understand how to find their market. None of them think that they, or their films, are entitled to get anywhere, but they make hundreds of decisions to ensure that they do so.

On *Acts of Godfrey* I got to direct Simon Callow, Celia Imrie, Harry Enfield and a host of tremendous actors speaking my lines, which was magical. We premièred at London's Raindance Festival, were nominated for the British Independent Film Awards and enjoyed a three-week cinema run. Having been to the première, a bunch of us bought tickets and went to see the film with other punters on Shepherd's Bush Green. We cheered through the credits. But the finest Act of Godfrey was introducing me to the woman who has shown the extraordinary resilience, patience and limitless love to help me finally begin to navigate my way out of the form I'd been forged into.

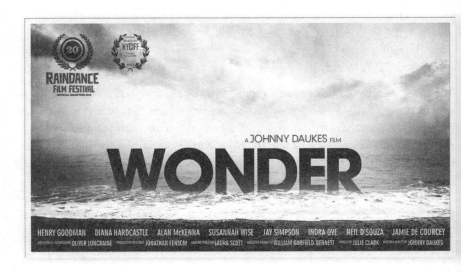

Wonder Has Finally Ceased

From this point onwards, I never wrote or made anything where I wasn't (at least on some level) aware of what I was writing. Over the decade from 2011 to the present I've made films, sitcoms, written screenplays and music, but none of it has blind-sided me with its meaning. Bananas hadn't gone anywhere, however, and there were still invitations to family events that, for the time being, I'd refuse if he was going to be present.

In order to process the breakdown of my marriage to Sarah, I wrote a series of songs that were duets between a man and a woman analysing their failed relationship. I recorded the songs with the producer Gareth Jones who'd worked with Depeche, Nick Cave and Mogwai. Gareth encouraged me to record the songs 'as live', playing and singing simultaneously, but my hands let me down. Not as badly though as I'd let my daughters down. It was (and has continued to be) a feeling that haunts me. The marriage had become impossible, our instincts and ideals absolutely at odds. Undoubtedly, we both wanted what was best for our children, but those desires were too strongly opposed, too often.

HIM	I fear that I'm a man who cannot see,
	your world of joy and possibility
	To turn, to spurn, to cry and walk away,
	and miss the dawning of a brighter day.
HER	I fear that you're a man of dying nerve,
	a humble servant to the ghosts you serve
	But what of flesh and blood, of skin and bone?
	The fragile seedlings of the seeds you've sown.

'The Man Who Cannot See', 2012

On all six songs, I dug deeply to try and represent both of our points of view and the inevitable repercussions. It was painful and exposing, not least on 'Fool'. As I wrote this song, from what I believed to be Sarah's point of view, I pictured the fool dressed as Santa, delivering mince pies whilst popping wheelies on a scooter.

> The Fool, dances gaily, fills my line of sight
> Fooled, I allowed his dreams to fill my nights
> And you – what were you thinking of, to do that?
> You fool, what were you dreaming of?
> 'Fool', 2012

I played the songs to Christian Ulf-Hansen (the husky-racing Dane), who suggested I should make a short film to go with the songs. I wrote a series of scenes between four different couples, all with relationships in disrepair. Each of the couples appeared at various times on a beach. We shot the scenes at Seatown in Dorset, just a few miles along the coast from Seaton in Devon which had been the destination of the Boys' Club cycle camp and where Bananas had taken the photo of me that's in the montage. The soundtrack was made from instrumental re-mixes of the songs (so not really promoting the songs at all – no change there). The film, *Wonder*, was shown at the New York Film Festival and at Raindance.

I don't think my children cared and I couldn't blame them.

Last Night I Dreamt

On 8 April 2010, in response to a text from Janet reminding me about it being Joely's silver wedding, I responded as follows:

> In case you haven't remembered, your husband raped my little brother and caused me untold damage. Now please stop texting me useless reminders and banal greetings. This is NOT an invitation to a discussion.

Following this, there are two texts from her in 2011 wishing me a happy birthday and Christmas. I didn't respond. But on 18 June 2013, there's this from me:

> Hi Janet, after my last response I'd understand if not, but if you fancy meeting in town, I'd be happy to. X

1167 days is a long time, but that was quite an emotional arc I'd travelled. In 2002, after the trial collapsed, I eventually reached a point where I could see Janet or Bananas in family social situations. I wouldn't seek their company, but time has a way of blunting emotions, especially when those emotions are as twisted and deformed as mine were. Even after the revelation of 2009 (which was clearly very raw in 2010), my brain had retreated from the position I'd held and begun to seek some kind of reconciliation.

I was prompted to send the text by a vivid dream in which I walked along a forest path and came upon a wooden house with a verandah. I knew that Janet was in the house and I lay down on the verandah and fell asleep. I felt safe and at peace. In the dream, there was no hint, suggestion or recollection of Bananas and I think the feelings were recalling those I'd felt as a child for my oldest sister. When I woke, I had an overwhelming sense that I needed to contact her, so I did.

During the period 2003–9 and then 2009–13, on some level my subconscious wanted everything to be alright. The rest of my family continued to have friendly relations with their family (and with ten children there were numerous interrelationships between cousins, uncles and aunts, godchildren etc.). It was as if everyone else had forgiven and forgotten and I suppose I wanted to prove myself magnanimous and capable of this degree of compassion. And yet I was continuing to write songs that clearly indicate my mind was, at best, conflicted. That conflict was explicitly explored in two drama scripts I wrote between 2011 and 2014.

Making Drama
Out of Crisis

In April 2011 I started sketching out some notes and voice recordings for something I called *Goodbye Mother*. It originally took shape as four kids and a husband gathering round the bed of their dying mother/wife and I proposed it to BBC Radio 4 as a 'musical play'. My proposal to commission ratio with Radio 4 was, until that point, one hundred per cent. After that point, the ratio fell.

My mum had died in January 2007. She woke up feeling a bit out of sorts, had a massive stroke and died around twelve hours later. During the course of the day, as the family arrived at the hospital and we were variously able to say what were obviously going to be goodbyes, a thing began to happen. Mum had a number of Opus Dei spiritual advisors over the years who became a huge influence in her life and who gave the type of shitty advice that celibates were uniquely placed to give to a woman with a husband and eight kids. These advisors had led our family to a situation where my dad felt estranged and we were frequently put at the back of a queue behind God, Opus Dei's founder The Blessed Josemaría, general praying and, increasingly, other families who represented an opportunity for Mum to practise the apostolate and ensnare other mums under the guise of helping them.

Throughout the day, a trio of Opus Dei members arrived at the hospital like a sort of crap Three Kings and there was a feeling of Mum's death being hijacked in a gradually tightening noose of piety and religious cosplay. A priest of Opus Dei turned up, as did candles and a creeping sense of 'ownership'. One inserted a crucifix into her hands, which Dad must have loved. As if it wasn't enough that they'd owned her life for forty years they now wanted to stage-manage her death too. Truly we were blessed!

I was asked to write my mum's eulogy and in the concluding paragraph I wrote the following.

This eulogy has been in praise of our friend, Gramma, sister, mother and wife. But it has also been, because of the way that life was lived, in praise of a marriage. The fundamental strength that our mother relied on and drew upon to sustain her faith and family, I believe came from our father, Colin Daukes.

So, while we remember Tess Daukes in prayer, let's combine those words with action. I invite you to stand and join me in a very physical tribute to that incredible love and that incredible life. (Applause)

The reference to 'our father' was a not very subtle dig at Opus Dei, who refer to their founder (the now Saint Josemaría) as 'Our Father' who, assuming he art in heaven, must be having some authority issues with The Big Man. I wanted to assert our dad, who'd been very much sidelined through Mum's devotion to Opus Dei and the Church. I followed that up with an invocation to applause – also anathema to the assembled Spiritual Stormtroopers.

Childish, possibly – but then, I was her child.

Less childish was the process of turning those experiences into the idea for *Goodbye Mother* and then adapting them a year later into the screenplay *The Seahorse and the Wolf*. The story was an allegory of how our family (and in particular my dad) had been affected and undermined by Opus Dei, which I represented in the character of a corrupt parish priest, who has an affair with the mother.

In the synopsis I described it like this:

'The Seahorse and the Wolf is a story about the battle for the soul of a family between its own father, Tom and the duplicitous Father Callum McDougall.

As the Sweeney family gather at their dying mother's bedside, they discover the dark truth of what has kept them apart for years and, ultimately, what makes them want to reconcile.

A gritty, yet ultimately uplifting, drama that explores themes of fidelity, faith and parenthood.'

The creation and development of this script was interspersed with making *Acts of Godfrey*, *Wonder*, a couple of albums and another BBC Radio 4 sketch show called *The Scanner*, so the script kept getting sidelined.

In July 2013 I spent a day recording four songs at The Pool Studios near Elephant & Castle. I'd written the songs as background to a further drama I was developing called *The Records*. The story was focused on a talent agent called Marc Chance, whose father Chaz Chance had been a minor glam-rock star in the 70s with his band, Chaz Chance & The Prophets, and I'd written several of Chaz's songs that had worked their way into the script as determining future events – The Prophets were *literally* prophets.

At the beginning of the script, Marc meets a journalist called Katia and their mutual attraction drives much of the plot and also proves a catastrophic and insurmountable final dilemma. As the script progresses, we learn that *The Records* refers not just to the recordings Chaz made in the 70s, but also to a diary that Katia has kept and the awful documentation therein, detailing the sexual abuse she's been subjected to by her father, Dieter. Dieter is a member of a Catholic sect called 'The Knights of the Light', who practise extreme forms of physical mortification and are obsessed with sexual propriety.

Another golden rule of drama: 'write what you know'.

In an almost Olympian act of *finding the silver lining round a cloud*, writing *The Records* had two positive side-effects. The first was that I collaborated with an excellent script editor who taught me a lot about structure, character motivation and pace. The second was that I got to record the songs with a band comprised of Gaz Coombes (*Supergrass*), Phil Manzanera (*Roxy Music*), Mat Osman (*Suede*) and Mike Joyce (*The Smiths*). For someone who'd tried (and largely failed) to write and record music at a certain level, to have these people investing their time and talent on songs that I'd written felt really rewarding. Someone who didn't like me observed

snidely at the time that I was 'confusing a hobby with an occupation'. I can't think of anything to aspire to *more* than being able to combine the two. A 'hobbupation', perhaps.

I didn't make any prolonged attempts to propagate either of these scripts, there was always something else more pressing. Or possibly it was that tendency to move on to something new, rather than persevering long enough to break through inevitable barriers.

Doctor Feelgood

I had been living with Julie and her two children for a few years now and had been more or less accepted in what I now felt was home. There were (and still are) stresses and strains inherent in living under the roof with step-children who know you're not their real dad, yet living apart from your own children who miss you and resent you living elsewhere. We all muddle through and at times can *almost* feel like a somewhat ramshackle unit. At other times, my heart feels like it's being wrenched in different directions. We did pan-European camper van trips with all six of us in 2013 and 2017 and these were probably the happiest five weeks of my life. Everyone I loved under one roof. Bliss.

Sarah and I continued trying our best to co-parent with diametrically opposed views about how to raise children in the twenty-first century. As the kids got older this gradually became easier as their opinions came to the fore and diluted our disagreements. We both, at times, felt we were running a three-legged race with someone who kept belting us in the face with a frying pan, but even that had begun to feel like a mild annoyance rather than something catastrophic.

Julie knew the entire history of Bananas and the family's attempts to deal with it. She was always one hundred per cent supportive of me and the position I took. She was also very wary of any contact with Bananas, Janet or their family. Unlike me, there was no weird sense of needing to reconcile. She saw it clearly for what it was and had an instinctive desire to protect me. At some point around this time (it may have been in 2014 as I was making a short film for Dad's eightieth birthday) Julie observed how often I'd included him in my work. Aside from basing Vic Timms on him in *Acts of Godfrey*, he'd also featured heavily in *The Message* (not least in the sketch about 'The Maida Vale Hunt' which was his idea). He'd featured in MTV titles, two music videos and was the central character in *The Seahorse and the Wolf.* I think in some way I was trying to place him more centrally than he'd ever been allowed to be. Or maybe I was fascinated by someone who'd always been such a closed book.

After Mum died, many of us feared the worst for how Dad would cope. He'd always played a supporting role in the relationship and probably said one word for every twenty of Mum's throughout their almost fifty years together. There was never any doubt how much he loved her; as I said, Dad was (as far as Mum was concerned) a *very* tactile man. But rather than succumbing to grief and loneliness, Dad adapted to his role of widower with ingenuity and enthusiasm.

Having always been an early adopter of technology, the potential complications of internet dating were swatted away with a swipe of his cordless mouse. A couple of relationships came and went before we were introduced to Wendy, who certainly released his inner Peter Pan.

They shared a love of logic, structure and good Scotch. All of a sudden we were presented with a Dad 2.0 who talked to and *with* his partner. After a few years of going steady they were married in November 2017 and it was my honour to be his best man.

It wasn't long after they were married that I got a phone call from Dad. In the course of a conversation that was hampered by his usual stilted delivery (although he'd started a new life, he still hadn't grasped the conversational pre-requisite of *asking questions of the other person*) he let me know how sorry he was for not offering his unequivocal support back in 2003. He wanted me to know that he understood the gravity of what Nick and I had gone through and that, thanks to some patient explanation from Wendy, he realised that he'd handled it badly. It was a short call, but it went a very long way.

Work had become a series of random projects comprised of branded content creation and writing/producing a Radio 4 sitcom called *Cracking Up*. I'd been shooting and editing a corporate film with Ian McKellen, for a director called Richard Loncraine. Richard had directed over a dozen movies including *Slade In Flame*, *The Missionary* and *Richard III*. In autumn 2017 he

had casually enquired about my making a promotional EPK (marketing clip) for his forthcoming movie, *Finding Your Feet*, but I'd heard nothing more. In early December, Richard called me. He was cutting the movie and it wasn't going well. He asked if I fancied editing it? I'd never cut a feature film in my life and said as much to Richard, but he was having none of it: 'Oh fuck off, you're a storyteller – come and cut my film, you'll be great.'

I cut *Finding Your Feet*, which wasn't without its challenges, not the least of which was that the ending didn't really work and was an anti-climax. One afternoon, I picked up a guitar and started tiddling around with some chords and words over the pictures. Quite soon I'd written a song that fitted in and around the end dialogue and action. Richard came over, I ran the cut with me singing the song and it made him cry. This really is another 'I had no idea' moment. The song was called 'Running To The Future' and besides fitting the final act of Imelda Staunton's character electing to take a leap of faith with Tim Spall, it was actually me writing from the heart about Julie and our lives together.

Though there's no changing what is in the past
The rest is mine to live at last
And so I'll take this chance - on you.
So I'm running to the future, and if this dream survives
I'll run along beside you through the best years of our lives
And it's calling me, yes it's calling me - to you
'Running To The Future', 2017

After the film finished, I made a second series of my sitcom *Cracking Up* for Radio 4, then Julie and I got married. My best men were John Coon and my step-son Elliot. Elliot's speech was funnier than anything I've ever written and I loved him for it. It was an unbelievable weekend, then Julie and I went to Mexico on honeymoon. We got on spectacularly well, apart from when we didn't. Despite my desire to run to the future alongside her, I was still the things that I'd been put through and my tendency to want to always be right could sometimes spill over. Nothing dramatic, largely due to her tolerance, but something was still boiling away inside me.

When we got back, I immediately started editing another movie, *Fisherman's Friends*. The cut went really well and I wound up with a co-producer credit, as well as that of editor.

On Wednesday, 27 February I took this picture on Kensal Rise – there were thousands of buses adorned with posters all across London. It was just past four o'clock in the afternoon and I was about to go home.

And Then There Were Four

This train careers with flapping sails
This supertanker's off the rails
As you deny the lives you've laid to waste. Bad taste.
'Anthem (For Wasted Youth)', 2008

When I was at home that evening, an idle glance at Facebook caused my heart to lurch, my blood pressure to soar and alarm bells to ring deafeningly loudly. So it wasn't just a birthday notification. My sister Janet had shared a *New York Post* article in defence of the (at that moment convicted*) sexual abuser Cardinal George Pell. This seemed a spectacular mis-step in the light of her being aware of the abuse suffered by me, Nick and a further individual at the hands of her husband. At the time, I was unaware that two of Bananas' and Janet's children had married Australian god-children of Pell and that the cardinal had conducted one of their weddings.

The post displayed a contemptuous lack of contrition and encapsulated the thinking of a couple who had somehow managed to rationalise the abuses that had taken place. And in this case 'somehow' involves a great deal of minimising and amelioration through notions of 'penance' and 'forgiveness' all seen through the prism of Catholic philosophy.

In the next few days following the Facebook post, I found myself arguing on social media with an enraged god-child of the (at that time convicted*) sexual

---

* Cardinal Pell subsequently had his conviction quashed in the Australian High Court who, whilst noting the credibility of the complainant and the unanimous verdict of the jury (and the upholding of his conviction by the Victoria Court of Appeal), summarised that this didn't establish the cardinal's guilt beyond reasonable doubt. Withheld from the original trial was the report from the Australian Royal Commission which gave details of the multiple occasions throughout his priestly career where Father Pell had turned a blind eye or offered protection to fellow priests in his orbit who had committed gross acts of sexual abuse.

abuser Cardinal George Pell. He became quite incensed and threatening towards me and my description of the (at that time convicted*) sexual abuser Cardinal George Pell as a 'convicted sexual abuser'. This seemed reasonable to me as the cardinal had (at that time*) been prosecuted for sexually abusing children and (following my sister posting the *NYP* article) I'd spent a significant amount of time reading up on the evidence and even watching some of the police interviews with the (at that time convicted*) sexual abuser Cardinal George Pell.

What Mr Angry wasn't aware of was that the person he was arguing with (the brother of his mother in-law: me) had been sexually abused by the man who was now his own father-in-law. And worse was to come.

I can pinpoint the exact time and date of 'worse', as I discovered it following the fall-out of the previous circumstances, in an email from one of my sisters. It was at 11:21am on Saturday, 2 March 2019 that I learned Bananas had also abused a fourth different individual and was clearly a serial offender. If you're thinking *he'd already abused you, your brother and a further third individual, wasn't that a bit of a clue?* then you're right. But this is indicative of the muddled thinking implicit in the awful mess that we'd arrived at through our various botched attempts as a family attempting to administer to this terrible situation 'in-house'. Translation: beyond fucked-up.

Over the next few days there were emails flying back and forth between my brothers and sisters. Several of these emails resembled campaign material for what looked to be quickly establishing itself as *PedoFudge3*. The most comprehensive and far-reaching of all of these emails (however well-intentioned) was from my older brother. In a phone conversation we had shortly afterwards, he informed me that I wouldn't 'find anyone who doesn't think that you're the most passive aggressive and controlling person they know'. This may or may not have been true but, as with so much throughout this debacle, it wasn't *really* the point. Needless to say, the thing that was boiling away inside me came out and I lost my shit with him, doing my argument no good whatsoever. Nick, with my full agreement, stepped into the email blizzard and shut down any and all further joint communication.

At this point, Nick and I came into possession of the full assessments of Bananas and Janet that had been made in 2009. As we trawled through these documents we discovered numerous factual inaccuracies, attempts to minimise, mistaken assumptions by the therapist in charge, and evidence of an 'investigation' that had been conducted in a manner that had been allowed, in part, to sanitise the perpetrator. Many of the recommendations of the report had been allowed to relapse or had not been adhered to at all.

Dad's Dying (etc. etc.)

On Friday, 5 June 2020 Dad was taken into hospital and it quickly became obvious that he wouldn't be coming back out – and not because he liked it so much. He had a massive tumour in his bowel and, on top of his heart condition, it was inoperable. All of his children were called and told to get to Frimley Park Hospital promptly to say our goodbyes.

The day was surreal. I went into Dad's room to see him alone for my allotted fifteen minutes. He was sat up, as alert and communicative as ever (which, admittedly, wasn't saying much). I told him I loved him and he told me he loved me, which was a first – and made me cry. Then he gave me a cuddle, which wasn't a first but hadn't happened since I was five.

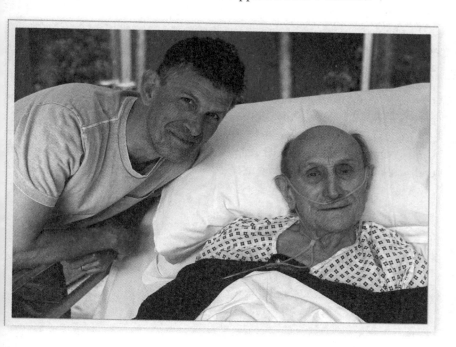

When I came out, I said to one of my sisters that it felt like he was about to be executed. A man with no real signs of illness, yet we were told with certitude he wouldn't last the night. Bizarre. He did last the night and, extraordinarily, the next eight days. I was able to bring my daughters to come and say goodbye to Grandad, which felt good for all of us.

It was in these last few days that another piece of Dad's jigsaw puzzle was slotted into place, one that significantly altered much of what I'd understood of him all my life. I can't remember how the information was shared as the scales of my emotions were teetering under quite a weight, but at some point Wendy told me that she believed my dad had always been mildly Aspergic. I immediately flipped through my mental Rolodex: Dad struggling to understand the sarcasm and mockery at the dining table, Dad standing apart from the other dads on the sidelines at football, Dad finding making friends and social situations cripplingly awkward, Dad fighting *any and all* change. It certainly explained a lot, though it seemed a shame that after a life of eighty-five years, we might only have a few hours in which to make allowances for it.

Just before I arrived at the hospital, I was texted and asked if I had a problem with Janet being there? I said no, but I'd rather we didn't cross over. Shortly after that I was asked if I'd be OK with Bananas being there. I very much wasn't and also felt very strongly that the question shouldn't have been asked. It simply shouldn't have been a consideration. It led to a fierce argument between me and most of my siblings.

On 15 June Dad died and I spent the next few weeks composing two things. One was a song that I recorded with my oldest daughter about our dads called 'No One's Son Anymore'.

Same eyes as me. Same size as me. Same blood in my veins.
Time's wire, aim, fire.
Rushing to an end-point that's been written in the stars.
Climb, fall. That's all. And I'm no one's son anymore.
'No One's Son Anymore,' 2020

The other was a letter to my siblings following the argument we'd had. I sent the letter on 20 July and their reaction has, in no small part, led to my writing this book. It has also caused a schism that will never heal as long as Bananas is allowed to be shielded by a cloak of secrecy and anonymity. That cloak is finite in that it is composed of the shame, compromises and distorted lives of his victims.

This is the text of the letter.

Dear brothers and sisters,

I originally planned to write at least some of this just after Christmas as I was in a train of thought that was rattling along in a direction hitherto untravelled. It was prompted by a song I was writing that provoked some questions. Or was it the questions that had led to the song? More of that anon, for now I'll stick to the mindset I was in on December 30th. The song is called 'A Winter Son' and besides being a fairly awful pun, travels over ground I've traversed fairly consistently since I first put pen to paper aged 16.

Like Autumn leaves - So does he
His final fall - Will be the death of me.
The light gets burned - Inside and not returned
And all is spent - Always before it's earned

And here I am, brothers and sisters.
And here I am, the fourth in line.
Here I am....waiting, to tell another lie.

A winter son - So full of fun
Transparently - Looks after number one
A frozen vein - With the mark of Cain
The vanity - To verbalise the 'pain'.

And here I am, brothers and sisters.
And here I am, the fourth in line.
Here I am....waiting, to tell another lie.

It has its sights trained unerringly on its target and is as comprehensive a self-laceration as one could imagine. It's taken minutes to finish that sentence. 'as one could hope for?' 'as one could wish for?' I realised as I toyed with these that they likely wouldn't make sense because why would you 'hope' or 'wish' for a destruction of yourself? In tandem with this, a realisation began to grow and it slowly occurred to me that I have had a tendency to exaggerate, to 'sweeten the pill', to put a spin on things. In the lyrics there's a hint to that in the line 'waiting to tell another lie...' although when I wrote that, I didn't really know why. There's another giveaway there too and this has literally occurred to me right now. It's 'pain' in parenthesis, ridiculing the notion that there might be actual pain.

I wasn't born a fibber, but at some point, it crept in. I'm glad however, that I didn't write this early in the New Year, as it would have been packing filler into age old cracks that, rather than requiring concealment, need quite the opposite. You'll all have been party to some variation of this at some point from me; verbal, behavioural, transactional, residual (as this sentence descends into a bad parody of 'Cats' I'm tempted to end 'fantastical individual!') because that's always been there too, as it so often is alongside self-loathing and inadequacy, an overweening sense of excellence and exceptionalism. A(nother) quick digression at this point. I'm imagining Francis (who has always been dismissive of what he sees as 'navel-gazing') rolling his eyes as I gaze at my navel, cut round and detach it, then fashion into a hat, that I parade down the high street wearing at a jaunty angle.

I feel that through our upbringing and beyond, I have been at times evasive, arrogant, dismissive and all manner of combinations therein. I'd like to apologise to each of you for any occasions where interaction with me has led to your feeling less of yourselves or of me. Where this becomes problematic is, unsurprisingly, in relation to ▓▓▓ ▓▓▓▓ and the events of 7th June which for now need to sit outside of what I've just acknowledged. ▓▓▓ ▓▓▓▓ however can now sit front and centre, as he has done in my amygdala (I think that's where the brain stores trauma?) since his ritual and thorough destruction of my confidence, sense of self and ongoing character development between the ages of 10 and 16. That's aside from the sheer terror, powerlessness and physical pain that can still return at any point on any night.

In recent months I've begun to undertake an examination of my role in shaping the key events and relationships in my life. It's ongoing, fascinating, humiliating, enlightening and upsetting. One of the first things I needed to admit to was my propensity to verbally cut people to shreds, a facet pointed out to me in my mid-teens by John Shanks who, having served some up, received it back twice as hard - prompting him to remark that I'd 'swallowed razorblades'. Those razorblades have been spat liberally over the years. Never unprompted and in most cases the disagreement has initially been justifiable but (and as was the case with the greedy bus-driver, it's a big but) there's a point at which I tip. Even as I'm doing it, alongside the feeling of richly-justified sweet relief there's a tiny realisation that I'm 'running my mouth'. It stems from anger obviously and the root of that anger is possibly more complex and difficult to access than you might imagine. It also has the effect of negating what I started out trying to say. This is all difficult to explain and I am not appealing for clemency, seeking mitigation nor trying to subvert what I've already acknowledged. As I said at the start, I had an inkling I needed to engage in this with all of you at the end of last year. I began to suspect the possibility of my own weakness in this regard several years ago and thankfully have been aided by a partner with immense reserves of fortitude, bravery, compassion and patience.

In the process of this Character Archaeology, rather than digging the foundations, I instead went into the loft of my flat in NW10 and there, in a storage box was a black lever-arch folder containing virtually every lyric I've ever written, the spine fittingly emblazoned with the sticker 'Toxic Hazard'. Around 300 pieces of paper (I know - 'the trees!') some headed 'Habitat', some 'Crow', coffee stains, hand written notes and phone numbers starting 01 Endless scrawled ramblings which amounted to an extraordinarily accurate and illuminating illustration of my mental development, best summed up as:

'1980 - I'm shit' to '2018 – I'm shit with better vocabulary and use of metaphor'.

I started to set aside everything that was riddled with self-loathing or self-criticism but stopped. Because it was nearly all of them.

This is fairly typical. It's FIN from 1992.

I should have learned to shut my mouth, to stop this nonsense coming out.
But is it that that makes me me? Or would it be much better to be...
My life's been a merry dance, of strange chance and circumstance.
A cracked childhood veiled in tears, and now I'm losing years and gaining fears.

The collection of lyrics is a diary (it's not Pepys, more clangs and squonks) and aside from being a bit *cringe* in places, it's really upsetting. Because a lot of what I thought was 'feel my pain' undergrad poetry is actually a genuine cry for help, albeit an unconscious one. I can remember writing 'a cracked childhood veiled in tears' and thinking 'hmm, that's a bit much - sounds like an image in search of an experience' such is one's mechanism for self-protection. My childhood wasn't cracked, it was torn apart.

████ ███████'s 'process' with me was one of deconstruction. He would constantly chide and undermine me; 'don't be a bighead', 'stop boasting', 'you're so cocky', 'don't be like your big brother'. At the same time as responsibility for me was all but handed over to him, he did everything he could to ensure my confidence was destabilised. At 10, in my last year at St Amands I was happy, confident, popular, doing well academically and in sport and drama. John Bosco was tough but what made it, at times, impossible to navigate were the confusing messages about *how to be*. My internal compass was knocked sideways. I might have been bullied anyway (though I never had been) and I think I became a more obvious target. Around this time was, as far as I remember, when the exaggeration kicked in and the boy with a highly active imagination became a bit 'Billy Liar'. In part trying to say things that would play well to others, in part trying to counteract the beginnings of a hatred of what I was being told not to be. Myself.

███ █████ the man who, in my key formative development from childhood to adulthood, was advising, mentoring and perverting that journey. A man whose toolkit included guilt, coercion, physical threat and bribery; and that's just what he used to break me down. His modus operandi in the pursuit of his own physical gratification included all of that and much more. You might be thinking 'yes, yes - I know all of that', but the magnitude of it and the profound effect it has wrought - is proving to be more fundamental than I had imagined. I have been running from this, bent out of shape in an attempt to accommodate and deny it, changed beyond recognition from what I should have been allowed to be. Melodramatic? To you maybe, but I feel a desperate and dam-bursting sadness for that 10-year-old boy, whose following five years encompassed endless nights in bedrooms and tents, in bathrooms, showers and toilets. To say nothing of the continued presence of my abuser for decades afterwards.

I began my recent odyssey having been woken in the middle of the night by a question: *Am I a toxic narcissist?* So, I did what any reasonable person would do. I got up and made a cup of tea, then Googled 'Am I a toxic narcissist?' It didn't look good, so I sought expert help. It's going to take quite a while (as odysseys do) because whilst I'm likely not a toxic narcissist (too much empathy, prepared to engage with possibility of being a toxic narcissist) I am all manner of things that I'd rather give myself a chance to be much less of. One of those (and there's something of an irony here, writing a document about yourself in which you confess to being attention seeking) is attention seeking. To most of you, that sentence will be as enlightening as a bag of nuts emblazoned with the slogan 'may contain nuts' but as Sam Jackson said at the end of Pulp Fiction 'I'm trying Ringo - I'm trying real hard'.

I'm ashamed of quite a lot in my life, not least the trail of domestic chaos. Ten years with a partner whose past is equally chequered and who believes very much in making things right in the here and now is progressively helping. I'm hoping that my meteoric rise through Bad Decisions Inc. to become Head of Bad Decisions might have been curtailed. Time will tell.

So, bear with me, or if not, I'll call back in a year or two.

Johnny x

The Odyssey Continues

I sent the letter at around the same time as I embarked on a course of psychotherapy. I'd dabbled twice before but had only made superficial progress due to an innate fear of 'looking bad'. It's my Achilles' heel.*

* This suggests that my area of weakness and vulnerability is small and hidden away. In fact, my fear of looking bad demands a new Greek myth wherein a warrior child is being washed by his mother in the Styx to confer invincibility on him but she has enormous hands and elects to hold him around his entire torso, rendering him vulnerable across a good fifty per cent of his surface area.

Undergoing psychotherapy whilst trying to maintain a veneer of something other than truth makes about as much sense as having a bath with your coat on and so my previous interactions had resulted in a steaming, sodden pile on the bathroom floor (at least metaphorically speaking) and little else. This felt different, having something of a 'last chance saloon' feel about it and was brought about by several factors coinciding:

1. I was on my third marriage, and was finding myself increasingly being the person who had not helped in the continuance of the previous two.

2. I was in the tenth year of a relationship with someone who I loved deeply and who, in spite of my myriad faults and flaws, loved me completely and unconditionally.

3. I was increasingly being a person incompatible with the continuance of point 2.

4. I was a father to two teenagers and step-father to two others and was too wrapped up in my own psycho-drama to be what they needed me to be.

5. The arrival of the 'A Winter Son' song had provoked me to think about things I'd ignored and/or been unaware of.

6. Now Dad had died, and Mum having died in 2007, I was somehow free to explore some issues in a way that began to feel more possible.

I knew of a psychotherapist locally, Dr M, who my partner and I had occasionally visited to discuss co-parenting issues (which are as frequent and apparently insoluble as parenting issues with the added spice that two of them *aren't your fault*).

Full disclosure: I have never been violent, threatening or even bordered on these. If you were to discuss the above with any of the three women I've been married to, they would all corroborate that. They'd also corroborate that I can be opinionated, argumentative, intolerant, judgmental and other variants of what I admitted to in the letter to my siblings. They would further add that there were occasions where my opinions and intolerance would bleed into my being critical of them, and that once this criticism started it could (especially if there had been Kronenbourg or Wyborowa taken) become unnecessarily destructive. These behaviours haven't been restricted to wives and partners, but have been enacted equally on male and female friends, work associates and family members. It was admitting to all of this with Dr M that led to conversations about the origins of the anger. At one point, she asked me: 'How would it feel to direct this anger toward Bananas?'

There's a Larson cartoon with two mosquitos; one is blown up like a balloon and the other is screaming, 'Pull out! You've hit an artery!'

We had, as the expression goes, struck the mother lode.

'Shame is the lie someone told you about yourself'

When Dr M and I decided that it was probably a good place to pause the psychotherapy, I mentioned that I'd been thinking of writing about my journey. 'Well of course you should,' she said, 'you've written about everything else.' And I have. As I acknowledged in 'The Virus' in 2010:

> Dreams, journeys – Flow through my mind
> And the songs you seeded – Saved my life

I realise that to you, having read this book, that's stating the bleeding obvious, but when I started writing I had no idea what I was going to discover. I shudder to think how many times I've written 'no idea' (actually it's only sixteen, which doesn't seem too bad), but this has been a constant process of surprise and enlightenment. The notion of Self-Psychotherapy is not unusual (apparently) but I wonder how common Unconscious Self-Psychotherapy is? Who knows – it could be my USP.

In the guts of the songs, sketches and screenplays were the shrapnel from the experiences of my childhood, but also the beginnings of the antidote. All this time I was healing myself and yet I had 'no idea' (seventeen).

At one point in the writing, I researched the significance and impact of shame on victims of child sexual abuse. I found a website that detailed it clearly and concisely and it was like looking in a mirror. As I read each sentence and paragraph, I felt an internal contraction at every point I recognised. The recognition wasn't painful, it was actually incredibly reassuring and comforting.

Yes. I feel this.
Yes, that's what has happened.
Yes, Yes, Yes.

'Let me go... No – no – no – no'

From an article in *Psychology Today*
Written by Beverly Engel L.M.F.T.
(**annotated** by me)

If you were a victim of childhood abuse or neglect, you know about shame.
[Yes, I do] You have likely been plagued by it all your life without identifying it
as shame **[Yes, I have]**

While those who were **sexually** abused tend to suffer from the most shame,
those who suffered from physical, verbal or **emotional** abuse blame themselves
as well **[Yes, I do]**

Conversely, when good things happen to you, you may actually become
uncomfortable, because you feel so unworthy **[Yes, I do]**

Emotional, physical, and sexual child abuse can so overwhelm a victim with
shame that it actually comes to define the person, keeping him from his full
potential. **[Yes, possibly]**

Unbeknownst to them, adults who were abused as children often express the
overwhelming shame they feel by pushing away those who try to be good to
them **[Yes]** by sabotaging their success **[Yes]** or by becoming **emotionally** or
physically abusive to their partners **[Yes]**

Shame can affect literally every aspect of a former victim's life, from self-confidence
[Yes] self-esteem **[Yes]** and body image **[Yes]** to the ability to relate to others
[Yes] to navigate intimate relationships **[Yes]** to be a good parent **[I try]** to work
effectively **[No]** to learn new things **[No]** and to care for yourself. **[No]** Shame
is responsible for myriad personal problems, including self-criticism and self-blame

[Yes] self-neglect **[No]** self-destructive behaviours (such as abusing your body with food, alcohol, drugs, or cigarettes **[Yes]** self-mutilation, being accident-prone **[No]** perfectionism (based on fear of being caught in a mistake) **[Yes]** believing you don't deserve good things, **[Yes]** believing that if others really knew you they would dislike or be disgusted by you (commonly known as the 'imposter syndrome') **[Yes]** people-pleasing and co-dependent behaviour **[Yes]** tending to be critical of others (trying to give shame away) **[Yes]** intense rage **[Yes]** and acting out against society (breaking rules or laws). **[Not so far]**

Luckily, when you've realised the origins of that shame, you're in a better position to be able to help yourself escape the effects of it. When Wendell (the accidental shaman) began that process with me, it was extraordinarily painful because the sexual abuse and the emotional abuse through the character rewiring were inextricable. What that process and much of my work with Dr M had in common was the volume of consequent tears. The tears were provoked by compassion for myself and what I'd endured.

That compassion, having given myself such a hard time for such a long time, brings a very moving sense of regret, but also relief. Better to have arrived here than not at all. Since the Christmas of 2019 when I wrote 'A Winter Son', I've been lucky to have gained a degree of enlightenment and understanding as to why I wrote what I did for forty-odd years.

Epilogue

I started writing this book a year ago in spring 2021. The process has been cathartic and illuminating, but not without negatives. The armour I've had to strap on has left me, at times, impenetrable to those around me. As I've rooted through the viscera and shit of a life that was so fundamentally perverted, the writing has often felt like being engaged in some terrible betrayal and I've been besieged by thoughts of what I'm divulging and its repercussions.

On a practical level, the act of writing is always riddled with self-doubt and writers frequently share with readers close to them as they go. That becomes a minefield when what you're writing is as explosive and exposing as this.

When I reached what I felt was a first draft, I needed some feedback and decided to share the manuscript. In doing so, I revealed some of the intimate personal details and admissions that are at the heart of this story for the first time. In a couple of cases, this disclosure wasn't entirely well received. But then a response came back that I wasn't expecting: 'This is closer to me than I've ever admitted'. Then another and then another.

At the time of writing, having shared around sixty copies of the manuscript with friends, editors, lawyers, publishers etc. I've had seven responses of this nature, enough to confirm that my experiences of child abuse are horribly common and widespread.

It was never my intention for *Shadowman* to have any kind of purpose beyond an initial desire to heave it out, that I might rid myself of feelings I'd carried for far too long. However, if you've read the experiences in this book and found yourself taken back to the memory of a bedroom, a classroom, a changing room, a park – anywhere where someone has done or said something to you that they had no right to, please try and tell somebody close to you. In the light of the reception I got from my parents, that might not seem the greatest advice in the world, but times have changed.

You need to know that what has been done or said to you is not OK and is not, in any way, shape, or form, your fault – however it may have come to feel. If there isn't someone you can share with, then contact the Lucy Faithfull Foundation via the details opposite. You'll be listened to and taken seriously. And that's a start.

Johnny

The Lucy Faithfull Foundation

0808 1000 900

www.lucyfaithfull.org.uk

@StopItNowUK

About the Author

Johnny Daukes is a writer, musician, film editor and voice artist. He was the singer/songwriter of 90s indie-band FIN, became a comedy writer with sketch shows on BBC Radio 4 (*Radio9 & The Scanner*), BBC Three (*The Message*) and voiced sixteen series of Channel 4's *Eurotrash*. He wrote and directed the 2011 feature film *Acts of Godfrey* (starring Simon Callow), released solo albums including *Promise* that was album of the week in *The Sunday Times* and *Rough Trade*. His sitcom *Cracking Up* ran for two series on BBC Radio 4 and he has latterly cut feature films including *Finding Your Feet*, *Fisherman's Friends* and *Settlers*. *Shadowman* is his first book, he's hoping it won't be his last.